THE COLLECTED COURSES OF
THE ACADEMY OF EUROPEAN LAW

Series Editors
PROFESSOR NEHA JAIN
PROFESSOR CLAIRE KILPATRICK
PROFESSOR SARAH NOUWEN
PROFESSOR JOANNE SCOTT
European University Institute, Florence

Assistant Editor
JOYCE DAVIES
European University Institute, Florence

Volume XXXI/1

Revisiting the Fundamentals of the Free Movement of Persons in EU Law

THE COLLECTED COURSES OF
THE ACADEMY OF EUROPEAN LAW

Edited by Professor Neha Jain, Professor Claire Kilpatrick,
Professor Sarah Nouwen, and Professor Joanne Scott

Assistant Editor: Joyce Davies

The Academy of European Law is housed at the European University Institute in Florence, Italy. The Academy holds annual advanced-level summer courses focusing on topical, cutting-edge issues in Human Rights Law and The Law of the European Union. The courses are taught by highly qualified scholars and practitioners in a highly interactive environment. General courses involve the examination of the field as a whole through a particular thematic, conceptual, or philosophical lens or look at a theme in the context of the overall body of law. Specialized courses bring together a number of speakers exploring a specific theme in depth. Together, they are published as monographs and edited volumes in the Collected Courses of the Academy of European Law series. The Collected Courses series has been published by Oxford University Press since 2000. The series contains publications on both foundational and pressing issues in human rights law and the law of the European Union.

OTHER TITLES IN THE SERIES INCLUDE:

Data at the Boundaries of European Law
Edited by Deirdre Curtin and Mariavittoria Catanzariti

Legal Mobilization for Human Rights
Edited by Gráinne de Búrca

The UK's Withdrawal from the EU
A Legal Analysis
Michael Dougan

Justifying Contract in Europe
Political Philosophies of European Contract Law
Martijn W. Hesselink

Contemporary Challenges to EU Legality
Edited by Claire Kilpatrick and Joanne Scott

Reframing Human Rights in a Turbulent Era
Gráinne de Búrca

New Legal Approaches to Studying the Court of Justice
Revisiting Law in Context
Edited by Claire Kilpatrick and Joanne Scott

EU Law Beyond EU Borders
The Extraterritorial Reach of EU Law
Edited by Marise Cremona and Joanne Scott

Revisiting the Fundamentals of the Free Movement of Persons in EU Law

Edited by
NIAMH NIC SHUIBHNE

Great Clarendon Street, Oxford, OX2 6DP,
United Kingdom

Oxford University Press is a department of the University of Oxford.
It furthers the University's objective of excellence in research, scholarship,
and education by publishing worldwide. Oxford is a registered trade mark of
Oxford University Press in the UK and in certain other countries

© The multiple contributors 2023

The moral rights of the authors have been asserted

First Edition published in 2023

All rights reserved. No part of this publication may be reproduced, stored in
a retrieval system, or transmitted, in any form or by any means, without the
prior permission in writing of Oxford University Press, or as expressly permitted
by law, by licence or under terms agreed with the appropriate reprographics
rights organization. Enquiries concerning reproduction outside the scope of the
above should be sent to the Rights Department, Oxford University Press, at the
address above

You must not circulate this work in any other form
and you must impose this same condition on any acquirer

Public sector information reproduced under Open Government Licence v3.0
(http://www.nationalarchives.gov.uk/doc/open-government-licence/open-government-licence.htm)

Published in the United States of America by Oxford University Press
198 Madison Avenue, New York, NY 10016, United States of America

British Library Cataloguing in Publication Data

Data available

Library of Congress Control Number: 2023934395

ISBN 978–0–19–888627–3

DOI: 10.1093/oso/9780198886273.001.0001

Printed and bound in the UK by
TJ Books Limited

Links to third party websites are provided by Oxford in good faith and
for information only. Oxford disclaims any responsibility for the materials
contained in any third party website referenced in this work.

Table of Contents

Table of Cases	vii
Table of Legislation	xiii
Notes on Contributors	xxi

1. Introduction: Revisiting EU Law on the Free Movement
   of Persons   1
   Niamh Nic Shuibhne

2. Is Free Movement (Law) Fully Emancipated from Migration (Law)?   6
   Ségolène Barbou des Places

3. Posted Workers Are Persons Too! Posting and the Constitutional
   Democratic Question of Fair Mobility in the European Union   39
   Sacha Garben

4. Economic Activity and EU Citizenship Law: Seeding Means-based
   Logic in a Status-based Freedom   87
   Niamh Nic Shuibhne

5. Free Movement and European Welfare States: Why Child Benefits
   for EU Workers Should Not Be Exportable   127
   Martin Ruhs and Joakim Palme

6. Brexit and the Free Movement of Persons: What Is EU Citizenship
   Really About?   158
   Eleanor Spaventa

Index   187

Table of Cases

For the benefit of digital users, table entries that span two pages (e.g., 52–53) may, on occasion, appear on only one of those pages.

EUROPEAN UNION

Court of Justice of the European Union

Case 4/73, Nold (EU:C:1974:51) 79n.156
Case 36/74, Walrave (EU:C:1974:140) 58–59n.73
Case 41/74, Van Duyn (EU:C:1974:133) 34n.134
Case 32/75, Cristini (EU:C:1975:120) 91n.16
Case 48/75, Royer (EU:C:1976:57) 114n.135
Case 151/78, Sukkerfabriken Nykøbing (EU:C:1979:4) 79n.156
Case 230/78, SpA Eridiana and others (EU:C:1979:216) 79n.156
Case 279/80, Criminal proceedings against Alfred John Webb
    (EU:C:1981:314) 52–53, 53n.55
Joined Cases 62/81 and 63/81, Seco (EU:C:1982:34) 47, 47n.33
Case 65/81, Reina (EU:C:1982:6) 92n.17, 98n.53
Case 152/82, Forcheri (EU:C:1983:205) 101n.64
Case 238/83, Meade (EU:C:1984:250) 14n.30
Case 249/83, Hoeckx (EU:C:1985:139) 97n.45
Case 293/83, Gravier (EU:C:1985:69) 91n.15
Case 137/84, Mutsch (EU:C:1985:335) 98, 98n.52
Case 59/85, Reed (EU:C:1986:157) 121, 121n.167, 123–24
Case 66/85, Lawrie-Blum (EU:C:1986:284) 50–51, 50n.44, 100, 109–10, 131n.10
Case 139/85, Kempf (EU:C:1986:223) 6n.3, 97n.46
Case 316/85, Lebon (EU:C:1987:302) 94n.31
Case 39/86, Lair (EU:C:1988:322) 92n.18, 101n.64
Case 197/86, Brown (EU:C:1988:323) 101–2, 101n.65
C-113/89, Rush Portuguesa
    Judgment (EU:C:1990:142) 39–40, 40n.4, 41, 46–47, 48–50,
        48n.36, 49n.39, 52–53, 54–56, 54n.59, 54n.60
    Opinion (EU:C:1990:107) 47–48, 47n.34, 48n.35, 49–50,
        49n.37, 53n.58, 54, 55n.64, 57
C-292/89, Antonissen (EU:C:1991:80) 50n.43, 114–17, 114–15nn.136–37,
        115n.138, 117n.147
C-363/89, Roux (EU:C:1991:41) 117n.151
C-237/91, Kus
    Opinion (EU:C:1992:427) 32, 32nn.125–27
C-292/92, Hünermund and Others
    Opinion (EU:C:1993:863) 53n.57
C-43/93, Vander Elst (EU:C:1994:310) 49n.39
C-308/93, Cabanis-Issarte (EU:C:1996:169) 96n.37
C-415/93, Bosman (EU:C:1995:463) 58–59n.73

viii TABLE OF CASES

C-214/94, Ingrid Boukhalfa v. Bundesrepublik Deutschland (EU:C:1996:174) 51n.47
C-278/94, Commission v. Belgium (EU:C:1996:321) 94n.31
C-85/96, Martínez Sala (EU:C:1998:217) 19, 19n.57, 87–88n.2, 92n.21, 97n.42,
98n.49, 98n.51, 101n.64, 114, 114n.134, 117n.147
C-369/96 and C-376/96, Arblade and Others (EU:C:1999:575) 54–55, 55n.62
C-240/97, Spain v. Commission (EU:C:1999:479) 79n.156
C-340/97, Nazli (EU:C:2000:77) 106nn.93–94
C-378/97, Wijsenbeek (EU:C:1999:439) 20–21, 20–21nn.62–63
C-35/98, Verkooijen (EU:C:2000:294) 107n.98
C-49/98, C-50/98, C-52–54/98 and C-68–71/98, Finalarte (EU:C:2001:564) 40n.4, 41,
49, 49nn.38–39, 49n.40, 52, 54–55, 55n.61, 55n.63, 57, 58–59, 83–84
C-165/98, Mazzoleni and ISA (EU:C:2001:162) 54–55, 55n.62
C-224/98, D'Hoop (EU:C:2002:432) 96n.41
C-411/98, Ferlini
   Opinion (EU:C:1999:442) 101n.64
C-184/99, Grzelczyk (EU:C:2001:458) 2n.1, 29n.109, 32–33, 87–88n.2, 90n.11,
107n.100, 171n.61, 175–76, 175n.79
C-257/99, Givane
   Judgment (EU:C:2003:8) 101–2, 101–2nn.67–69, 108, 108n.106
   Opinion (EU:C:2002:297) 102, 102n.70
C-309/99, Wouters (EU:C:2002:98) 58–59n.73
C-413/99, Baumbast (EU:C:2002:493) 87–88n.2, 95–96, 96n.38, 163–64, 164n.26, 172
C-60/00, Carpenter (EU:C:2002:434) 102–3
C-112/00, Schmidberger (EU:C:2003:333) 58–59n.73
C-299/01, Commission v. Luxembourg (EU:C:2002:394) 118n.154
C-413/01, Ninni-Orasche (EU:C:2003:600) 50, 50nn.45–46
C-482/01 and C-493/01, Orfanopoulos and Oliveri (EU:C:2004:262) 106, 106n.95
C-138/02, Collins (EU:C:2004:172) 94–95, 94nn.31–32, 113–14, 113n.131
C-148/02, Garcia Avello (EU:C:2003:539) 18–19, 18n.53
C-200/02, Zhu and Chen (EU:C:2004:639) 107n.99
C-442/02, CaixaBank France
   Opinion (EU:C:2004:187) 53n.57
C-456/02, Trojani (EU:C:2004:488) 19, 19n.58, 87–88n.2, 97n.42
C-65/03, Commission v. Belgium (EU:C:2004:402) 50n.42
C-147/03, Commission v. Austria (EU:C:2005:427) 50n.42
C-209/03, Bidar (EU:C:2005:169) 19, 19n.58, 96n.40, 102, 102n.71
C-380/03, Federal Republic of Germany v. European Parliament and Council of
   the European Union (Tobacco Advertising) (EU:C:2006:772) 68, 68n.114
C-109/04, Kranemann (EU:C:2005:187) 52, 52n.50, 82, 83–84
C-145/04, Spain v. United Kingdom (EU:C:2006:543) 182n.96, 183n.100
C-212/05, Hartmann
   Judgment (EU:C:2007:437) 104–5, 105nn.84–85
   Opinion (EU:C:2006:615) 105n.85
C-213/05, Geven (EU:C:2007:438) 103n.78
C-325/05, Derin (EU:C:2007:442) 35, 35n.137
C-341/05, Laval
   Judgment (EU:C:2007:809) 39–40, 40n.5, 41, 54–55, 58–59, 58–59nn.73–74,
59nn.76–78, 60n.79, 60n.83, 61–62, 63–64, 65–66, 72, 73–74, 84, 85
   Opinion (EU:C:2007:291) 58–59n.73
C-438/05, Viking Line (EU:C:2007:772) 61, 61n.86
C-294/06, Payir, Akyuz and Ozturk (EU:C:2008:36) 31–32, 31n.123
C-319/06, Commission v. Luxembourg (EU:C:2008:350) 61, 61n.88, 65–66
C-346/06, Rüffert (EU:C:2008:189) 61, 61n.87, 64–66, 85n.171

TABLE OF CASES ix

C-353/06, Grunkin and Paul (EU:C:2008:559) 18–19, 18n.54
C-158/07, Förster (EU:C:2008:630) 50n.42, 101–2, 101n.66, 111–12, 112n.121
C-269/07, Commission v. Germany (EU:C:2009:527) 104n.82
C-484/07, Pehlivan (EU:C:2011:395) 35, 35n.138
C-22/08 and C-23/08, Vatsouras and Koupatantze (EU:C:2009:344) 87–88n.2, 94n.32,
113–14, 114n.132
C-73/08, Bressol (EU:C:2010:181) 26n.92, 50n.42
C-127/08, Metock (EU:C:2008:449) 23n.81, 32, 32n.124
C-310/08, Ibrahim (EU:C:2010:89) 120–21, 120nn.163–64
C-462/08, Bekleyen (EU:C:2010:30) 35, 35n.139
C-480/08, Teixeira (EU:C:2010:83) 97n.47
C-34/09, Ruiz Zambrano (EU:C:2011:124) 88n.3, 166–67, 166n.36, 178–80,
179n.89, 180n.91, 181
C-97/09, Schmelz (EU:C:2010:632) 67n.110
C-348/09, P.I. (EU:C:2012:300) 26–27, 26n.94, 28
C-434/09, McCarthy (EU:C:2011:277) 88n.3
C-542/09, Commission v. Netherlands (EU:C:2012:346) 88–89n.4, 99, 99nn.54–56,
104n.83, 107–8, 108n.104, 109n.111
C-188/10 and C-189/10, Melki and Abdeli (EU:C:2010:363) 21, 21n.65, 21n.67,
21–22nn.69–70
C-424/10 and C-425/10, Ziolkowski and Szeja (EU:C:2011:866) 106n.97, 121n.166
C-611/10 and C-612/10, Hudziński and Wawrzyn (EU:C:2012:339) 52, 52nn.51–54,
82, 83–84
C-40/11, Lida
Judgment (EU:C:2012:691) 38n.150
Opinion (EU:C:2012:296) 38n.150
C-147/11 and C-148/11, Czop and Punakova (EU:C:2012:538) 118n.153
C-256/11, Dereci and Others (EU:C:2011:734) 88n.3, 103n.76
C-367/11, Prete (EU:C:2012:668) 29n.109
C-523/11 and C-585/11, Prinz and Seeberger (EU:C:2013:90) 93n.24, 96n.39
C-20/12, Giersch
Judgment (EU:C:2013:411) 29n.115, 103n.78, 104–5, 104n.80, 105nn.86–87
Opinion (EU:C:2013:70) 106n.92
C-140/12, Brey
Judgment (EU:C:2013:565) 7n.5, 87–88n.2, 107nn.99–100, 124–25, 164n.26
Opinion (EU:C:2013:337) 124–25, 125n.179
C-159/12–C-161/12, Alessandra Venturini v. ASL Varese and Others; Maria Rosa
Gramegna v. ASL Lodi and Others; Anna Muzzio v. ASL Pavia and Others
Opinion (EU:C:2013:529) 53n.57
C-378/12, Nnamdi Onuekwere v. Secretary of State for the Home
Department (EU:C:2014:213) 172n.65
C-456/12, O and B (EU:C:2014:135) 88n.3, 161n.16, 166n.35
C-457/12, S and G (EU:C:2014:36) 102–3, 103nn.74–75
C-507/12, Saint Prix (EU:C:2014:2007) 106, 106n.96, 111–13, 112nn.123–25,
113n.129, 114, 116–19, 117n.147, 123–24
C-81/13, UK v. Council (EU:C:2014:2449) 32–33, 32n.128
C-333/13, Dano (EU:C:2014:2358) 6–7, 7n.5, 25–26, 29–30, 36, 37, 50n.43,
87–88n.2, 92n.22, 100, 163–64, 164nn.25–26, 169,
169n.50, 171–72, 174–75, 176, 177–78
C-396/13, Elektrobudowa
Judgment (EU:C:2015:86) 52, 63–64, 65–66, 83
Opinion (EU:C:2015:2236) 63–64
C-474/13, Pham (EU:C:2014:2096) 16–17, 17n.44

X   TABLE OF CASES

C-549/13, Bundesdruckerei GmbH v. Stadt Dortmund (EU:C:2014:2235) 64, 64n.99, 65–66
C-554/13, Z. Zh. (EU:C:2015:377) 28n.102
C-562/13, Abdida (EU:C:2014:2453) 17n.47
C-673/13, Relu Adrian Coman and Others v. Inspectoratul General pentru
    Imigrări and Ministerul Afacerilor Interne (EU:C:2018:385) 161n.16, 166n.35
C-67/14, Alimanovic
    Judgment (EU:C:2015:597) 7n.5, 25, 29–30, 92–93n.23, 95n.35, 100, 107n.101,
                                                            112–14, 113n.129, 114n.133, 115n.139,
                                                            116–17, 169n.50, 171–72, 171n.63
    Opinion (EU:C:2015:210) 100n.61
C-115/14, RegioPost (EU:C:2015:760) 64–66, 64n.98, 64nn.100–1
C-153/14, K and A (EU:C:2015:453) 15n.37, 29nn.110–12
C-165/14, Rendón Marín (EU:C:2016:675) 88n.3
C-218/14, Singh (EU:C:2015:476) 171n.64
C-299/14, García-Nieto (EU:C:2016:114) 7n.5, 50n.43, 95n.35, 169n.50, 171n.63, 172
C-308/14, Commission v. UK (EU:C:2016:436) 7n.5, 87–88n.2
C-515/14, Commission v. Cyprus (EU:C:2016:30) 107–8nn.102–3
C-115/15, Secretary of State for the Home Department v. NA
    (EU:C:2016:487) 88n.3, 171n.64
C-133/15, Chavez-Vilchez (EU:C:2017:354) 88n.3
C-201/15, Anonymi Geniki Etairia Tsimenton Iraklis (AGET Iraklis) v.
    Ypourgos Ergasias, Koinonikis Asfalisis kai Koinonikis
    Allilengyis (EU:C:2016:972) 78–79n.152
C-238/15, Bragança Linares Verruga
    Judgment (EU:C:2016:949) 103–4, 104n.79, 105n.88
    Opinion (EU:C:2016:389) 105–6, 105–6nn.89–91
C-401/15–C-403/15, Depesme and Kerrou (EU:C:2016:955) 121–22, 122nn.168–69
C-82/16, KA and Others (EU:C:2018:308) 88n.3, 103n.76
C-156/16, Lounes (EU:C:2017:862) 165–66, 165n.32
C-184/16, Petrea (EU:C:2017:684) 24–25, 24nn.86–87
C-316/16 and C-424/16, B and Vomero (EU:C:2018:256) 89n.8, 116n.146, 172n.65
C-331/16 and C-366/16, K. and H.F. (EU:C:2018:296) 27–28, 27n.97, 27nn.99–100
C-442/16, Gusa (EU:C:2017:1004) 117–18, 117n.148, 117n.150, 124–25, 124n.177
C-578/16, C. K. (EU:C:2017:127) 17n.47
C-618/16, Prefeta (EU:C:2018:719) 118–20, 119n.161, 119n.162
C-638/16, X and X v. Belgium (EU:C:2017:173) 15n.36, 38n.151
C-163/17, Jawo (EU:C:2019:218) 17n.47
C-221/17, M.G. Tjebbes and Others v. Minister van Buitenlandse
    Zaken (EU:C:2019:189) 178–80, 179n.89
C-247/17, Raugevicius (EU:C:2018:898) 93n.24, 96n.39
C-257/17, C.A. (EU:C:2018:876) 29n.113
C-412/17, Touring Tours (EU:C:2018:1005) 21, 21n.64, 21n.69
C-483/17, Tarola (EU:C:2019:309) 107–8, 108n.105, 109–10,
                                                            118–20, 119n.160, 173n.72
C-93/18, Bajratari (EU:C:2019:209) 172n.67
C-174/18, Jacob and Lennertz (EU:C:2019:205) 118n.156
C-380/18, E.P. (EU:C:2019:1071) 28, 28nn.103–4
C-410/18, Aubriet (EU:C:2019:582) 29n.115, 103nn.77–78, 104
C-544/18, Dakneviciute (EU:C:2019:761) 117–18, 117nn.151–52
C-620/18, Hungary v. Parliament and Council (EU:C:2020:1001) 39–40, 40n.7, 51–52,
                                                            67n.111, 68–72, 68n.115, 68nn.116–17,
                                                            69nn.119–21, 70–71nn.124–25, 85n.174, 86

TABLE OF CASES xi

C-755/18 P, Shindler (EU:C:2019:221) 184n.102
C-830/18, Landkreis Südliche Weinstraße v. PF and Others (EU:C:2020:275) 50n.41
C-836/18, Subdelegación del Gobierno en Ciudad Real (EU:C:2020:119)...........88n.3
C-181/19, Jobcenter Krefeld
    Judgment (EU:C:2020:794) 87–88n.2, 97, 97nn.43–44, 99nn.57–58,
        100nn.59–60, 101–2, 116–17, 119n.159, 120–21, 120n.165, 122–23,
        122nn.170–71, 123n.172, 163, 163n.23, 164n.25, 169n.50, 172n.68
    Opinion (EU:C:2020:377) 122–23, 123nn.173–75, 125n.179
C-451/19, Toledo (EU:C:2022:354) 88n.3
C-535/19, A
    Judgment (EU:C:2021:595) 87–88n.2, 164n.27, 169n.50, 172n.66
    Opinion (EU:C:2021:114) 169n.50
C-710/19, G.M.A. (EU:C:2020:1037) 87–88n.2, 114, 115, 115nn.139–41,
        116–17, 116nn.142–44, 162–63, 162n.19, 163n.21
C-718/19, Ordre des barreaux francophones et germanophone
    (EU:C:2021:505) 24–25, 24n.85, 25n.88, 172n.69
C-719/19, FS v. Staatssecretaris van Justitie en Veiligheid (EU:C:2021:506) 172n.69
C-897/19 PPU, Ruska Federacijia v. I.N. (EU:C:2020:262) 32–33, 32–33nn.129–31
C-930/19, X v. Belgian State (EU:C:2021:657) 171n.64
C-118/20, JY v. Wiener Landesregierung (EU:C:2022:34) 179n.89
C-163/20, AZ (pending) 109n.109
C-168/20, BJ and OV (EU:C:2021:907)............ 94nn.29–30, 118n.155, 118nn.157–58
C-247/20, VI v. Commissioners for Her Majesty's Revenue and Customs (Assurance
    maladie complète) (EU:C:2022:177) 87–88n.2, 164nn.26–27, 174n.75
C-328/20, Commission v. Austria
    Judgment (EU:C:2022:468) 109–10, 109n.110, 109nn.112–13, 125–26,
        125nn.181–82, 130n.5, 138–39
    Opinion (EU:C:2022:45)....... 108–9, 109n.109, 110n.114, 138, 138n.27, 139, 177n.84
C-368/20 and C-369/20, Landespolizeidirektion Steiermark
    Opinion (EU:C:2021:821) 28n.105
C-490/20, V.M.A. v. Stolichna obshtina, rayon 'Pancharevo' (EU:C:2021:1008) 179n.89
C-574/20, XO (pending) 109n.109
C-673/20, Préfet du Gers
    Judgment (EU:C:2022:449) 89n.7, 159–60, 160n.10, 180,
        180n.93, 183–84, 183n.100, 185
    Opinion (EU:C:2022:129) 182–83, 182n.97, 183n.100, 184
C-709/20, CG (EU:C:2021:602) 87–88n.2, 96–97, 97n.42, 111, 111n.119,
        164n.29, 165n.31, 173–76, 174n.76, 175n.78
C-499/21 P, Silver (pending)...184n.102
C-501/21 P, Shindler (pending) 184n.102
C-502/21 P, Price (pending) 184n.102
C-637/21 P, K.R. (pending)..168n.45

Opinion 1/91 of the Court of 14 December 1991 pursuant to the second
    subparagraph of Article 228(1) of the Treaty (EU:C:1991:490) 4n.3
Opinion 2/13 of the Court (Full Court) of 18 December 2014 pursuant to
    Article 218(11) TFEU (EU:C:2014:2454) 4n.3

General Court

Case T-198/20, Shindler (EU:T:2021:348) 184n.102
Case T-231/20 Price (EU:T:2021:349) 184n.102
Case T-252/20, Silver (EU:T:2021:347) 184n.102

xii TABLE OF CASES

OTHER SUPRANATIONAL COURTS

European Committee of Social Rights

Swedish Trade Union Confederation (LO) and Swedish Confederation of
Professional Employees (TCO) v. Sweden, No 85/2012 (3 July 2013) . . . 61–63, 62n.93

European Court of Human Rights

Norwegian Confederation of Trade Unions (LO) and Norwegian Transport
Workers' Union (NTF) v. Norway, Application no. 45487/17, Judgment
of 10 June 2021 . . . . 62n.95

NATIONAL COURTS

France

Cour de Cassation Pourvoi n° 20-16.901 (FR:CCASS:2020:C201153) 182n.98

United Kingdom

Ahmad v. The Secretary of State for the Home Department
[2014] EWCA Civ 988 . . . . 174n.75
Fratila and another (AP) v. Secretary of State for Work and Pensions
[2021] UKSC 53 . . . . 174n.76, 176, 176n.80
R (Gureckis) v. Secretary of State for the Home Department
[2017] EWHC 3298 (Admin) 159n.5

Table of Legislation

For the benefit of digital users, table entries that span two pages (e.g., 52–53) may, on occasion, appear on only one of those pages.

EUROPEAN UNION

Treaties and Conventions

Treaty establishing the European Coal
and Steel Community (ECSC)
(Treaty of Paris), 1951 10–11
Treaty establishing the European
Economic Community (EEC)/
European Community (EC)
(Treaty of Rome), 1958 . . . 1, 10, 11–12,
108, 130–31
Article 7 . . . . 101n.64
Article 17
Article 17(1) 13–14
Article 48 . . . . 11, 14n.30, 15–16,
47–49, 49n.39
Article 48(1) 12n.22
Article 48(2) 12n.22
Article 48(3) 12n.22
Article 128 . . . . 101n.64
Article 226 . . . . 11, 11n.20
Treaty of Amsterdam amending the
Treaty on European Union, the
Treaties establishing the European
Communities and certain related
acts, OJ 1997 C 340/1 11–12
Charter of Fundamental Rights of
the European Union, OJ 2000
C 164/1 . . . . 12, 13, 15n.36, 38,
72–73n.128, 79, 81n.161,
174–76, 183–84
Article 15
Article 15(2) 74–75, 79–81
Article 16 . . . . 78–81, 78–79n.152
Article 17 80–81
Article 24 147–48
Article 40 182–83
Article 52
Article 52(2) . . . 78–79n.152, 81n.161,
112n.126

Treaty of Lisbon amending the Treaty
on European Union and the
Treaty establishing the European
Community, OJ 2007 C 306/1 . . . . 12, 81
Treaty on European Union (TEU)
(Maastricht Treaty), OJ 2012
C 326/13 (consolidated
version) 130–31
Article 2 . . . . 27–28, 44–45
Article 3 . . . . 4n.3, 27–28, 68–69
Article 3(2) 32–33
Article 3(3) 85
Article 9 . . . . 89n.7
Article 50 . . . . 158n.1, 182–83
Article 50(3) 178
Protocol No 2 on the application
of the principles of subsidiarity
and proportionality, OJ 2008
C 115/206 . . . . 66n.106
Treaty on the Functioning of the
European Union (TFEU),
OJ 2012 C 326/47 (consolidated
version) 23, 68–69, 68n.116,
111–12, 118, 146, 163
Article 7 . . . . 69n.118
Articles 8–13 . . . . 69n.118
Article 9 . . . . 68n.116
Article 18 . . . . . 92–93, 96–97, 98, 98n.49,
111, 117–18, 168–69,
169n.50, 174–75, 175n.78
Articles 20–24 . . . . 90n.10
Article 20 . . . . 18, 24, 87–88, 89n.7,
102–3, 110–11, 124–25
Article 20(1) 166–67
Article 21 . . . . . 18, 24, 25n.90, 38, 87–88,
90, 94–95, 96–97, 98n.49, 99,
102, 108, 110–12, 113, 114,
116–17, 124–25, 161–62,
165–67, 174–75, 175n.78
Article 21(1) 89–90, 94

xiv TABLE OF LEGISLATION

Articles 22–24 87–88
Article 45 . . . . 3, 18, 49–50, 52–53,
62–63, 88–89, 90n.9, 94–97, 98–99,
98n.49, 101–3, 106, 107–8, 108n.106,
110–13, 114–15, 116–18, 120–21,
124–26, 130–31, 146, 161–62
Article 45(2) 94–95, 99
Article 45(3) 116–17
Article 45(3)(c) 123–24
Article 48 . . . . 117n.149, 125–26
Article 49 . . . . 88–89, 94, 95, 99, 110–11,
113, 117–19, 120–21,
124–25, 161–62
Article 53 70–72
Article 56 . . . . 52–54, 64–65, 85, 94, 95n.36
Article 57 . . . . 52–54, 85
Article 61 85
Article 62 71–72
Title V, Chapter 2 (Articles 77–80) . . . 12
Article 77 12
Article 78
Article 78(2) 15–16
Article 79 12
Article 114 70–71
Article 153 . . . . 67–68, 70–72,
124–25, 161n.16
Article 153(2)
Article 153(2)(b) 70–71
Article 153(5) 67–68
Article 155 70–71

Directives

Directive 68/360/EEC on the abolition
of restrictions on movement and
residence within the Community
for workers of Member States and
their families, OJ 1968 Sp. Ed.
L 257/13 . . . . . 91n.14, 130–31, 130n.7
Directive 73/148/EEC on the abolition
of restrictions on movement and
residence within the Community
for nationals of Member States
with regard to establishment
and the provision of services,
OJ 1973 L 172/14 . . . . 91n.14
Directive 90/364/EEC on the right of
residence, OJ 1990 L180/26 . . . 91n.15
Directive 90/365/EEC on the right
of residence for employees and
self-employed persons who have
ceased their occupational
activity, OJ 1990 L 180/28 . . . . . 91n.15

Directive 93/96/EEC on the right of
residence for students, OJ 1993
L 317/59 . . . . 91n.15
Directive 96/71/EC of the European
Parliament and of the Council of
16 December 1996 concerning
the posting of workers in the
framework of the provision of
services (Posted Workers
Directive, or PWD),
OJ 1996 L 18/1 . . . . 55–58, 56n.65,
60–61, 63–66, 72, 84, 85, 85n.171
Preamble 57
Recital 5 . . . . 57n.67
Recital 17 . . . . 60n.82
Article 3 . . . . 56–57, 60–61
Article 3(1)–(6) 56, 60–61
Article 3(1)–(8) 56–57
Article 3(1) 60–61, 63–65, 66, 69
Article 3(1)(c) 66
Article 3(7) 56, 60–61
Article 3(8) 56, 64
Article 3(9) 56–57
Article 3(10) 56–57, 61
Directive 2003/86/EC of 22 September
2003 on the right to family
reunification (Family Reunification
Directive), OJ 2003 L 251/12 17
Directive 2003/109/EC of 25
November 2003 concerning
the status of third-country
nationals who are long-term
residents (Long-Term Residents
Directive), OJ 2004 L 16/44 . . . . 14n.31,
15–16, 16n.39, 16n.41, 17, 17n.46
Chapter III 181n.94
Article 22 . . . . 17n.46
Directive 2004/18/EC of 31 March
2004 on the coordination of
procedures for the award of public
works contracts, public supply
contracts and public service
contracts (Public Procurement
Directive), OJ 2004 L 134/114 64
Directive 2004/38/EC of 29 April 2004
on the right of citizens of the
Union and their family members
to move and reside freely within
the territory of the Member States
(Citizens Directive), OJ
2004 L 158/77 . . . 2, 3, 10n.12, 23n.81,
24–25, 28–29, 34, 36–37,

87n.1, 88–89n.4, 89–90, 89n.8,
91n.14, 92–93, 96–97, 107–8, 111–12,
112n.126, 113–15, 115n.138, 116–17,
118–24, 130–31, 160–62, 161n.13,
161n.16, 163–64, 165–69, 167n.40,
170, 171–76, 175n.77, 177–78

Preamble
Recital 3 .... 2n.2, 36n.146
Recital 4 ..... 2n.2, 37n.149, 89–90, 120
Recital 17 120–21
Article 2 .... 91n.14, 121–22
Article 2(2) 121–22
Article 3 .... 91n.14, 121
Article 3(2) 121
Article 3(2)(b) 121, 122–23
Article 6 .... 114, 115–17
Article 6(1) 88–89n.4
Article 7 .... 37, 89n.8, 111–12, 114,
115, 116–17, 120–21, 131n.8,
161n.15, 169n.50
Article 7(1) 88–89n.4, 106n.97,
118–19, 120–21, 165–66
Article 7(1)(a) 87–88, 93, 95,
95n.36, 98, 117, 118
Article 7(1)(b) 88–89n.4, 92–93,
95, 95n.36, 96–97, 111,
120–21, 174n.75
Article 7(1)(c) 92–93, 95,
96–97, 120–21
Article 7(3) 93, 93n.27, 106, 111–14,
117, 118–19, 120–21, 123–24
Article 7(3)(a) 118–19
Article 7(3)(b) 118–19, 164n.28
Article 7(3)(c) 119, 164n.28
Article 7(3)(d) 118–19
Article 12 .... 34n.135
Article 12(3) 118n.153
Article 13 .... 34n.135
Article 14 116–17
Article 14(1) 116–17
Article 14(2) 116–17
Article 14(4) 116–17
Article 14(4)(a) 93, 93n.28
Article 14(4)(b) 93n.28, 94n.33,
96–97, 114–15, 116n.143, 120–21,
162n.18, 163n.21, 168–69
Article 16 ...... 104–5, 165–66, 167n.40
Article 16(1) 106n.97, 120–21
Article 16(3) 167nn.41–42
Article 17 93
Article 24 .... 92–93, 97, 111, 168–69
Article 24(1) 92–93, 118–19,
122–23, 174–75

Article 24(2) 93, 94n.33, 96–97,
98–99, 101n.66, 103–4,
113–14, 122–23, 169n.50
Articles 27–33 107
Article 27 24–25
Article 27(3) 170n.56
Directive 2008/115/EC of 16
December 2008 on common
standards and procedures in
Member States for returning
illegally staying third-country
nationals (Return Directive),
OJ 2008 L 348/98 .... 13, 13n.27,
16–17, 24–25, 28
Preamble
Recital 2 .... 17n.45
Article 3
Article 3(3) 13–14
Directive 2009/50/EC of 25 May
2009 on the conditions of entry
and residence of third-country
nationals for the purposes of
highly qualified employment
(Blue Card Directive),
OJ 2009 L 155/17 ..... 15–16, 16n.39
Preamble
Recital 15 .... 16n.40
Directive 2013/33/EU of 26 June
2013 laying down standards for
the reception of applicants for
international protection (recast),
OJ 2013 L 180/96
Preamble
Recital 24 .... 16n.40
Article 2 .... 13, 13n.29
Directive 2014/54/EU on measures
facilitating the exercise of
rights conferred on workers in
the context of freedom of
movement for workers,
OJ 2014 L 128/8 .... 122n.169
Preamble
Recital 1 121–22
Article 2
Article 2(2) 122n.169
Directive 2014/66/EU of 15 May
2014 on the conditions of entry
and residence of third-country
nationals in the framework of
an intra-corporate transfer,
OJ 2014 L 157/1
Preamble
Recital 18 .... 16n.40

xvi   TABLE OF LEGISLATION

Directive 2014/67/EU of 15 May 2014
on the enforcement of Directive
96/71/EC concerning the posting
of workers in the framework of
the provision of services and
amending Regulation 1024/
2012/EU on administrative
cooperation through the Internal
Market Information System,
OJ 2014 L 159/11 ..... 65–66, 65n.105
Directive 2016/801/EU of 11 May
2016 on the conditions of entry
and residence of third-country
nationals for the purposes of
research, studies, training,
voluntary service, pupil exchange
schemes or educational projects
and au pairing, OJ 2016 L 132/21
Preamble
Recital 41 .... 16n.40
Directive 2018/957/EU of 28 June
2018 amending Directive 96/71/EC
concerning the posting of
workers in the framework of
the provision of services (Revised
Posted Workers Directive, or
RPWD), OJ 2018 L 173/16 39–41,
40n.6, 65–66, 66n.106, 67–68,
69, 70–72, 83, 84–85, 86
Preamble 66
Recital 6 .... 66, 66n.107
Recital 10 .... 67, 67n.108
Recital 24 70–71

Regulations

Regulation 1612/68/EEC of the Council
of 15 October 1968 on freedom of
movement for workers within the
Community, OJ 1968 L 257/2 28–29,
28n.106, 35–36, 47–48, 49–50, 91n.14,
101–2, 120, 121, 123–24, 130–31, 130n.6
Preamble
Recital 3 .... 92n.18
Recital 4 .... 36n.143
Article 7
Article 7(2) 91–92, 94–95, 121
Article 10..................... 91n.14
Article 11..................... 91n.14
Regulation 1251/70/EEC on the
right of workers to remain in the

territory of a Member State after
having been employed in that
State, OJ 1970 L 142/24 ...... 101n.67
Article 2..................... 111–12
Article 3
Article 3(2) 101–2
Regulation 1408/71/EEC of the Council
of 14 June 1971 on the application of
social security schemes to employed
persons and their families moving
within the Community,
OJ 1971 L 149/2..... 14n.30, 52, 140, 144
Regulation 883/2004/EC of the
European Parliament and of the
Council of 29 April 2004 on the
coordination of social security
systems (Social Security
Regulation), OJ 2004 L 166/1 18,
18n.50, 104–5, 104n.81,
125–26, 128n.3, 131, 135–36,
137–38, 140, 144, 151
Preamble
Recital 8 104
Article 6..................... 18n.50
Article 7....................... 132
Chapter 8 (Articles 67–69) 132
Article 67..................... 132
Article 68..................... 132
Article 68(1) 132
Article 68(1)(a) 132
Regulation 593/2008/EC of the
European Parliament and of the
Council of 17 June 2008 on the
law applicable to contractual
obligations (Rome I Regulation),
OJ 2008 L 177/1 .... 51nn.48–49
Article 20..................... 51n.49
Regulation 987/2009/EC of the
European Parliament and of the
Council of 16 September 2009
laying down the procedure for
implementing Regulation 883/2004,
OJ 2009 L 284/1 .... 128n.3, 131
Regulation 492/2011/EU on freedom
of movement for workers within
the Union, OJ 2011 L 141/1 88–89,
89n.5, 90, 91–92, 97, 98n.49,
99, 104–6, 111, 113, 117–24,
122n.169, 132n.13, 138
Preamble
Recital 4 .... 92n.18

TABLE OF LEGISLATION   xvii

Articles 1–6 119–20
Article 7 117–18
    Article 7(1) 99, 132n.13
    Article 7(2) 95–98, 98n.49, 99,
        103–4, 103n.78, 105–6, 113, 117–18,
        121–24, 132n.13, 137–38, 169n.50
    Article 10 . . . . 97–98, 100, 117–18,
        120, 122–23, 164n.25, 169n.50
Regulation 1051/2013/EU of the
    European Parliament and of the
    Council of 22 October 2013
    amending Regulation 562/
    2006/EC in order to provide for
    common rules on the temporary
    reintroduction of border control
    at internal borders in exceptional
    circumstances, OJ 2015
    L 295/1 . . . . 22n.71
Regulation 2016/399/EU of the
    European Parliament and of the
    Council of 9 March 2016 on a
    Union Code on the rules
    governing the movement of
    persons across borders
    (Schengen Borders Code),
    OJ 2016 L 77/1 . . . . . . 10n.11, 14n.32,
        21–23, 28, 28n.105
    Preamble 22–23
    Recital 26 22–23
    Article 8 . . . . 9–10, 10n.12
    Article 2
    Article 2(5) 13–14
    Article 20 . . . . 21, 21n.66
    Article 21 21
    Article 21(a) 21–22
    Article 25 . . . . 22, 28n.105
    Article 25(1) 28n.105
    Article 25(4) 28n.105
    Article 26 22
    Article 27 . . . . 28n.105
    Article 28 22
    Article 29 22–23

Decisions

Commission Decision 2011/833/EU
    of 12 December 2011 on the reuse
    of Commission documents, OJ
    2011 L 330/39 . . . . 133*f*, 134*f*
Council Decision 2020/135/EU of 30
    January 2020 on the conclusion of

the Agreement on the withdrawal
    of the United Kingdom of Great
    Britain and Northern Ireland from
    the European Union and the
    European Atomic Energy
    Community, OJ 2020 L 29/1 . . . 182–83,
        182n.99, 184

Recommendations, opinions and other instruments

Act concerning the conditions of
    accession of the Kingdom
    of Spain and the Portuguese
    Republic and the adjustments
    to the Treaties (Act of Accession),
    OJ 1985 L 302/23 . . . . . . 47–49, 83–84
    Article 216 48
Commission Opinion 2015/7100/EC
    of 23 October 2015 on the necessity
    and proportionality of the controls
    at internal borders reintroduced
    by Germany and Austria pursuant
    to Article 24(4) of Regulation
    562/2006/EC (Schengen Borders),
    C(2015)7100 . . . . 23n.76
Council Recommendation of 8
    November 2019 on access to
    social protection for workers
    and the self- employed,
    OJ 2019 C 387/1 . . . 124–25, 125n.180
Council Recommendation 2020/912/EU
    of 30 June 2020 on the temporary
    restriction on non-essential
    travel into the EU and the
    possible lifting of such restriction,
    OJ 2020 L 208I/1 . . . . 30, 30n.116

OTHER SUPRANATIONAL CONVENTIONS

Council of Europe

European Convention on Human
    Rights and Fundamental
    Freedoms (ECHR) 1950 . . . . . 62n.95,
        72–73n.128, 182
    Article 11 . . . . 62n.95
European Social Charter (ESC) 61–62
    Article 19 62–63
    Article 19(4) 62–63

xviii TABLE OF LEGISLATION

United Nations

Convention on the Rights of the
Child 1989 147–48
Article 12 147–48
Article 24 .... 147–48, 147n.46
Convention relating to the Status of
Refugees 1951 27–28
Article 1F(a) 27–28

BILATERAL/MULTILATERAL AGREEMENTS

Agreement on the European Economic
Area (EEA Agreement),
OJ 1994 L 1/3 .... 32–33, 94–95
Agreement creating an Association
between the European Economic
Community and Turkey (Ankara
Agreement), OJ 1977 L 361/29 31,
31n.121, 32–33, 35
Article 12 .... 31n.122
Additional Protocol
Article 37 .... 31n.122
Agreement on the Withdrawal of
the United Kingdom of Great
Britain and Northern Ireland
from the European Union and
the European Atomic Energy
Community (Withdrawal
Agreement), OJ 2019
C 384I/01 .... 158–69, 159n.7,
161–62n.17, 163n.21, 165n.31,
166n.36, 168n.44, 170–74,
173–74n.74, 175–77, 178–79,
179n.87, 180, 182–83, 183n.100, 184
Article 4 .... 161n.14
Article 4(4) 176
Part II (Articles 9–12) 160, 168–69
Article 10 .... 161–62n.17, 163
Article 10(1) 168n.47
Article 10(1)(b) 179n.87
Article 10(1)(c) 161–62n.17
Article 10(1)(d) 161–62n.17
Article 10(1)(e)
Article 10(1)(e)(iii) 168n.46
Article 10(2) 168n.48
Article 10(3) 168n.49
Article 10(4) 168n.49
Article 10(5) 168n.49

Article 12 163
Article 13 161–62
Article 13(1) 161–62
Article 15 .... 161n.12
Article 18 .... 161n.12, 162–63
Article 18(1) 170n.54
Article 18(1)(b) 162n.20
Article 18(1)(c) 162n.20
Article 18(1)(d) 170n.55
Article 18(1)(h) 165n.31
Article 18(1)(p) 170n.56
Article 18(1)(r) 165n.30,
170n.53, 175–76
Article 20
Article 20(1) 170n.58
Article 20(2) 170n.58
Article 23 168–69
Article 24
Article 24(2) 163
Article 25
Article 25(2) 163
Article 127 182
Article 158 .... 161n.14
Article 164
Article 164(5)
Article 164(5)(d) 168n.44
Decision 1/80 of the Association
Council of the EEC and Turkey
of 19 December 1980 on the
development of the
Association 31–32
Article 6 .... 31n.123
Article 6(1) 106
Decision of the Heads of State
or Government of 18 and
19 February 2016, meeting
with the European Council,
concerning a New Settlement
for the United Kingdom
within the European Union,
OJ 2016 C 691/1 25–26,
26n.91, 30–31, 108–9, 108n.108,
125–26, 136, 136n.20, 184
Trade and Cooperation Agreement
between the European Union
and the European Atomic
Energy Community, of the one
part, and the United Kingdom
of Great Britain and Northern

Ireland, of the other part (Trade
and Cooperation Agreement, or
TCA), OJ 2021 L 149/10 158–59,
159n.8, 181

NATIONAL LEGISLATION

Czech Republic

Act No 117/1995 Coll. on State
Social Support 152

Estonia

Income Tax Act of 1999 152

Germany

Arbeitnehmer-Entsendegesetz
[Posted Workers Law] 64–65

The Netherlands

Algemene Kinderbijslagwet [General
Child Benefit Act] of 1962,
as amended 157
Act on Child-Related Allowance 157

United Kingdom

Human Rights Act 1998 176

Notes on Contributors

Ségolène Barbou des Places is Professor of Public and European Law at the Sorbonne Law School, Paris 1 University. She is one of the joint editors of *European Papers: A Journal on Law and Integration*, and co-director of the *GIS-Eurolab*, an interdisciplinary network of 200 researchers on the European Union. Her research examines questions of substantive EU law with a particular focus on free movement law, European Union citizenship, and migration law. She analyzes the different ways in which the different forms of mobility organized at EU level are articulated, and she investigates the way in which EU law 'constructs the person' and the European society.

Sacha Garben is Professor of EU Law at the Legal Studies Department of the College of Europe, Bruges. She is furthermore an official in the European Commission, currently on leave to be at the College of Europe full time. She has published widely on a range of constitutional and substantive aspects of EU law, and takes a special interest in Social Europe.

Niamh Nic Shuibhne is Professor of EU Law at the University of Edinburgh. Her research examines substantive EU law from a constitutional perspective, with particular focus on principle-based analysis of free movement and Union citizenship. She was awarded a Leverhulme Trust Major Research Fellowship (2016–2019) to examine how protection of the commitment to equal treatment in EU law came to represent an ideological challenge for the Union: how it became a 'confounding' rather than founding EU value. Her current research explores the integrity of the EU legal order as well as the concepts and principles that both constitute and distinguish it. Niamh is a Joint Editor of the *Common Market Law Review*.

Joakim Palme is Professor of Political Science at Uppsala University. He has published extensively on the welfare state and inequality as well as social investment. Joakim is the co-editor of *Welfare and the Great Recession* (2019). He was the Director of the Institute for Future Studies in Stockholm in 2002–2010. Since 2013, he has been the Chairman of Delmi, the independent Migration Studies Delegation (www.delmi.se) appointed by the Swedish Government in 2013, which is actively engaged in migration policy discussions.

Martin Ruhs is Professor of Migration Studies and Deputy Director of the Migration Policy Centre (MPC) at the European University Institute in Florence. Martin is the author of *The Price of Rights: Regulating International Labor Migration* (2013) and co-editor (with Kristof Tamas and Joakim Palme) of *Bridging the Gaps: Linking Research to Public Debates and Policy Making on Migration and Integration* (2019). He was a Member of the UK's Migration Advisory Committee in 2007–2014.

Eleanor Spaventa is Professor of European Union Law at Bocconi University, Director of the Bocconi Lab for European Studies (BLEST), and Visiting Professor at the College of Europe in Bruges. Her areas of interest include Union citizenship and Brexit, as well as fundamental rights and the constitutional dimension of the EU.

1

Introduction: Revisiting EU Law on the Free Movement of Persons

Niamh Nic Shuibhne

1. Introduction

How 'free' is the free movement of persons? And why, and in what respects, does the law that enables and supports it need to be 'revisited'? This collection of essays, curated by Claire Kilpatrick and Joanne Scott for the European University Institute's (EUI) 2020 Academy of European Law, was conceived to address these questions.

Ironically, the Academy courses on which the chapters are based had to pivot to online delivery in the early summer of 2020. The follow-up Authors' Workshop was also convened virtually, in the spring of 2021. This meant that we were considering what it means to move freely within the meaning of EU law from our own respective homes and the perspective of *not* being able to do something that we had all come to take for granted. Nevertheless, we could connect, something that we did not take for granted. Following the individual delivery of each of the courses, a wider conversation was facilitated through the Workshop by bringing the convenors, authors, and EUI researchers acting as discussants together for collective reflection. Over the course of that day, we considered complexity and concepts; exclusion and inclusion; context and narratives; convergence and asymmetries; risks and tensions; control and fairness; integration and solidarity. We identified and evaluated changes over time. We were also alert to the tendency towards self-referentialism, both in terms of how we frame and assess EU free movement law with reference primarily to EU legal texts (including EU case law) and EU-centric scholarship; and of how we still use the European Economic Community (EEC) Treaty's conception of the free movement of persons, even if later progressed by the creation of Union citizenship, as the barometer for whether we have 'achieved—or betrayed—the "real" and "original" objectives of its founding fathers', as Ségolène Barbou des Places puts it in her chapter (Chapter 2).

We considered too how the free movement of persons connects to and is shaped by the EU legal spaces beyond the free movement of persons. For example, several chapters engage with how EU citizenship law intersects with the protection of fundamental rights. Eleanor Spaventa, in Chapter 6, identifies a sharp mismatch

---

Niamh Nic Shuibhne, *Introduction: Revisiting EU Law on the Free Movement of Persons* In: *Revisiting the Fundamentals of the Free Movement of Persons in EU Law*. First Edition. Edited by: Niamh Nic Shuibhne, Oxford University Press.
© Niamh Nic Shuibhne 2023. DOI: 10.1093/oso/9780198886273.003.0001

between the Court of Justice's emphasis on Member State nationality as the key to free movement rights, on the one hand, and the boundary-free ethos of the EU's internal market and Union citizenship's insistence on the territory of the Union as a composite space, on the other. Martin Ruhs and Joakim Palme take us to the space beyond law in Chapter 5, holding a mirror up to entrenched legal perspectives that do not necessarily fit with political or economic conceptions of 'free' movement. In their view, focusing on the Union as an entity divorced from its Member States only compounds longstanding tensions. They emphasize that 'it is necessary to explore the role of institutional characteristics and reforms of European welfare states as sources of discontent with the current rules for free movement'. Their chapter also forces us to think about mechanisms for addressing minority political views when such views *persist*, given that a minority of Member States cannot bring about legislative change within the EU system.

Most remarkably, though, since we had been given considerable freedom to shape our individual courses, two themes emerged both organically and strongly over the Workshop discussions as well as the written contributions that we present here, as we seek to revisit some of the fundamentals of EU free movement (law)—its *categories* and its *fragility*.

2. Revisiting the Categories of EU Law on the Free Movement of Persons

EU citizenship law communicates a deceptively simple message of regulatory streamlining in two related ways. First, there is the assertion that Union citizenship is 'the *fundamental status* of nationals of the Member States, enabling those who find themselves in the same situation to enjoy the same treatment in law irrespective of their nationality, subject to such exceptions as are expressly provided for'.[1] Second, one of the central aims of Directive 2004/38 was therefore 'to codify and review the existing Community instruments dealing separately with workers, self-employed persons, as well as students and other inactive persons in order to simplify and strengthen the right of free movement and residence of all Union citizens', with 'a view to remedying this sector-by-sector, piecemeal approach to the right of free movement and residence and facilitating the exercise of this right' by adopting 'a single legislative act'.[2] And yet, and in large part independently of each other, the chapters in this volume identify and confront persisting *categories* in EU law on the free movement of persons.

[1] Case C-184/99, *Grzelczyk v. Centre public d'aide sociale d'Ottignies-Louvain-la-Neuve* (EU:C:2001:458), para. 31 (emphasis added).
[2] Directive 2004/38/EC on the right of citizens of the Union and their family members to move and reside freely within the territory of the Member States, OJ 2004 L 158/77, recitals 3 and 4.

They do so in several ways. First, notwithstanding the 'fundamental status' of Union citizenship or the aims of the Directive, categories continue to fulfil a function of *allocation or assignment* so that the 'correct' basis of Treaty or legislative protection can be identified. However, in her exploration of the optimal Treaty home for posted workers, Sacha Garben (Chapter 3) challenges how the formal categories of 'persons' are drawn in EU law and shows why people can end up being problematically 'misplaced'. Similarly, my contribution (Chapter 4) explores the extent to which the category of economically active Union citizen is shaped, both positively and negatively, by developments in EU citizenship law. Spaventa examines the category of Union citizenship itself, in terms of the limited extent to which EU law protects former Union citizens following the UK's withdrawal from the EU. Thus, while Garben calls for existing categories to be reconsidered, my chapter shows how they interrelate, and Spaventa's work shows how new categories are created.

Second, there is the idea of categories as establishing *boundaries*; illustrated, for example, by Barbou des Places' unpacking of the normative and legal qualities of migration and free movement in EU law and by Spaventa's critique of the extent to which Member State nationality fixes a boundary so rigid that it diminishes the prospects of protecting former Member State nationals. However, third, there is, at the same time, significant evidence of *cross-fertilization* in a substantive sense across categories that are formally more distinct—demonstrated revealingly, through Barbou des Places' account of the entwined pasts, presents, and futures of EU free movement law and EU migration law; aspirationally, through Garben's argument that posted workers are workers within the meaning of Article 45 of the Treaty on the Functioning of the European Union (TFEU); and problematically, through my concern about the increasing prevalence of citizenship-oriented integration requirements and financial means questioning in economic free movement law as well as through Ruhs and Palme's account of how categories collide in their juxtaposition of the different foundational principles of national social security protection and EU free movement law.

How well are we served now, therefore, by the conventional categories of EU free movement law? Do they still represent meaningful differences? Do they act as valuable compass points or inhibitors of innovation in the task of navigating complex legal frameworks? Do they ensure comprehensive or fragmented protection of the person? Do the categories of EU law on the free movement persons enable proper account to be taken of the rights and freedoms of others? Do they sustain protective legal threads through periods of political and social volatility, or do they constrain our thinking about optimal ways to reform free movement law? Above all, considering how the categories of free movement law, those both obvious and more subtle, are constructed, sustained, or transgressed enabled all of us to call attention to tensions that we have not yet properly resolved: between appropriate differentiation and problematic discrimination, for example, and between

4 NIAMH NIC SHUIBHNE

the mythology and the experienced reality of free movement for the people who actually move.

3. The Fragility of the Free Movement of Persons

In EU law, the free movement of persons presents itself through a series of apparently indissociable linkages: for example, between the person and the EU's internal market; between Union citizenship and the nationality of the Member States; and perhaps most profoundly, as we reflected on each other's contributions at the Authors' Workshop, between the means of free movement and the ends of what we often refer to as the project of European integration.[3] The interconnectedness of free movement and the Union's objectives as a polity means that, as Garben argues in her exploration of 'fair' mobility, 'without a legitimate methodology to debate and decide on it, the topic becomes explosive and has the potential to blow up the entire enterprise'. Addressing fairness in a different way, Ruhs and Palme reflect on the 'fairness concerns that arise from the clash of institutional logics at the heart of the current system'. More specifically, they argue that 'EU policies with institutional logics that are fundamentally different from prevailing national policies and norms are likely to be seen as "fundamentally unfair" by the publics ... of Member States ... [thereby] not only feed[ing] political tensions about the exportability of child benefits but also potentially threaten[ing] the political sustainability of free movement itself'.

Do we take the foundations of EU free movement law for granted? Do we presume shared commitment to its distinctiveness, without rigorous questioning of its implications? For, as observed by Barbou des Places, '[f]ree movement is no longer unanimously viewed as a metric of progress in the human condition for those crossing international borders in Europe'.

The contributors to this volume do not shy away from provoking a rethink of fundamental principles or the presumed conceptual, even moral, underpinnings of the free movement of persons. As a starting point, there are legal arguments to consider here: for example, the 'changed (constitutional) context of the post-Lisbon EU legal order', as highlighted by Garben. From a more normative perspective, we have been grappling for some time with central features of the free movement paradigm, and notably its (conferred rather than inherent) exclusionary nature both with

---

[3] The Court expressed this means/ends idea in Opinion 1/91 (EU:C:1991:490), esp. at para. 50; as developed further in Opinion 2/13 (EU:C:2014:2454), para. 172 ('The pursuit of the EU's objectives, as set out in Article 3 TEU, is entrusted to a series of fundamental provisions, such as those providing for the free movement of goods, services, capital and persons, citizenship of the Union, the area of freedom, security and justice, and competition policy. Those provisions, which are part of the framework of a system that is specific to the EU, are structured in such a way as to contribute—each within its specific field and with its own particular characteristics—to the implementation of the process of integration that is the *raison d'être* of the EU itself').

respect to nationality and also in terms of economic capacity, as Spaventa under-lines. There are other critical questions that we have not faced up to yet to anything like the same extent, such as the Union's colonial history and the implications of taking a narrow approach to Member State nationality in that light. If Europe is a space where 'free movers can dream different lives', as Barbou des Places suggests, what kind of dreams are—will in the future be—supported for those who also in-habit (or wish to inhabit) the European space? In that light, she raises challenging questions for all of us about the 'exceptionalism' embedded in free movement law, which necessarily then shapes the 'European venture as a whole'.

At the same time, Barbou des Places reflects on *why* free movement law is dis-tinctive and she outlines a case for why it should remain so by highlighting and appealing for the furthering of European integration's progressive purpose. Importantly, this perspective, she argues, encourages—requires, even—ways to make free movement law *better*, not to abandon freedom of movement. In essence, the chapters in this volume interrogate the underpinning models and (changing) objectives of the free movement of persons to take up precisely the challenges and the ambition to do free movement law better. Revisiting free movement law en-tails disruption, so perhaps the central message is this: while the authors engage with and propose different ways to revisit the fundamentals of EU free movement law, there are shared aims of making it both more protective of people and more resilient in ethical, systemic, and sociological senses; and a shared sense too of the free movement of persons as a worthwhile and distinctive ligament of the EU. In short, we want to do free movement better.

2

Is Free Movement (Law) Fully Emancipated from Migration (Law)?

Ségolène Barbou des Places[*]

1. Introduction

This chapter questions the 'exceptionalism' of free movement and free movement law. Every student of European Union (EU) law is educated to believe that the EU has constructed its own and exceptional—i.e. unparalleled—regime of human mobility. There exists nowhere else, in either international or regional law,[1] even in the systems that have created regional citizenship,[2] such a legal regime: one that allows non-nationals to cross a border freely; to enjoy non-discrimination on grounds of nationality for civil, economic, and social rights; and to benefit from the host society's solidarity. Free movement is thus considered the main expression of European identity and is accordingly deemed the main pillar of the EU construction. There is indeed an intimate link between the rights granted to individuals under EU law, in particular the right to free movement, and the nature and *ethos* of European integration.[3] This is why the perceived threat of Schengen's demise—which resurfaced with the reintroduction of internal borders controls in the context of the 2015 crisis and, more recently,

---

[*] The very first draft of this chapter was read and discussed by Nina Hetmanska, to whom I dedicate the text in memory of her passion for intellectual reflection and her commitment to migrants' rights. I am grateful for all those who have commented on the work during its gestation and on papers in draft: the participants of the Academy of European Law, the researchers of the *Centre de droit européen* (Université Libre de Bruxelles), and Niamh Nic Shuibhne, for their very helpful remarks. The usual disclaimer applies.

[1] For a presentation of the EU as the 'forefront' of workers' mobility, followed suit by the ASEAN, see Rubrico, 'Free Flow, 'Management Movement: Labour Mobility Policies in ASEAN and the EU', 2015/03 European Institute for Asian Studies Briefing Paper (October 2015). See also R. Hansen et al. (eds), *Migration, Nation States, and International Cooperation* (2011).

[2] Weinrich, 'Varieties of Citizenship in Regional Organisations: A Cross-Regional Comparison of Rights, Access, and Belonging', 24(4) *International Area Studies Review* (2021) 255.

[3] See de Witte, 'The Liminal European: Subject to the EU Legal Order', 1 *Yearbook of European Law* (2021) 26. Since Case 139/85, *Kempf* (EU:C:1986:223), at para. 13, the Court holds that 'freedom of movement for individuals is one of the foundations of the European Union'.

Ségolène Barbou des Places, *Is Free Movement (Law) Fully Emancipated from Migration (Law)?* In: *Revisiting the Fundamentals of the Free Movement of Persons in EU Law*. First Edition. Edited by: Niamh Nic Shuibhne, Oxford University Press. © Ségolène Barbou des Places 2023. DOI: 10.1093/oso/9780198886273.003.0002

of the Covid-19 pandemic—led many observers to worry for the European venture as a whole.[4] For the same reason, the 'Dano quintet'[5] provoked strong backlash as the Court of Justice ended a period of construction, and expansion, of free movement rights.[6] In a similar vein, Brexit was a seismic shock in the European landscape, particularly for the millions who lost their EU citizenship and so came to the harsh realization that free movement was a very fragile *acquis*. It is thus generally acknowledged that the past decade has been characterized by regression, rather than progression, with regard to free movement and EU citizenship law.

Simultaneously, an increasingly critical narrative around free movement law has surfaced.[7] Free movement is no longer unanimously viewed as a metric of progress in the human condition for those crossing international borders in Europe. Rather, its critics would argue, free movement law supports a process of 'disaffiliation' of the individuals, and takes no consideration of national communities, or their coherence and identity. The 'elitist' nature of free movement law[8] is also seen as undermining the development of a more robust conception of EU citizenship, which would strengthen rather than destabilize national welfare systems, and so

---

[4] Salom and Rijpma, 'A Europe Without Internal Frontiers: Challenging the Reintroduction of Border Controls in the Schengen Area in the Light of Union Citizenship', *German Law Journal* (2021) 1; De Somer, Tekin, and Meissner, 'Schengen under Pressure: Differentiation or Disintegration?', 2020/7 *EUIDA Policy Papers* (September 2020); Comte and Lavenex, 'Differentiation and De-Differentiation in EU Border Controls, Asylum and Police Cooperation', 57 *The International Spectator. Italian Journal of International Affairs* (2002) 124; Guild, 'Schengen Borders and Multiple National States of Emergency: From Refugees to Terrorism to COVID-19', 23 *European Journal of Migration and Law* (2021) 385. For a very different approach, Votoupalova, 'The Wrong Critiques: Why Internal Border Controls Don't Mean the End of Schengen', 27 *New Perspectives. Interdisciplinary Journal of Central & East European Politics and International Relations* (2019) 7.

[5] I.e. Case C-140/12, *Brey* (EU:C:2013:565); Case C-333/13, *Dano* (EU:C:2014:2358); Case C-67/14, *Alimanovic* (EU:C:2015:597); Case C-308/14, *Commission v. UK* (EU:C:2016:436); and Case C-299/14, *Garcia-Nieto* (EU:C:2016:114).

[6] For a very critical reading, O'Brien, 'Civis Capitalist Sum: Class as the New Guiding Principle of EU Free Movement Rights', 53 *Common Market Law Review* (2016) 937. See also Nic Shuibhne, 'Limits Rising, Duties Ascending: The Changing Legal Shape of Union Citizenship', 53 *Common Market Law Review* (2015) 889; Spaventa, 'Earned Citizenship – Understanding Union Citizenship Through its Scope', in D. Kochenov (ed.), *EU Citizenship and Federalism: The Role of Rights* (2017) 204. Differently Carter and Jesse, 'The "Dano Evolution": Assessing Legal Integration and Access to Social Benefits for EU Citizens', 3(3) *European Papers* (2018) 1179. Finally, for a very different approach, Davies, 'Has the Court Changed or Have the Cases? The Deservingness of Litigants as an Element in Court of Justice Citizenship Adjudication', 25(4) *Journal of European Public Policy* (2018) 1442. And the response, by Hoogenboom, 'CJEU Case Law on EU Citizenship: Normatively Consistent? Unlikely! A response to Davies "Has the Court Changed or Have the Cases?"', 13 November 2018, available online at EU Law Analysis, eulawanalysis.blogspot.com (last accessed 4 July 2021).

[7] The most prominent critique has come from Somek, 'The Individualisation of Liberty: Europe's Move from Emancipation to Empowerment', 4 *Transnational Legal Theory* (2013) 258. See also Somek, 'Alienation, Despair and Social Freedom', in L. Azoulai, S. Barbou des Places, and E. Pataut (eds), *Constructing the Person in EU Law. Rights, Roles, Identities* (2016) 5. See on a different note the critical approach by Menendez, 'Which Free Movement? Whose Free Movement?', in S. Borelli and A. Guazzarotti (eds), *Labour Mobility and Transnational Solidarity in the European Union* (2019) 7.

[8] Davies, 'How Citizenship Divides: The New Legal Class of Transnational Europeans', 4(3) *European Papers* (2019) 675.

8 SÉGOLÈNE BARBOU DES PLACES

in turn the sense of belonging to the European Community. The criticism is becoming increasingly significant.

However, whether these appraisals are positive or negative, the description of free movement law that we find in the EU law literature tends to remain self-referential.[9] Most academic analyses revolve around determining whether the legislator and the Court of Justice have achieved—or betrayed—the 'real' and 'original' objectives of its founding fathers. But the degree of achievement of free movement (law) is predominantly evaluated on the basis of its effect on the EU itself and on Europeans alone. Such a reading tends to neglect the fact that free movement (law) was not created in a vacuum, and moreover, that it does not operate in a territory where EU citizens are the only people to move. The EU also regulates the mobility of people who are not 'free movers'. Hence arises the necessity to understand how free movement and migration relate, interact with, and influence each other.

This chapter thus aims to show that free movement is part of a larger system of international mobility. Considering free movement in this broader context enables us to devise an analytical framework that aligns more closely with reality because, as mentioned previously, free movement is not insulated from external influence. As different groups of people move into a single territory, free movement and migration constantly interact. Therefore, legal regimes constructed for migrants and free movers interact with and influence each other. The chapter thus identifies different kinds of relationships between free movement and migration in EU law: these range from separation and opposition, in contrast to influence and convergence. However, the objective is not to build a typology of the relationships that exist between free movement and migration. Rather, the goal is to understand how free movement was 'constructed' as an exceptional form of mobility (which has very little in common with ordinary regimes of 'migration') and then to address the exception hypothesis. The chapter asks simple, yet provocative questions: Is free movement (still) as exceptional as it is claimed to be? Is not free movement an ordinary type of migration after all?

Asking these questions does not equate to a plea for limiting or eroding free movement in EU law. The goal of the chapter is not to support the idea that *free movement* should be reduced to *fair mobility* in the sense supported by Catherine Barnard.[10] On the contrary, it aims to show that the exceptionalism of free movement (law) is a fragile construction. Absent the narrative underpinning *free* movement law, the regime of free mobility enshrined in the Treaty, and implemented by

---

[9] This is different in sociology or political science. For instance, Ruhs, '"Migrants", "Mobile Citizens" and the Borders of Exclusion in the European Union', in R. Baübock (ed.), *Debating European Citizenship* (2019) 163, argues that we need to connect debates about the free movement of EU citizens with discussions about immigration policies towards people from outside Europe.

[10] Barnard, 'Free Movement Vs. Fair Movement: Brexit and Managed Migration', 55(3) *Common Market Law Review* (2018) 203.

secondary law norms, could indeed turn out to be a banal regime of economic migration law. This is why the chapter aims to understand how and why the European regime of mobility has been progressively emancipated from migration law. It thus investigates the exceptionalism of free movement law, as well as its limitations.

The chapter is divided into four further parts. In the first, it assumes a constructivist perspective. The roles of the legislator, of the Court of Justice, and of EU legal scholarship in the construction of exception are scrutinized. The objective is to understand how and why free movement has been developed and conceived as a special and unequalled regime of human mobility. The chapter analyses how the divide between free movement and migration in EU law was constructed, and explains how and why they have progressively become separate regimes of mobility, each based on a specific domain of EU law. On a conceptual level, the chapter shows that free movement was constructed as a fundamentally different form of mobility, which was constantly contrasted with the default form of mobility: migration.

In its second part, the chapter questions the 'exceptionalism' of EU free movement law. It aims to show that free movement and migration are intertwined realities: that they are indeed connected at both structural and conceptual levels. Recent crises, which remind us that turbulences in migration management have a direct impact on free movement, have forced us to reinvestigate the overlap between free movement and migration in EU law. Looking at recent case law, moreover, it also becomes more apparent that many notions of free movement law are borrowed from the realm of migration law.

Stemming from these considerations, the third part of the chapter shows that what makes free movement law so unique was the evolution and the progressivism supported by the EU institutions, including but not only the Court of Justice's dynamic interpretation of both Treaty provisions and secondary legislation. As the context has changed, however, the dominant narrative has evolved, and free movement now appears to be a more fragile reality. Absent the logic of evolution and progression, which underpinned the EU institutional approach, what in fact separates free movement and migration in EU law could well be a difference in intensity, rather than in substance. Part four provides concluding remarks. It draws attention to the risk inherent in proposals that aim to recalibrate free movement (law). The narrative underpinning free movement law is part of its exceptionalism and breaking with it comes with consequences.

2. The Making of Exception

The two-lines division at European airports symbolizes the divide between 'migration' and 'free movement' in EU law, with different groups of people following different rules of entry into the EU. The separation even lies at the heart of the

Schengen system, as Article 8 of the Schengen Borders Code (SBC)[11] distinguishes between 'thorough checks' on entry for third country nationals and 'minimal checks' as 'the rule for persons enjoying the right of free movement under Union law'.[12] Years after the entry into force of the Schengen agreements, this division has become part of our mental representation of migration versus free movement; it underpins our vision of people's mobility in the EU.

It is, nonetheless, a mere construct. The making of exception is indeed the fruit of a collective work of, first, those who drafted the Treaty; second, of the legislator; and, third, of the Court of Justice and EU legal scholarship. Free movement law was first invented as a new way to organize labour mobility (A). It was then progressively separated and insulated from migration law, thus drawing a clear-cut line which increasingly divided these two spheres of EU law (B). Over time, a dominant narrative has emerged, grounded in the scholar's interpretation of the Court's case law. This narrative stresses the peculiarities of free movement, which is deemed 'new' and 'progressive': it has been characterized as a *distinct form* of international human mobility (C).

A. Invention. Conceiving a New Regime of Labour Mobility

In 1951 and in 1957, the drafters of the Paris Treaty and of the European Economic Community (EEC) Treaty were not in unanimous agreement that a completely new regime of international mobility had to be created. Indeed, apart from Italy, the Member States' negotiators were not convinced that a regime of 'freedom of movement', rather than of economic migration, had to be promoted.[13] The other Member States indeed aimed to retain the logic of classic international migration law:[14] at the beginning of the negotiations of the Schuman Plan, France and the Benelux countries wished to remain in full control of labour inflows.

In contrast, the Italian government supported a system of free movement of workers, broadly defined as including 'free job-seeking circulation' (migration would be allowed before the migrant was employed) and free movement for all workers (rather than restricted to skilled workers). Gradually, some other Member

---

[11] Regulation 2016/399/EU of 9 March 2016 on a Union Code on the rules governing the movement of persons across borders (Schengen Borders Code), OJ 2016 L 77/1.

[12] The sixth paragraph of Article 8 also underlines the separation between the two procedures applicable at border crossings, as checks on a person enjoying the right of free movement shall be carried out in accordance with Directive 2004/38/EC on the right of citizens of the Union and their family members to move and reside freely within the territory of the Member States, OJ 2004 L158/77.

[13] On the Treaty negotiations, see S. Goedings, *Labor Migration in an Integrating Europe* (2005).

[14] At the Conference in Messina (June 1955), the Foreign Affairs Ministers adopted a resolution, which stresses the need to gradually set up the common market and to progressively open the national markets to the workers from the other Member States. In November 1955 a note was prepared by the Inter-Governmental Committee which recognized the need for certain safeguards clauses in case of an influx of workforce that would cause risk to certain industries.

States followed suit: Germany[15] and Belgium started supporting the inclusion of a free movement of workers agreement in the Paris Treaty. In the end, the 'conflict between the two expressions of the expression "free movement of workers" however remained unsettled',[16] and the Paris Treaty only mentioned, in neutral terms, the abolition of restrictions based on nationality permitting the employment of skilled workers from within the Community.[17]

The concept of free movement of workers, Goedings shows,[18] changed during the Treaty of Rome negotiations. In the Spaak Report, unemployment was no longer seen as a hindrance but rather as a source for European growth. Progressively, the positions of the negotiators evolved, and 'Spaak won'.[19] As he managed to convince his partners that there was no excess migration in the EEC but rather too little, the Treaty opted for a regime of 'free movement of workers' and not of privileged economic migration. A free movement clause was indeed incorporated in the Treaty and free movement of workers held an equal position to the other freedoms. Article 48 EEC contained neither reference to quotas of EEC workers nor an emergency brake in case of 'deterioration of the economic situation' of a given area. In addition, Article 226 EEC,[20] which created the 'original' common market safeguard mechanism, was only a transitional mechanism.

All together, these elements support the idea that there was something 'different' from the ordinary economic migration that international law intended from the outset. A regime of 'free movement' was created and its beneficiaries had to be limited. The free movement clause (Article 48 EEC), Emmanuel Comte explains, was indeed formulated as excluding many Member States nationals. The reason why Article 48 referred to 'workers'—and not 'national workers' as intended in the preliminary version—was indeed to 'exclude colonies':[21] France's partners opposed the free movement of labour for Algerians and inhabitants of France's Overseas Territories.

It is the case that we can find no trace of a separation between free movement and migration in 1957, migration not being mentioned in the EEC Treaty. At the same time, the Treaty does not stipulate any clear-cut divide between Member States' nationals, who enjoy the right to free movement, and third country nationals, who

---

[15] On the German position during negotiations, see E. Comte, *The History of the European Migration Regime. Germany's Strategic Hegemony* (2018).

[16] Goedings (n. 13).

[17] As for unskilled workers, their migration was to be facilitated in case production in the coal and steel sectors was restricted by a shortage of suitable workers.

[18] Goedings (n. 13) 107.

[19] Barnard (n. 10).

[20] Article 226 EEC provided: 'If, during the transitional period, difficulties arise which are serious and liable to persist in any sector of the economy or which could bring about serious consideration in the economic situation of a given area, a Member State may apply for authorisation to take protective measures in order to rectify the situation and adjust the sector concerned to the economy of the common market ...'.

[21] Comte (n. 15) 50.

remain categorized as migrants.[22] The divide between free movement and migration became apparent in the Treaties produced in later years, namely in 1999, when the drafters of the Amsterdam Treaty agreed to place migration policy under a new and specific title.

B. Separation. Insulating Free Movement Law from Migration Law

Since the Treaty of Amsterdam, free movement and migration have been explicitly divided into two different and separate regimes of human mobility, based on two different Treaty chapters. Two very different and insulated sets of secondary law norms have also been adopted since that time. As they are based on different legal sources, free movement law and migration law are logically destined to pursue different objectives. While EU free movement law is both a means to achieve an internal market, as well as a freedom attached to European citizenship, it promotes and favours mobility, thus granting mobile citizens more rights than those who are firmly settled in one Member State. The contrast is striking when compared to Chapter 2 of Title V of the Treaty on the Functioning of the European Union (TFEU), which pursues the traditional objective of migration management. Article 77 mentions 'checks' on persons and 'monitoring of the crossing of external borders', while Article 79 is about the 'action against illegal immigration and trafficking of human beings', 'repatriation', and 'removal'. The Treaty drafters have agreed on a strategy of control, which also applies to economic migrants. Migration policy has progressively become a self-sufficient policy with its own rules and objectives, which do not follow the single-market paradigm.[23]

Logically the same divide is used to structure EU secondary law, with distinct legal regimes deriving from the two Treaty chapters. Those who can rely on the free movement regime are granted a very privileged legal situation: directly applicable norms in primary EU law confer rights (of entry, residence, protection against expulsion, access to work, access to social subsidies, non-discrimination, etc.). Exceptions to free movement are narrowly interpreted and must be proportionate. Moreover, since the Treaty of Lisbon, the EU Charter of Fundamental Rights comes to be seen as an autonomous source of rights protecting EU citizens in free movement context.

---

[22] While Article 48(2) EEC signals nationality indirectly, ('[s]uch freedom of movement shall entail the abolition of any discrimination based on nationality between workers of the Member States as regards employment, remuneration and other conditions of work and employment'), Article 48(1) does not differentiate between EU Member State nationals and third country nationals: 'Freedom of movement for *workers* shall be secured within the Community' (emphasis added). Article 48(3) does not refer to nationality either.

[23] Thym, '"Citizens" and "Foreigners" in EU Law. Migration Law and its Cosmopolitan Outlook', 22(3) *European Law Journal* (2016) 296.

There is an immense discrepancy between the 'regime of rights' and the regime of administrative authorization and obligation established for migrants.[24] The latter are conferred with a limited number of subjective rights, granted to them mainly by secondary law norms. EU primary law empowers the EU legislator to define the scope and limits of their rights in situations of cross-border migration. Thus, while the legislator may opt for a generous migration regime, 'it is not constitutionally obliged to do so'.[25] Third country nationals may invoke safeguards, including human rights granted by the Charter of Fundamental Rights, but they leave much discretion for interpretation. The legal situation of migrants is mostly dependent on the national authorities' decisions on entry, residence, work, and other rights: generally speaking, national authorities are granted a significant margin of discretion. National discretion is, in contrast, much more limited in the case of free movement law.

Increasingly, EU institutions also consider that third country nationals (should) have obligations. This logic is present in the New Pact on Migration and Asylum put forward by the Commission in September 2020.[26] Already in the Return Directive,[27] obligations to report regularly to the authorities, to deposit an adequate financial guarantee, or to submit documents at a certain place have been imposed on third country nationals in order to avoid the risk of this person absconding during the period of voluntary departure. The same logic was dominant in the Dublin IV Regulation proposal,[28] which included the obligation for asylum seekers to apply in the Member State of first entry and to remain in the 'responsible State', but also to remain present and available for the authorities and to respect the transfer decision. The consequences of non-compliance range from the examination of the asylum application under an accelerated procedure to the deprivation of the reception conditions set out in Directive 2013/33.[29]

However, looking at the scope of free movement law and migration law indicates that free movement law and migration law are not only different regimes of mobility: they are also *separate* legal spheres, devised to govern the lives of different people. It was soon established that, despite the ambiguous wording of Article 48

---

[24] Shaw and Miller, 'When Legal Worlds Collide: An Exploration of What Happens when EU Free Movement Law meets UK Immigration Law', 39 *European Law Review* (2013) 137.

[25] Ibid. 316.

[26] See Commission Communication 2020/609 on a New Pact on Migration and Asylum, COM/2020/609 final.

[27] Directive 2008/115/EC on common standards and procedures in Member States for returning illegally staying third-country nationals, OJ 2008 L 348/98.

[28] Commission Proposal 2016/270 final for a Regulation establishing the criteria and mechanisms for determining the Member State responsible for examining an application for international protection lodged in one of the Member States by a third-country national or a stateless person (recast), COM/2016/0270 final.

[29] Directive 2013/33/EU of 26 June 2013 laying down standards for the reception of applicants for international protection (recast), OJ 2013 L 180/96.

14   SÉGOLÈNE BARBOU DES PLACES

EEC, migrants are excluded from free movement law.[30] Equally, EU citizens are explicitly excluded from the scope of application of EU migration law. The provisions that define the personal scope of migration directives[31] adopted in the 2000s all describe third country nationals as 'any person who is not a citizen of the Union within the meaning of Article 17(1) of the Treaty and who is not a person enjoying the Community right of free movement, as defined in Article 2(5) of the Schengen Borders Code.'[32] Accordingly, Article 3(3) of the Return Directive excludes from the scope of returns the 'persons enjoying the Community right of free movement'. This is a clear indication that those who enjoy free movement are not subject to those measures that are devoted to regulating (and denying) third country nationals' mobility.

In sum, after years of development, the EU's legal norms that organize human mobility within the EU are based on a deep divide that separates those who (have a right to) move freely and those who do not: the logic is one of differentiation between insiders and outsiders. Even legal scholarship tends to be separated along the divide as free movement lawyers and EU migration lawyers tend to form distinct groups of academics. This last element matters because EU scholarship has played a role in picturing 'free movement', in comparison with 'migration', as an unprecedented and disruptive 'form' of mobility.

C. Particularization. Portraying Distinctive 'Forms' of Mobility

Free movement and migration are not only different legal regimes of mobility: they are contrasting *forms* of mobility. By *form of mobility*, I mean that free movement and migration are not only sets of rights and obligations allocated to people, but also representations based on a certain narrative that goes hand in hand with the development of legal regimes. Free movement and migration are therefore portrayed as two distinct forms of mobility insofar as they are assumed to denote or project different aspirations and modes of life and so do not correspond to the same sense of justice.

The contrast between free movement and migration—once these are defined as *forms of mobility*—is readily perceptible when resorting to the 'key figures' of mobility, a notion I borrow from anthropological literature. Key figures, which connote a representation of an ideal-type person, indeed help us to understand what

---

[30] In its ruling in Case 238/83, *Meade* (EU:C:1984:250), the Court held that neither Regulation 1408/71/EEC of the Council of 14 June 1971 on the application of social security schemes to employed persons and their families moving within the Community, OJ 1971 L 149/2, nor Article 48 of the Treaty prevents family allowances from being withdrawn pursuant to national legislation on the ground that a child is pursuing its studies in another Member State, where the parents of the child are nationals of a non-member country.

[31] For example, Article 2 of Council Directive 2003/109/EC concerning the status of third-country nationals who are long-term residents, OJ 2004 L 16/44.

[32] Schengen Borders Code.

makes people mobile; specifically in terms of the relation they have to the places they come from and to those to which they move, as well as their reasons for migration.[33] Six key figures have emerged in the literature on mobility: the nomad, the exile, the pilgrim, the tourist, the pedestrian, and the 'flaneur'. Yet none of these can fully account for the particularity of those who are free movers and 'migrants' under EU law.[34]

By contrast, Adrian Favell,[35] who analysed the emerging patterns that are shaping Europe as a distinctive space of migration and mobility, has resorted instead to two figures, which help us to understand what distinguishes free movement from migration: 'Eurostars' and the 'traditional non-European "ethnic" (im) migrants'. In so doing, he has portrayed free movement as fundamentally different from migration. Favell's notion of 'traditional non-European "ethnic" (im) migrants' contains the idea that people are outsiders. They are assumed to have a different cultural background; coming 'from abroad', then they are supposed to remain outside the reach of protective norms.[36] These immigrants, Favell explains, raise issues of multiculturalism and inter-ethnic conflicts and they also permanently face integration injunctions. This description corresponds perfectly to the requirements present in migration law, i.e. obliging the migrants to provide evidence of x degree of integration in the host society as a condition to access rights.[37] Three other figures, 'immobilized' and 'obliged' wo/men (1) and 'augmented' wo/men (2), can be proposed as a means of complementing Favell's description. They provide an understanding of how EU law represents the lives of 'free movers' and of migrants.

1. 'Immobilized' and 'Obliged' Wo/men

A first useful figure for representing those people moving on the basis of EU migration law is that of the 'immobilized person'. As Loïc Azoulai rightly points out, 'migrants' are not destined to have a truly European life.[38] They can only project a one-way mobility (from a third State to one single Member State) and thus limit their expectations to a purely national (i.e. not more broadly *European*) life. It is

---

[33] Lindquist, 'Of Figures and Types: Brokering Knowledge and Migration in Indonesia and Beyond', 21(1) *Journal of the Royal Anthropological Institute* (2015) 162. See also Salazar, 'Theorizing Mobility through Concepts and Figures', 30(2) *Tempo Social* (2018) 153.

[34] These figures indeed aim to describe types of spatial and temporal movements and to capture the specific way in which people become part of networks and linkages. They also try to grasp what mobility means to the movers. But they do not aim to capture how legal rules shape mobility.

[35] Favell, 'Immigration, Migration and Free Movement in the Making of Europe', in J.C. Checkel and P.J. Katzenstein (eds), *European Identity* (2008) 167.

[36] The best example is the judgment in Case C-638/16, *X and X v. Belgium* (EU:C:2017:173), in which the Court denied access to the European territory to a Syrian family seeking protection in the EU. As a consequence, the situation of the claimants fell outside the scope of the Charter of Fundamental Rights.

[37] For instance, Case C-153/14, *K and A* (EU:C:2015:453).

[38] Azoulai, 'Le droit européen de l'immigration, une analyse existentielle', *Revue Trimestrielle de Droit Européen* (2018) 519.

true that Article 78(2) TFEU calls for the legislator to adopt measures aimed to facilitate third country nationals' intra-EU mobility. But even in the Long-Term Residents Directive and the Blue Card Directive—two texts that promote third country nationals' intra-EU mobility—there remain substantial limits to migrants' circulation.[39] EU migration law is also replete with references to 'secondary movements' that are generally associated with abuse.[40] 'Migrants' can thus be deemed 'immobile' persons because they are stopped in their trajectory: they are allocated to one single host society in which they are then supposed to live, and into which they are supposed to integrate.

The 'obliged person' is another key figure we can use to denote the highly institutionalized life of migrants under EU law. EU migration law constantly constrains migrants' life choices, as migrants are never viewed as (or allowed to be) autonomous agents. Control and surveillance are applicable to their entire life: from the capacity to move, which is subject to authorization; to work (including the choice of economic sector), which must be approved; to marriage, which is under surveillance (as EU law allows States to fight against fraudulent marriages), not to mention ordinary decisions like visiting friends abroad (since re-entering into the EU could mean visa obstacles). Migrants are also constrained to follow the 'migration trajectory', which results from the tubular structure of migration law. Once a person has entered the EU as an asylum seeker or student, there is very little possibility of her/him accessing another type of status in the future.[41] Like many other migration regimes in the world, EU migration law thus tends to increase what Vincent Chétail

---

[39] In the Long-Term Residents Directive (Directive 2003/109/EC concerning the status of third-country nationals who are long-term residents, OJ 2004 L 16/44), residence and access to work in a second (or third) Member State is subject to an important number of conditions: residence can be conditioned to the possession of resources and sickness insurance; proof of integration can be required; and access to the labour market can be limited by labour market tests. Even in the recently revised version of the Blue Card Directive, which aims at facilitating intra-EU mobility, there are important limits remaining. 'Long-term mobility' is allowed only after 12 months of legal residence in the first Member State as an EU Blue Card holder; the Directive provides that if the Blue Card holder moves from a non-Schengen to a Schengen State, the latter can ask for evidence at the border. Member States are required to decide on applications for an EU Blue Card within 30 days, but they can refuse if the Blue Card holder has been abusing the system.

[40] For example, recital 15 of Directive 2009/50/EC of 25 May 2009 on the conditions of entry and residence of third-country nationals for the purposes of highly qualified employment, OJ 2009 L 155/77 (Blue Card Directive); recital 18 of Directive 2014/66/EU on the conditions of entry and residence of third-country nationals in the framework of an intra-corporate transfer, OJ 2014 L 157/1; recital 41 of Directive 2016/801/EU of 11 May 2016 on the conditions of entry and residence of third-country nationals for the purposes of research, studies, training, voluntary service, pupil exchange schemes or educational projects and au pairing, OJ 2016 L 132/21; recital 24 of Directive 2013/33/EU of 26 June 2013 laying down standards for the reception of applicants for international protection (recast), OJ 2013 L 180/96.

[41] This was well evidenced by the first version of the Long-Term Residents Directive: even after years of legal and continuous residence asylum seekers and refugees remained outside the scope of the protective status of Long-Term Residents Directive.

names the 'normative ghetto'[42] in which refugees remain trapped: where a single legal regime of migration defines their entire life and future. Taken together, these different elements make it such that migrants' lives are highly 'institutionalized'.[43] In EU law, like in much national legislation, 'migration' is a restrictive form of mobility, which leaves little space for any preference-based decisions on the part of migrants themselves. Forum shopping by migrants is generally viewed as problematic (or, indeed, often as abuse or fraud), as illustrated by the Dublin system. And in *Pham*,[44] the Court of Justice relied on the wording of the Return Directive[45] yet went as far as denying a woman the right to be detained in prison with her fellow citizens rather than socially isolated in separate buildings.

All of this means that, in the dominant narrative, migration is assumed to denote a specific conception of justice. Migration law places most migrants outside the national spheres of solidarity, and the social protection granted to asylum seekers is thus minimal. Even the two most protective EU norms for migrants, namely the Family Reunification and the Long-Term Residents Directives, limit the scope of non-discrimination regarding social protection.[46] The case law of the Court of Justice follows this same logic: the rights granted to the most vulnerable migrants cover only their most basic needs.[47] EU law limits its ambition to guaranteeing a 'decent life', and the Court limits its protection to the migrants' 'naked life'.[48] The contrast between the life offered and guaranteed by EU law to those people who hold free movement rights, and that offered to migrants, is striking.

2. The 'Augmented Wo/men'

'Eurostars' is the name given by Favell to those persons who can rely on EU free movement law to conceive of their life within a broader framework of free movement: the ability to move, shop, work, live, and settle wherever they want. Eurostars, according to Favell, see Europe as a unique space for their cosmopolitan

---

[42] Chétail, 'International Legal Protection of Migrants and Refugees: Ghetto or Incremental Protection? Some Preliminary Comments', in K. Padmaja (ed.), *Law of Refugees: Global Perspectives* (2008) 31.

[43] Ibid.

[44] Case C-474/13, *Pham* (EU:C:2014:2096), paras 21–22.

[45] Which pursues the establishment of an effective removal and repatriation policy, guaranteeing the return 'in a humane manner and with full respect for their fundamental rights and dignity' (recital 2).

[46] Council Directive 2003/109/EC concerning the status of third-country nationals who are long-term residents, OJ 2004 L 16/44. Under Article 11, long-term residents shall enjoy equal treatment with nationals as regards access to employment, education and vocational training, social security, social assistance and social protection, but Member States 'may limit equal treatment in respect of social assistance and social protection to core benefits'.

[47] See Case C-562/13, *Abdida* (EU:C:2014:2453); Case C-578/16, *C. K. and Others* (EU:C:2017:127); Case C-163/17, *Jawo* (EU:C:2019:218).

[48] Azoulai (n. 38) 519. For authors like Carlier, these cases are the expression of charity rather than of dignity: Carlier, 'Les frontières de l'Europe sociale et le traitement des ressortissants de pays tiers: la dignité au risque de la charité?', in S. Barbou des Places, E. Pataut, and P. Rodière (eds), *Les frontières de l'Europe sociale* (2018) 115.

18   SÉGOLÈNE BARBOU DES PLACES

and postnational way of life. Given the specific and protective regime constructed for them (they do not need a visa, nor residence permits; they do not worry about citizenship or integration), borders are not synonymous with barriers of class, race, or ethnicity. In a sense, these free movers correspond to the notion of 'prototypical Europeans' given that they find little difficulty in combining their new European identity with those more specific identities rooted in both their nation of origin and nation of residence.

There is no denying that EU citizens who hold free movement rights are autonomous agents who can take advantage of the opportunities offered by EU law in order to develop their lives; they are the figures that embody the regime enshrined in Articles 20, 21, and 45 TFEU. However, in addition to the Eurostar, who emphasizes mobility, another key figure is implicit in the literature on free movement law: let us name them the 'augmented wo/man'. They are offered (by EU law) a 'European space of multiple opportunities',[49] as successive moves in different EU countries are facilitated by EU law provisions: the aggregation of periods in the Social Security Regulation allows an EU citizen who has successively lived in different Member States to have a full pension;[50] EU citizens can also imagine different types of family organization insofar as their children can expect to receive education subsidies independently of where they live: be that in their State of origin, or any other Member State. Europe is a space where free movers can dream different lives.[51]

Moreover, 'free movement' is increasingly described as a promise of a free—and better—life. The more enthusiastic reading is that of Floris de Witte, who describes free movement as emancipation. Free movement, he argues, liberates EU citizens as it allows individuals to 'live their lives unencumbered by the limits that their place of birth imposes on them'.[52] There is no denying that free movement is a legal regime which gives individuals the greatest possibility to find an environment that fits their preferences. Rulings such as *Garcia Avello*[53] or *Grunkin and Paul*[54] are paradigmatic examples of the 'de-subjugation' facilitated by EU law as EU citizens moving within the EU can escape the limitations generally deriving

---

[49]   Preuß, 'Problems of a Concept of European Citizenship', 1(3) *European Law Journal* (1995) 267.

[50]   This is made possible by the 'aggregation of periods' mechanism set up in the EU rules which coordinate social security systems (see Article 6 of Regulation 883/2004/EC of 29 April 2004 on the coordination of social security systems, OJ 2004 L 166/1).

[51]   On that view, 'EU citizenship was originally conceived as an exercise in de-territorialization within the territory of the Union. Its whole point is to facilitate the possibility of moving from one member territory to another, making national territories open to and onto on elsewhere ... the ambition of the ECJ was to offer Europeans and their family members a winded "social freedom". It is to allow them to find a location and to develop a set of relationships elsewhere, unburdened by the identification with a nation's people'. Editorial Comments, 'Europe Is Trembling. Looking for a Safe Place in EU Law', 57 *Common Market Law Review* (2020) 1675.

[52]   de Witte, 'EU Citizenship, Free Movement and Emancipation: A Rejoinder', in F. de Witte (ed.), *Debating European Citizenship* (2019) 169.

[53]   Case C-148/02, *Garcia Avello* (ECLI:EU:C:2003:539).

[54]   Case C-353/06, *Grunkin and Paul* (ECLI:EU:C:2008:559).

from their nationality. But de Witte goes one step further: freedom of movement would allow individuals self-understanding (and the possible 'realization of the self') in much more authentic terms. He argues that every individual has many meaningful relationships, ties, and identifications with different groups in a society, while the concept of single nation States reduces the incredibly complex individual to a one-dimensional being: a national. The added value of EU law is that 'it 'problematizes' the domination that the nation-State exerts over the individual's self-understanding and capacity for self-realization'.[55]

In that light, free movement is also assumed to denote a specific conception of justice. De Witte describes free movement as 'a recalibration of justice'. The right to free movement and non-discrimination 'can be understood to correct instances of injustice and promote the inclusion of outsiders'.[56] This view is rooted in the line of case law that began with the *Martínez Sala* case, in which the Court decided that EU citizens can expect a degree of solidarity from the host society.[57] In the Court's case law, free movement is not only physical movement: it is also an aptitude to call for protection; *Trojani* and *Bidar*[58] are the name for this EU's normative choice.

In sum, in EU institutional life and in the academic literature, both 'free movement' and 'migration' are conceived as ideal-types that (serve to) represent different kinds of human mobility organized by EU law. Nonetheless, emphasizing the difference between the two regimes of mobility, and claiming that the two kinds of mobility have a different nature, is not a purely descriptive operation. In the literature, highlighting this distinction serves to bolster the 'exceptionalism' narrative. Stressing the uniqueness of free movement law has led most EU commentators to conclude that the EU has invented a completely 'new form' of international human mobility, which projects a purely European mode of life. This can be taken seriously because, as Salazar points out,[59] the imaginaries attached to key figures are not only influential in academia, they also play a role in political circles. Free movement has become 'symbolically the emblem of the de-nationalized Europe that the EU has enabled'.[60]

However, despite its strengths, the exceptionalism hypothesis—which is based on the assumption that a clear-cut structuring divide separates free movement and migration in EU law—is fragile. The crises the EU has been facing in the last decade instead invite us to readjust our narrative and to engage in deeper enquiry regarding the patterns of organization of mobility in EU law. It is therefore clear

---

[55] De Witte, 'The Liminal European: Subject to the EU Legal Order', 40 *Yearbook of European Law* (2021) at 7.

[56] De Witte, 'Kick Off Contribution. Freedom of Movement Under Attack: Is it Worth Defending as the Core of EU Citizenship?', Robert Schuman Centre for Advanced Studies Research Paper No. RSCAS 2016/69, 2.

[57] Case C-85/96, *Martínez Sala* (EU:C:1998:217).

[58] Case C-456/02, *Trojani* (EU:C:2004:488); Case C-209/03, *Bidar* (EU:C:2005:169).

[59] Salazar, 'Theorizing Mobility through Concepts and Figures', 30(2) *Tempo Social* (2018) 162.

[60] Ibid. 153.

that the claim that free movement (law) is radically different, and separate, from migration (law) has to be challenged.

3. Questioning the 'Exceptionalism' Narrative

There exists another possible reading of the relationships between free movement and migration; one which emphasizes potential points of convergence, rather than their differences. Because both free movement and migration rely on a common 'infrastructure of mobility', the two regimes are structurally interdependent (A). These two regimes of mobility are also conceptually interdependent: EU free movement law was constructed upon notions borrowed from migration law. The logic of migration law is, therefore, likely to permeate free movement law (B). It is therefore the whole dichotomy between different regimes of mobility, created for distinct groups of people, which must be challenged: the dividing line between mobile EU citizens, and migrants under control, is unstable (C).

A. Structural Interdependency

By *structural interdependency* I mean that migrants and 'free movers' share the same 'infrastructure of mobility'. I borrow the term coined by Thomas Spijkerboer,[61] who argues that there is a 'global mobility infrastructure' that consists of different structures (physical structures, services, and law) and enables people to move across the globe. Spijkerboer's notion of 'infrastructure of mobility' sheds light on the different material and immaterial elements that either facilitate mobility or make it impossible. The daily operation of border controls is one of them; the administrative work of national authorities in charge of issuing residence or work permits is another. These examples help us to understand the extent to which free movement is dependent on migration management: the two types of mobility are equally restrained by controls at internal Schengen borders (1); at the national level, free movement and migration are often treated alike, by the same rules and the same administration (2).

1. The Impact of Migration Controls on Free Movement
Schengen State nationals and third country nationals share a same space of mobility. Therefore, Schengen States cannot control migrants within Schengen without having a negative impact on free movement. Already in 1994, the *Wijsenbeek* ruling[62] evidenced that the maintenance of controls for third country

---

[61] Spijkerboer, 'The Global Mobility Infrastructure: Reconceptualising the Externalisation of Migration Control', 20(4) *European Journal of Migration and Law* (2018) 452.
[62] Case C-378/97, *Wijsenbeek* (EU:C:1999:439).

nationals at internal borders requires that the national authorities distinguish these persons from Member State nationals, and that, consequently, the latter have to undergo controls: States can restrain free movement 'in order to be able to establish whether the person concerned is a national of a Member State, thus having the right to move freely within the territory of the Member State, or a national of a non-Member State, not having that right'.[63]

After the *Wijsenbeek* ruling, the expectation was that, with the adoption of EU rules unifying the conditions imposed on third country nationals for entry into the Schengen area, Member States would renounce their exercise of controls at internal borders, hence guaranteeing the effectiveness of free movement law. But this has not been the case, as judgments of the Court of Justice illustrate. In *Touring Tours*,[64] a German rule required that coach travel operators on routes crossing the internal borders of the Schengen area would check passengers' passports and residence permits. In *Melki and Abdeli*,[65] France authorized identity checks in the area between the land border of France with Schengen States, and a line drawn 20 kilometres inside that border. Of course, migration controls are, in principle, prohibited at internal borders.[66] This is why France and Germany grounded their control on Article 21 of the SBC, a provision which allows Schengen States to maintain controls ('police controls') related to the protection of their security at the borders—or near the borders—in different situations, and under the condition that these controls cannot be found 'equivalent to the border checks' prohibited by Article 20 SBC ('migration controls').

However, the dividing line between 'migration controls' and 'police controls' is fine and indeed uncertain.[67] Because the criminalization of illegal migration has been a general trend in the EU,[68] most Member States have started to penalize both irregular entry to and residence in their territory. Thus, when the police control mobile persons' documents, can we still distinguish between the 'exercise of police power' and prohibited 'border checks'? Governments constantly try to take advantage of the ambiguous wording of the SBC.[69] The effectiveness of free movement is therefore dependent on the Court's capacity to limit States' strategies

---

[63] Ibid., para. 43.

[64] Case C-412/17, *Touring Tours und Travel GmbH* (EU:C:2018:1005).

[65] Joined Cases C-188/10 and C-189/10, *Melki and Abdeli* (EU:C:2010:363).

[66] Article 20 of the Schengen Borders Code provides that internal borders may be crossed at any point without a border check on persons, irrespective of their nationality, being carried out.

[67] In the *Melki* judgment, the Court even acknowledged the need for 'legal certainty': Joined Cases C-188/10 and C-189/10, *Melki and Abdeli* (EU:C:2010:363), para. 74.

[68] V. Mitsilegas, *The Criminalization of Migration in Europe. Challenges for Human Rights and the Rule of Law* (2015).

[69] In *Touring Tours*, the government argued that the checking of travel documents could not be classified as a measure having an effect equivalent to border checks because its purpose was not to control the crossing of the border but to enforce provisions relating to entry into the territory. In *Melki and Abdeli*, the French government claimed that the purpose of the controls was to establish the identity of a person, either in order to prevent the commission of offences or disruption to public order, or to seek the perpetrators of an offence.

22 SÉGOLÈNE BARBOU DES PLACES

to circumvent the prohibition of 'migration controls' at internal borders. But the Court, interpreting the conditions established by Article 21(a) SBC, only requires that national legislation provides the 'necessary framework' for the power granted to the police authorities 'in order to guide the discretion which those authorities enjoy in the practical application of that power'.[70] This is not a very significant constraint for national authorities.

During the two main crises the Schengen area has undergone, in 2010 and 2015, the extent to which the effectiveness of free movement law is dependent on States' willingness to master migration was officially accepted. In 2010, in the context of the Arab Spring, Member States and EU institutions have admitted that the loss of control of migration movements could (or, rather, had to) justify restrictions on free movement. The significant numbers of migrants arriving in Italy, followed by what the French government viewed as uncontrolled secondary movement, first served as justification for the temporary reintroduction of controls at the France–Italy border. Shortly afterwards, Member States and the Commission amended Schengen law. A new provision (Article 29 SBC)[71] was adopted, whereby States could reintroduce controls at internal borders for up to six months where exceptional circumstances put the 'overall functioning of the area without internal border control' at risk 'as a result of serious deficiencies relating to external border control'. This was a significant change insofar as, previously, the SBC allowed controls at land borders to be reinstated only on the basis of Articles 25, 26, and 28;[72] three provisions which are not related to controlling migration, but to 'show[ing] the public that the state is protecting its citizens against undesired events'.[73] The adopted reform has codified the link between free movement and migration.

During the 2015 'migration crisis', many Schengen States reintroduced controls at internal borders.[74] The problem is, however, that the Commission has allowed a questionable interpretation of the SBC.[75] Despite recital 26 of the preamble, which states that 'migration and the crossing of external borders by a large number of third country nationals should not, per se, be considered to be a threat to public policy or

---

[70] Joined Cases C-188/10 and C-189/10, *Melki and Abdeli* (EU:C:2010:363), para. 74; see also van der Woude and van der Leun, 'Crimmigration Checks in the Internal Border Areas of the EU: Finding the Discretion that Matters', 14(1) *European Journal of Criminology* (2017) 27.

[71] European Parliament and Council Regulation 1051/2013/EU amending Regulation 562/2006/EC in order to provide for common rules on the temporary reintroduction of border control at internal borders in exceptional circumstances, OJ 2015 L 295/1.

[72] These provisions condition the decision to reintroduce controls on the presence of a serious threat to public policy or internal security in a Member State.

[73] See Groenendijk, 'Reinstatement of Controls at the Internal Borders of Europe: Why and Against Whom?', 10(2) *European Law Journal* (2004) 150.

[74] Carrera et al., *The Future of the Schengen Area: Latest Developments and Challenges in the Schengen Governance Framework since 2016* (2018) available online at https://www.europarl.europa.eu/thinkt ank/en/document.html?reference=IPOL_STU(2018)604943 (last accessed 12 February 2021).

[75] Guild et al., 'What Is Happening to the Schengen Borders?', 86 *CEPS Paper in Liberty and Security in Europe* (2015). On reform proposals, see de Somer, 'Schengen: Quo vadis?', 22(2) *European Journal of Migration and Law* (2020) 178.

internal security', the Commission[76] has admitted that massive and non-controlled movements of migrants can equate to putting at risk Member States' public policy, and so can justify limitation to free movement.[77] This interpretation is at odds with the wording of the preamble, and the general structure of the SBC: in principle, the legal basis to be used in case of massive arrivals of migrants at the EU's external borders is Article 29 SBC. By acknowledging that the uncontrolled arrival of migrants equates to a security problem, the Commission has extended States' capacity to limit free movement. Since then, the effectiveness of free movement has become contingent on the number of migrants arriving in the EU. In sum, within Schengen—the area within which every 'person' is allowed to circulate—limiting migrants' mobility generally impacts the situation of 'free movers' too.

2. The Unclear Separation of Free Movement and Migration in National Law

In the TFEU, there is a clear-cut divide between free movement (law) and migration (law). But at a national level, migration law existed before free movement law, and so the separation between the two regimes of mobility is not so obvious. Jo Shaw and Nina Miller even describe a system in which the two 'legal worlds' of free movement and migration collide.[78] Often the administration in charge of applying free movement law is not even separate from that in charge of migrants. As a consequence, in the absence of bureaucratic reorganization, national administrations tend to apply, by analogy, rules and practices aimed at managing migration. Often, as Shaw and Miller show, practitioners at national level continue asking, 'Has this person proved that they have a right?', rather than asking, 'Does this person have a right?'[79]

This administrative reality is part of what Anthony Valcke calls the 'implementation gap in free movement law',[80] which concerns the transposition, application, and enforcement of EU free movement rules.[81] Except when specific (and protective) free movement law rules are efficiently transposed or applied, the national legislation on foreigners tends to be applied by default to all non-nationals,

---

[76] Commission Opinion 2015/7100/EC on the necessity and proportionality of the controls at internal borders reintroduced by Germany and Austria pursuant to Article 24(4) of Regulation 562/2006/EC (Schengen Borders), C(2015)7100.

[77] It concluded that the measures taken by Germany provided an adequate response to the identified threat to the internal 'public policy consisting of the uncontrolled influx of exceptionally large numbers of undocumented persons and the risk related to organized crime and terrorist threats' (ibid., para. 3(28)).

[78] Shaw and Miller (n. 24).

[79] Shaw and Miller (n. 24) 155.

[80] Valcke, 'EU Citizens' Rights in Practice: Exploring the Implementation Gap in Free Movement Law', 21(3) *European Journal of Migration and Law* (2019) 289.

[81] An example of this gap can be found in the *Metock* case (Case C-127/08, *Metock* (EU:C:2008:449)), which was born from the situation of 'gold-plating' whereby transposition of Directive 2004/38/EC in national law led to the inclusion of additional conditions, for free movement, that are not required by the Directive.

24 SÉGOLÈNE BARBOU DES PLACES

including those persons who hold free movement rights.[82] But as Shaw and Miller show,[83] the problem is not only an issue of 'compliance gap' or of 'domestic interpretation gap': it has more to do with the socio-legal/cultural character of the encounter between EU free movement rules and national immigration law. In addition, the 'step-by-step strengthening of EU rights and associated procedural guarantees has run counter to a trend in many states – driven partly by a more general politicisation of the whole issue of "immigration" ... – towards greater use of the power to deport persons deemed undesirable by the executive authorities'.[84]

Sometimes the application of 'migration rules' to EU citizens is not a matter of facts but is enshrined in the national legislation. This happens, in particular, when Member States incorporate EU free movement rules within already existing legislation or codes devoted to the foreigners, or when migration rules are applied to EU citizens by analogy. The *Ordre des barreaux francophones et germanophone* case[85] is a good example of the latter situation. Belgian legislation, which was similar to the measures transposing the Return Directive in respect of third country nationals in order to avoid any risk of their absconding during the period in which they were allowed to leave the Belgian territory following a return decision, was applied to EU citizens. The Belgian judge asked whether the application of migration rules to EU citizens was permitted under Articles 20 and 21 TFEU, and Directive 2004/38 (the Citizens Directive). The judge also asked whether EU law precludes the application of provisions that impose treatment identical to that applied to third country nationals in relation to the maximum period of detention (eight months) for the purposes of removal.

Having observed that Directive 2004/38 does not make specific provision for the possibility of Member States adopting measures aimed at avoiding the risk of absconding during the period allowed to leave the territory of the host State, the Court held, in line with *Petrea*,[86] that it is for the Member States to lay down rules enabling them to ensure that expulsion decisions based on Article 27 of Directive 2004/38 are enforced, provided that this is not precluded by any provisions of EU law. The mere existence of national rules that are applicable in the context of the enforcement of a decision to expel Union citizens, and that are based on the rules applicable to the return of third country nationals whose purpose is to transpose Directive 2008/115 into national law, while 'not, in itself, contrary to EU law, such rules must nevertheless comply with EU law'.[87] In light of the 'fundamental status'

---

[82] Heindlmaier, 'Social Citizenship at the Street Level? EU Member State Administrations Setting a Firewall', *Journal of Common Market Studies* (2020) 1, analyses how Member State administrations handle the social rights of mobile EU citizens in practice in case they are granted discretion and shows that Member State administrations tend to make the access to social benefits difficult.

[83] Shaw and Miller (n. 24) 139.

[84] Shaw and Miller (n. 24) 143.

[85] Case C-718/19, *Ordre des barreaux francophones et germanophone* (EU:C:2021:505).

[86] Case C-184/16, *Petrea* (EU:C:2017:684), para. 52.

[87] Ibid., para. 39.

of Union citizenship, these rules must be examined in the light of the specific provisions applicable to Union citizens in relation to free movement and residence and Union citizens must be treated no less favourably than third country nationals with respect to measures aimed at avoiding the risk of absconding in the context of the former's expulsion.[88] Yet, in making such judgments, the Court admits, as a matter of principle, that rules devoted to migration management can in fact be applied by analogy to EU citizens. It may even be inferred from the Court's choice to reason by analogy that the separation between the scope of migration and free movement regimes is not a given. At national level, there is often no such thing as clearly separated legal or administrative spheres; migration and free movement are interdependent realities. Migrants and free movers share the same infrastructure of mobility.

B. Conceptual Interdependency

The claim that free movement law is radically different from migration law assumes that the former regime is constructed upon specific and original concepts. The very notion of 'free movement', which combines the semantics of freedom and 'circulation', rather than that of 'migration', gives weight to the argument that free movement law is a *sui generis* regime of mobility.[89] However, the *Dano* and *Alimanovic* cases have incited EU legal scholars to admit that the EU Citizens Directive, the main text organizing EU citizens' free movement, is full of conditions and limits.[90] The Directive is also replete with words and notions that belong to the realm of migration: the unreasonable 'burden' on social assistance, 'abuse of rights' or 'fraud', 'marriages of convenience', the notion of 'integration', etc.

For years, these notions carried only negligible weight in the reasoning of the Court, but in the wake of the *Dano* ruling, they progressively re-emerged. The conceptual influence that migration law can have on free movement law has even become more apparent in the context of the Brexit crisis. In his letter to the then President of the European Council Donald Tusk on November 2015, the British Prime Minister, David Cameron, albeit speaking of EU citizens, repeatedly employed the terms 'migration' and 'migrants'. His letter was about more 'control' of the 'flows of population', and EU citizens were described as a threat to the national system. Cameron asked for 'stronger power to deport criminals', in order to 'reduce the numbers coming',

---

[88] Case C-718/19, *Ordre des barreaux francophones et germanophone* (EU:C:2021:505), para. 57.

[89] In the literature on transnational and postnational citizenship, the European free mobility regime is regularly described as a model: S. Soysal, *Limits of Citizenship* (1994), ch. 8; A. Schachar, *The Birthright Lottery* (2009).

[90] Article 21 TFEU ensures that those 'conditions and limits' imposed by the legislator have constitutional significance.

and so in turn 'reduce the draw that [the national] welfare system can exert across Europe'. While the vocabulary employed could be justified by Mr Cameron's political agenda, the tone of the response by the heads of State or government of the Member States was more surprising. Adopting the 'New Settlement of the United Kingdom within the EU',[91] the latter resorted to the same semantics of migration: section D of the Decision refers to the 'scale' of the 'flows' of workers that have 'negative effects' for Member States. Envisioning free movement as a problem rather than as a means to achieve certain objectives served, in fact, to justify proposals for the most radical limitations to free movement law the EU had ever seen.

This episode is an example of migration semantics being imported into free movement texts. Increasingly often, governments also evoke the 'excess of mobility' of EU citizens before the Court.[92] Even in academic literature, some authors describe EU citizens as 'migrants'.[93] This must be taken seriously because, as free movement law is replete with notions borrowed from migration law, the logic of migration law is also likely to infiltrate the substance of free movement law. The notions of 'public policy' (1) and 'integration' (2) can serve as examples to show the possibility of this influence.

1. Public Policy, a Notion Imported from Migration Law

Public policy (and public security) clauses, which justify rights limitations and give administrative authorities a margin of discretion, are core elements of migration law. The 'threat to public policy' is indeed a notion that serves to deny entry and residence. Under international law, only nationals of a given territory have a right to enter said territory; so too, public policy clauses embody the difference between nationals and foreigners. This is why constructing an EU regime of free movement has required neutralizing States' capacity to invoke public policy and security. The Court of Justice has imposed a narrow definition of the 'threat to public policy', which is restricted to individual conduct representing a genuine, present, and sufficiently serious threat affecting one of the fundamental interests of the Member State concerned.

The recent evolution of the case law suggests, however, that the Court has chosen to nuance its canonical interpretation of the notion of public policy. *P.I.* is the most notorious case[94] in which the Court has (re)defined public security: it has 'advanced a social, rather than a classic, institutional vision of public security'.[95] Given

---

[91] Decision of the Heads of State or Government, meeting with the European Council, concerning a new settlement for the United Kingdom within the European Union, EUCO 1/16, 18 and 19 February 2016, A, ex I.

[92] For example, the Belgium Government in Case C-73/08, *Bressol* (EU:C:2010:181).

[93] For example, Davies, 'Migrant Union Citizens and Social Assistance. Trying to be Reasonable about Self-Sufficiency', 2 *Research Paper in Law, College of Europe* (2016); Barnard (n. 10).

[94] Case C-348/09, *P.I.* (EU:C:2012:300).

[95] Azoulai and Coutts, 'Restricting Union Citizens' Residence Rights on Grounds of Public Security. Where Union Citizenship and the AFSJ Meet: Case C-348/09, P.I. v. Oberbürgermeisterin der Stadt Remscheid, judgment of the Court of Justice (Grand Chamber) of 22 May 2012', 50 *Common Market Law Review* (2013) 553.

the atrocity committed by P.I., who had sexually abused his stepdaughter, it was society itself, and its normative foundations, which was perceived as being under threat. The host State was thus allowed to take a measure of expulsion. The ruling is important because, in *P.I.*, the Court has accepted the 'gradual dismantling of the difference between Union citizens and nationals through the establishment of a regime of permanent residence'.[96] The atrocity of his crime placed *P.I.* outside the (European) society of co-citizens: this is why he cannot be treated like a 'quasi-national' anymore. This case is a strong reminder that even in free movement law, public policy clauses are destined to keep away those who do not 'belong' to national society, either because they are legally foreigners or because they are sociologically 'outsiders'. While for years, the public policy clauses had been deactivated or neutralized, the notion of 'threat to public policy' remains present in EU free movement law. This leaves open the possibility to reactivate the exclusionary potential of the public policy clause, as evidenced by the *P.I.* ruling.

In *K.*,[97] the Court had to address the situation of a Croatian national who held the status of long-term resident in the Netherlands but was declared an 'undesirable immigrant in the Netherlands', as he was found guilty of conduct within the scope of Article 1F(a) of the 1951 Geneva Convention relating to the Status of Refugees.[98] The Court acknowledged that K. had been peacefully residing in the Netherlands for many years; his crimes were committed long ago and were unlikely to reoccur outside their specific historical context. The fact that he has been the subject, in the past, of a decision excluding him from refugee status, does not enable the Netherlands to consider automatically that his mere presence constitutes a threat to public policy. The finding that there is such a threat must be based on an assessment of his personal conduct, taking into account the factors on which the decision to exclude him from refugee status was based.[99] However, such an assessment must take account of the time that has elapsed since the date when the acts were allegedly committed, and the subsequent conduct of K., 'particularly in relation to whether that conduct reveals the persistence of a disposition hostile to the fundamental values enshrined in Articles 2 and 3 TEU, capable of disturbing the peace of mind and physical security of the population'.[100] Time, therefore, plays an important role in the reasoning of the judge.[101] The idea of 'persistence in K. of a disposition hostile to the fundamental values' portrays him as the migrant he was

---

[96] Ibid.

[97] Joined Cases C-331/16 and C-366/16, *K. and H.F.* (EU:C:2018:296).

[98] In that he had knowledge of war crimes and crimes against humanity committed by special units of the Bosnian army and in that he had personally participated in those crimes.

[99] The nature and gravity of the crimes that he is alleged to have committed, the degree of his involvement in them, and whether or not he has been convicted, C-331/16 and C-366/16, *K. and H.F.* (EU:C:2018:296), para. 66.

[100] Ibid.

[101] Benlolo Carabot, 'Citizenship, Integration, and the Public Policy Exception: B and Vomero and K. and H.F.', 56(3) *Common Market Law Review* (2019) 771.

years ago, when he first sought refugee status, and was subsequently found to have breached the Geneva Convention. After years of integration in the Netherlands, and in spite of Croatia's accession to the EU, it is nonetheless as if K's double position of 'migrant' and 'potential criminal' had been frozen in time. He thus remains represented as being both legally and sociologically a foreigner, and so deemed undeserving of protection against public policy measures.

The *P.I.* and *K.* rulings reveal that the dominant interpretation of the notion of 'threat to public policy' is not immutable in free movement law. Moreover, there is a degree of convergence with the Court's interpretation of 'threat to public policy' in migration law. When the Return Directive[102] or the provisions of Schengen on external borders are at stake, the Court tends indeed to retain a broader definition of the 'threat to public policy'. In *E.P.*,[103] the Court accepted an important degree of discretion granted to national immigration authorities in the determination of threats to public security. The Court found the safeguarding of public policy to be one of the objectives pursued by the SBC, and that 'the EU legislature intended to combat all threats to public policy'.[104] In light of these considerations, the SBC cannot be interpreted as precluding a national practice under which a return decision is issued to a third country national who is present on the territory of the Member States for a short stay, if that national is only suspected of having committed a criminal offence, without it having been established that their conduct represents a genuine, present, and sufficiently serious threat that affects one of the fundamental interests of the host society.[105]

2. The Two Meanings of 'Integration'
'Integration' is another notion of free movement law that has been borrowed from migration law. In national legislation, proof of integration can be required to acquire nationality, or for family reunification, or invoked as a protection against termination of residence. The notion of integration was introduced to EU free movement law with Regulation 1612/68,[106] but has since become a central notion

---

[102] Case C-554/13, *Z. Zh.* (EU:C:2015:377).

[103] Case C-380/18, *E.P.* (EU:C:2019:1071).

[104] Ibid., para. 45.

[105] In the *Landespolizeidirektion Steiermark* judgment (C-368/20 and C-369/20), the Court was asked to determine the States' capacity to limit free movement in the situation in which controls at Schengen internal borders controls have been prolonged several times after the expiry of the six-month period mentioned in Article 25(1) SBC. According to AG Saugmandsgaardøe (EU:C:2021:821), the SBC not only ensures the absence of any control at internal borders, but also the maintenance of public policy and the combating of all threats to public policy. Therefore, the Member States' powers and responsibilities in that area cannot be framed by absolute periods. However, the enhanced proportionality condition becomes even stricter each time it is reapplied. The Court held that Article 25(4) of the SBC must be interpreted as precluding border control at internal borders from being temporarily reintroduced on the basis of Articles 25 and 27 of that code where the duration of its reintroduction exceeds the maximum total duration of six months, set in Article 25(4) and no new threat exists that would justify applying afresh the periods provided for in Article 25.

[106] Regulation 1612/68/EEC of 15 October 1968 on freedom of movement for workers within the Community, OJ 1968 L 257/2.

of free movement.[107] Progressively, the Court has resorted to the notion of 'integration' as a 'counter-limit'[108] to be used to prevent Member States from restricting EU citizens' access to social rights.[109] In Directive 2004/38, Union citizens' integration serves to limit the host States' capacity to terminate their residence. Defined in this way, integration is 'inclusive': it is an objective to be realized through the recognition of rights accorded to EU citizens.

However, the Court has increasingly privileged a more 'exclusive' sense of the notion of integration; one which is more familiar to the specialists of migration law. 'Integration' has progressively become a condition to fulfil prior to being granted rights. This evolution first started at national level, with States imposing integration injunctions on third country nationals in order for them to access residence or to ask for family reunification. These 'integration tests' began in the Netherlands and were then effectively copied and pasted by other Member States. These tests aimed to evaluate language skills and knowledge of society, institutions, or culture, and must be passed before migrants can receive residence permits or authorization to enter. The Court of Justice has found that integration tests are legitimate,[110] even when required from long-term residents, because the acquisition of knowledge of the language of the host Member State, for example, 'facilitates communication between third country nationals and nationals of the Member State concerned and encourages interaction and the development of social relations between them'.[111] True, the condition imposed to pass the integration test must not lead to denial of residence permits to third country nationals, but they must demonstrate 'their willingness to pass the examination and have made every effort to achieve that objective'.[112] The focus is thus very much on the efforts migrants must make to prove that they want to belong to the society.[113]

Progressively, the exclusive conception of integration has permeated free movement law. Niamh Nic Shuibhne has rightly described the 'rise of duties',[114] which increasingly characterizes free movement case law. The judgments on Luxembourg's refusal to grant aid to students,[115] like the *Dano* and *Alimanovic* rulings, show that the function of the notion of integration is evolving in free movement law. Its

---

[107] Barbou des Places, 'The Integrated Person in EU Law', in L. Azoulai, S. Barbou des Places, and E. Pataut (eds), *Constructing the Person in EU Law. Rights, Roles, Identities* (2016) 179.

[108] Azoulai, 'La citoyenneté européenne, un statut d'intégration sociale', in *Mélanges en l'honneur de Jean-Paul Jacquet* (2010) 1.

[109] For example, Case C-184/99, *Grzelczyk* (EU:C:2001:458) and Case C-367/11, *Prete* (EU:C:2012:668).

[110] Case C-153/14, *K and A* (EU:C:2015:453).

[111] Ibid., para. 53.

[112] Ibid., para. 56.

[113] Case C-257/17, *C.A.* (EU:C:2018:876).

[114] Nic Shuibhne (n. 6) 889.

[115] For example, Case C-20/12, *Giersch e.a.* (EU:C:2013:411) and Case C-410/18, *Aubriet* (EU:C:2019:582). In these cases, the Court has allowed Luxembourg to take into account 'different elements potentially representative of the actual degree of attachment of the applicant with the society'.

exclusive sense, which is dominant in migration law, is increasingly important in free movement law. Who indeed, except for a foreigner, is asked to give evidence of their integration in the host society?

The binary opposition between free movement and migration thus fails to provide an adequate description of the reality. Even in EU law, the borderline between the two regimes of mobility is unclear.

C. The Unclear Border between Free Movement and Migration

At the beginning of the Covid-19 crisis, rights of mobility were redistributed according to criteria other than nationality. The difference between 'essential' and 'non-essential' workers became predominant, as rights of mobility were redistributed on the basis of the contribution to the national economy and specifically to the health sector. A new dividing line thus emerged, which distinguished between persons allowed to cross the EU's external[116] and internal[117] borders, and those persons excluded from such mobility. The different texts adopted at that time (e.g. Council Recommendation 2020/912 on the temporary restriction on non-essential travel into the EU) can be deemed to have created a new model of mobility—a regime of 'selective mobility'[118]—which is based on the difference between those who are 'essential' and 'non-essential' to the society in question, and not on the basis of nationality. The Covid-19 crisis thus helped to blur the line that separates free movement and migration in EU law. But in reality, the dichotomy between EU citizens, holding free movement rights, and third country nationals, subject to controls and limitations to mobility, is already a fragile construction. Three categories of persons illustrate the difficulty in drawing a line between migrants and free movers.

The first group is composed of EU citizens who are nationals of non-Schengen EU Member States. As EU citizens, these nationals are granted the exact same rights of entry, residence, work, and social protection as any other EU citizen. But because border controls and documents are part of their European life, they can hardly share the conception held by other EU citizens that the EU is a space of unrestricted mobility, of the EU as a territory in which the symbolic and the legal effects of borders have been eliminated.

EU citizens from eastern Member States compose the second group of people who, despite being EU citizens, are often represented as migrants. Limitations on

---

[116] Council Recommendation (EU) 2020/912 of 30 June 2020 on the temporary restriction on non-essential travel into the EU and the possible lifting of such restriction, OJ 2020 L 208I/1.

[117] See, for example, the Covid-19 Guidelines for border management measures to protect health and ensure the availability of goods and essential services, OJ 2020 C 86I/1.

[118] Robin-Olivier, 'Free Movement of Workers in the Light of the COVID-19 Sanitary Crisis: From Restrictive Selection to Selective Mobility', 5(1) *European Papers* (2020) 613.

their freedom of movement were included in their nation's treaty of accession. But even after the period of application of the limitation clauses, these 'Eastern European' citizens, described by Adrian Favell as an intermediate category between Eurostars and ethnic immigrants,[119] have continued to face legal and sociological obstacles to free movement. In the 'New Settlement of the United Kingdom within the EU' adopted in 2016, the EU accepted, in breach of EU primary law, exceptions to free movement that were aimed at specifically targeting Eastern European EU citizens. The New Settlement, which contained significant departures from the principle of equal treatment, envisaged an 'emergency brake' on contributory in-work benefits for up to four years, and indexed child benefit to the standard of living of the child's State of residence. In sum, Eastern European EU citizens have not been conceived as fully mobile EU citizens, but rather as people in transition towards full EU citizenship. Worse, the New Settlement enshrined the possibility of permanent exception to their freedom of movement.[120]

Turkish workers and European Economic Area (EEA) nationals comprise the third category of person who cannot easily be classified as belonging to one of the two forms of mobility that are free movement and migration. As third country nationals, Turkish nationals are assumed to be migrants, and thus have more obligations than they do rights. However, under the Ankara Agreement,[121] the EEC Member States and Turkey agreed that Turkish workers would be accorded privileged status in the territories of the contracting parties. Signed at a time when it was agreed that Turkey would soon become a Member State, the Agreement aimed to approximate the legal status of Turkish workers in the EEC with that of Member States nationals.[122]

The Court of Justice has played a prominent role in broadly interpreting these different provisions. In the *Payir* case,[123] the reasoning the Court used was surprising, as it ignored the balance that was found in Decision 1/80 between the objective to support circulation and the respect given to Member States' capacity to regulate migration. The Court's mode of reasoning is characteristic of the interpretation of free movement rules: while the Court retained a broad definition of the 'worker', it privileged a strict interpretation of the conditions required to enjoy

---

[119] Favell (n. 35) 178.

[120] See Barbulescu, 'From International Migration to Freedom of Movement and Back? Southern Europeans Moving North in the Era of Retrenchment of Freedom of Movement Rights', in J.-M. Lafleur and M. Stanck (eds), *South-North Migration of EU Citizens in Times of Crisis*, IMISCOE Research Series (2017) 15.

[121] Agreement creating an association between the European Economic Community and Turkey, OJ 1977 L 361/29.

[122] Article 12 mentions the 'freedom of movement' of workers, while Article 37 of the 1970 Additional Protocol to the Ankara Agreement lays down a right to non-discrimination on grounds of nationality.

[123] Case C-294/06, *Payir, Akyuz and Ozturk* (EU:C:2008:36). The case was about a Turkish national entering the UK to work as an au pair and invoking Article 6 of EEC–Turkey Association Council Decision 1/80 in order to remain in the UK and work. For the Court, the fact that Mrs Payir was granted leave to enter the territory as an au pair could not deprive her of the status of worker.

32 SÉGOLÈNE BARBOU DES PLACES

free movement rights and refused to take into consideration the underlying motivations for movement. In sum, the Court brought a situation of migration within the scope of the rules that organize free movement.

In *Metock*,[124] the Court considered that the distinction between 'internal' (inside the EU) and 'external circulation' (from a third country into the EU) did not apply. As the Union derives from the Treaty's competence to enact the necessary measures to bring about freedom of movement for EU citizens, it has competence to regulate the conditions of entry and residence of their family members, because EU citizens would be discouraged from exercising their freedom of movement if their family members could not accompany or join them. In accepting that a third country national can enter and reside in the territory of a Member State as the spouse of an EU citizen without having first resided with them in another Member State, the Court encompassed Mr Metock's legal situation in the realm of free movement law. Like *Payir*, the *Metock* case is a good example of the Court moving the line that separates the domains of free movement law and migration law. Once they had entered a Member State, Turkish workers were, at the time, treated not like 'migrants', but like quasi-EU nationals. In the *Kus* case,[125] immediately after claiming that 'Turkish workers cannot be assimilated to Community nationals',[126] AG Darmon added that 'Turkish workers are no longer in the situation of nationals of other non-member countries'.[127] Therefore, the neat picture presented in the first part of this chapter, which separates freely moving EU citizens and much less mobile third country nationals, was blurred.

EEA nationals can also be described as belonging to an in-between category between migrants and free movers. Within the scope of the EEA Agreement, citizens and economic operators from the 'EEA EFTA' (European Free Trade Association) States (Iceland, Liechtenstein, and Norway) enjoy essentially the same rights in the EU as EU citizens. In *UK v. Council*, differentiating the EEA Agreement from the EEC–Turkey Association Agreement, the Court held that the three participating EFTA States find themselves 'on the same footing as Member States of the European Union' for the purposes of the application of internal market rules.[128] In *I.N.*,[129] a case in which an Icelandic citizen sought protection in the EU from extradition to

---

[124] Case C-127/08, *Metock* (ECLI:EU:C:2008:449). The case was about the Minister for Justice refusing to grant a residence card to a third country national married to a Union citizen residing in Ireland. At the time of the ruling, no provision of the Directive imposed a requirement on a spouse to previously reside in a Member State before joining his/her spouse. Yet the intervening governments claimed that for the first entry into the EU, family members were to be considered as third country nationals, whose situation is covered by migration law.

[125] Case C-237/91, *Kus* (EU:C:1992:427).

[126] At para. 64 of the Opinion delivered on 10 November 1992 (EU:C:1992:427).

[127] At para. 65 of the Opinion. On the evolution of the Court's case law on Turkish workers, in relation to the accession negotiations, Barbou des Places, 'La Cour de Justice et l'accord d'Ankara: variations jurisprudentielles sur la vocation européenne des travailleurs turcs', in B. Bonnet (ed.), *L'Union européenne et la Turquie: Etat des lieux* (2012) 19.

[128] Case C-81/13, *UK v. Council* (EU:C:2014:2449), para. 59.

[129] Case C-897/19 PPU, *Ruska Federacijia v. I.N.* (EU:C:2020:262).

Russia, the Court of Justice construed his free movement rights and their protection in the light of the instruments governing the 'special relationship'[130] between Iceland and the EU. The Court held that although I.N. was a national of an EFTA State, the fact that his State of nationality, which is a party to an EEA Agreement, together with the fact that that State implements and applies the Schengen *acquis*, renders the situation of that person 'objectively comparable with that of an EU citizen to whom, in accordance with Article 3(2) TEU, the Union offers an area of freedom, security and justice without internal frontiers, in which the free movement of persons is ensured'.[131] For Halvard Haukeland Fredriksen and Christophe Hillion,[132] the essence of the judgment may be that the Grand Chamber 'is prepared to consider not only the EEA EFTA States but also (and perhaps even primarily) their citizens as "insiders" rather than "outsiders"'. The case could thus be seen, the authors argue, 'as a *Grzelczyk* moment' for nationals of the EEA EFTA States in terms of their position under EU law. The special relationship between the EU and the EEA-Schengen States 'establishes a citizen-like status for nationals of those countries within the EU legal order (as free movement is concerned, not political rights)'.[133]

The example of both Turkish workers and EEA nationals shows that the border between free movement and migration is constantly moving. In the name of proximity between the EU and a third country, non-EU nationals can be included in the realm of free movement law and become insiders. The dynamic of inclusion of third country nationals within the scope of free movement has an explanation: free movement is a regime and a form of mobility based on evolution and progressivism.

4. What is Left of Free Movement (Law) without Evolution and Progressivism?

In its inception, free movement law was not, either structurally or conceptually, fundamentally different from migration law. The provisions organizing free movement law have, however, been interpreted in a progressive way. The logic of evolution (A) and the objective of social progress (B) have guided the Court's

---

[130] Ibid., para. 44. The relationship is deemed special because it goes beyond economic and commercial cooperation; Iceland implements and applies the Schengen *acquis*, and is also a party to the EEA agreement; it participates in the common European asylum system; and has concluded an Agreement on the surrender procedure with the EU.

[131] Ibid.

[132] Fredriksen and Hillion, 'The "Special Relationship" between the EU and the EEA EFTA States and Free Movement of Persons in an Extended Area of Freedom, Security and Justice. Case C-897/19 PPU, *Ruska Federacijia v I.N.*, judgment of the CJEU (Grand Chamber) of 2 April 2020, EU:C:2020:262', 58 *Common Market Law Review* (2021) 14.

[133] Ibid.

34 SÉGOLÈNE BARBOU DES PLACES

interpretation of free movement law provisions. One may thus ask what would remain from free movement if we were to remove these two guiding principles.

A. What Is Left of Free Movement (Law) without Evolution?

The story of free movement law can be deemed a linear evolution: more rights have been granted to more people, and, as a result, free movement law has been applied to an increased number of situations. The reason why EU institutions have pushed forward the development and the evolution of free movement law is that free movement is symbolically significant of the ideas of the unified Europe conceived by the founders of European integration. Free movement is part of a broader ambition: achieving the internal market and European citizenship are both objectives that shape the future of the European project. In other terms, facilitating EU citizens' mobility allows them to change the direction of their life and, at the same time, to participate in the realization of the European project.

As free movement is both a 'fundamental right' of the person and a 'fundamental principle',[134] it required further development. Expansionism has characterized free movement law for more than four decades. EU institutions have even gone as far as expanding the scope of free movement over the sphere of migration. The most striking example is that of EU citizens' family members. Despite being third country nationals, they are granted rights to accompany or join the citizen who is exercising free movement. Directive 2004/38 even recognizes a certain degree of autonomy: they can live their life away from the citizen of the Union or even separated from him/her.[135] Similarly, once admitted to a Member State, Turkish workers were granted by the Court, at least in the first period of its case law, a regime of mobility constructed 'by analogy' with that of EU workers. The expansion of concepts and principles of free movement to Turkish workers went as far as to lead some authors to consider that the Court had 'obliterated'[136] the distinction that was thought to exist between Turkish workers and EU workers.

Nevertheless, a look at the case law on Turkish nationals reveals what happens when the evolutionist paradigm fades away. The Court's interpretation of the Ankara Agreement has changed over time and, in turn, its progressive approach has lost ground. Gradually, it has become apparent that the Court was not

---

[134] Case 41/74, *Van Duyn* (EU:C:1974:133).

[135] Article 12 is about retention of the right of family members to remain in the host State in the event of death or departure of the Union citizen; Article 13 addresses retention of the right of residence in the event of divorce, annulment of marriage, or termination of registered partnership.

[136] See Martin, 'Le traitement privilégié des ressortissants turcs', 1 *Revue du droit du travail* n°1, (2011) 62.

anticipating the accession of Turkey anymore. As a consequence, Turkish workers' mobility has progressively been (re)conceived as being a 'migration' issue.

In cases like *Derin*,[137] *Pehlivan*,[138] or *Bekleyen*[139] the judiciary started underlining the differences between EU workers and Turkish workers. Finally, it concluded that EU citizens enjoy free movement rights while Turkish workers have their situation governed by the Ankara Agreement, which is an external agreement devoted to workers' mobility and not to free movement, even once allowed to enter into the EU.[140] In other words, when the Court abandoned the idea that Turkish workers would become EU citizens, their legal status regressed: from a regime that aimed to prepare Turkish workers to become actual free movers after Turkey's accession, it turned back to an ordinary regime of migration. It remains a regime of privileged mobility, since Turkish workers can rely on the rights granted by the Ankara Agreement, but under EU law, there remains a substantial gap between the regime of the most privileged migrants and free movement law.

B. What Is Left of Free Movement (Law) without Progressivism?

The evolution of free movement law was not purely formal: evolution meant social change and progress in the social condition of Member States' nationals. Already in 1950, Schuman and Monnet had the ambition to raise the standard of living of EEC workers.[141] The willingness to contribute positively to European social change is also intrinsic to Regulation 1612/68, the text that played a pivotal role in the construction of free movement of workers. The Regulation extended the scope of freedom of movement and the list of rights to be granted to workers, and also allowed new beneficiaries (namely the worker's family members) to enjoy free movement rights. Particularly, the legislator acknowledged that free movement had to go beyond physical or work mobility, and explicitly linked mobility to the prospect of a better life: 'whereas mobility of labour within the Community must be one of the means by which the worker is guaranteed the possibility of improving their living and working conditions and promoting his social advancement'. Progressivism has therefore been central in the development of the regime of free movement law.[142]

---

[137] Case C-325/05, *Derin* (EU:C:2007:442).

[138] Case C-484/07, *Pehlivan* (EU:C:2011:395).

[139] Case C-462/08, *Bekleyen* (EU:C:2010:30).

[140] Repeatedly, the Court holds that, unlike workers from the Member States, Turkish nationals are not entitled to freedom of movement within the EU but can rely only on certain rights in the territory of the host Member State alone.

[141] Goedings (n. 13) 58.

[142] The notion of progressivism is employed here as a means to emphasize that progress is the fuel for the evolution of the human condition.

36 SÉGOLÈNE BARBOU DES PLACES

The fact that intra-EEC movement was associated with upward social mobility explains why the scope of equality of treatment granted to EEC workers has expanded over time. Equality had to apply not only to access to work and working conditions, but also to fiscal and social advantages. States agreed that 'the right of freedom of movement, in order that it may be exercised ... in freedom and dignity, requires that equality of treatment shall be ensured in fact and in law in respect of all matters relating to ... eligibility for housing, and also that obstacles to the mobility of workers shall be eliminated, in particular as regards the worker's right to be joined by his family and the conditions for the integration of that family into the host country'.[143] Regulation 1612/68 even addressed difficulties in finding a job and a house to host workers' families. Family members were enabled to profit from rights that contribute to the individual's social advancement. Children were given access to education. As for the worker's spouse and children, they were granted the right to take up any activity as an employed person throughout the territory of the host State. On the whole, these rights favour social mobility; education, for instance, is the condition for social emancipation, and work the condition for women's autonomy.

In fact, Regulation 1612/68 outlines a model of society in which individuals are granted rights in support of their efforts to improve their economic and social condition. The same idea of social progression can be found in Directive 2004/38. The Commission[144] followed the line of conclusions produced by the Cardiff European Council, which recognized that 'a sustained effort is needed ... to bring the Union more relevant to daily life'.[145] Directive 2004/38 expresses the EU's willingness to develop free movement rights: its aim was to 'strengthen the right of free movement and residence of all Union citizens'.[146]

Unsurprisingly, when progressivism fades, there is not much left of the exceptionality of free movement. When, with the *Dano* case, the Court put an end to the expansion of free movement law, its resemblance to instruments and principles of migration law suddenly becomes self-evident. In those rulings in which the Court accepts new limits to social protection, there is no consideration for EU citizens' upward social mobility. The Court has therefore made social advancement conditional upon the efforts of each person.

In curtailing the logic of progression, the Court has even reactivated the role of the 'categories' of persons mentioned in Directive 2004/38. Categories are crucial in migration law: they serve to classify types of migrants, and so in turn to define the

---

[143] Recital 4 of Regulation 1612/68/EEC.

[144] Commission Proposal 2001/257 for a Directive on the right of citizens of the Union and their family members to move and reside freely within the territory of the Member States, OJ 2001 C 270/150.

[145] Explanatory memorandum of the Commission proposal, para. 1.

[146] Directive 2004/38/EC on the right of citizens of the Union and their family members to move and reside freely within the territory of the Member States, OJ 2004 L 158/77, recital 3.

legal regime to be attributed to each of them. Categories also serve to create differential treatment,[147] and they enable States to control migrants.[148] The EU legislator, in 2004, chose to depart from this logic. Directive 2004/38 was aimed at 'remedying [the] sector-by-sector, piecemeal approach to the right of free movement and residence';[149] its ambition was to go beyond the fragmented approach to various types, or categories, of EU citizens. To achieve this aim, two macro-categories ('worker' and 'Union citizen') were superimposed onto the different categories of EU citizens (workers, jobseekers, students, and other inactive persons), thus aiming to create a mobility regime common to them all.

It therefore came as a surprise when, in the *Dano* case, the categorization of mobile EU citizens re-emerged. In emphasizing that Mrs Dano had to comply with the conditions of residence enshrined in Article 7 of the Directive, the Court reintroduced a distinction among different categories of EU citizens on the basis of their length of residence in the host State. Progressively, in the case law, the differences between students, family members, and active and inactive citizens, have become more tangible. Absent the progressive interpretation of Directive 2004/68, its resemblance with ordinary migration law instruments can no longer be denied.

In other words, when the logic of progressivism becomes secondary, what separates free movement law from migration law is a difference in intensity rather than substance. Because recent developments allow for the fact that progression and evolution do not guide the Court's interpretation of free movement provisions, what is indeed left of the 'exceptionalism' of free movement (law) is highly uncertain. This is a cruel reminder that the emancipation of free movement law is a fragile pursuit.

5. Conclusion

In recent decades, the transformation of free movement law has led commentators to describe it as an unequal regime of human mobility. In the narrative underpinning this construction, 'free movement' is conceived as a distinctive *form* of mobility. Free movement law is deemed an exceptional regime of international human mobility, one which is both distinct and separated from migration law. Nevertheless, recent developments have required that this narrative be adjusted and reworked, which is why this chapter has sought to describe the intricacies of

---

[147] Differences of rights granted to migrants are legal insofar as migrants do not belong to the same category. To treat refugees and the beneficiaries of subsidiary protection differently, for instance, is not deemed to breach equality, as long as the two groups of people are said (by the law) to be in different situations.

[148] 'Highly skilled workers' is a category which serves to define a group of migrants which States (or the EU) aim to attract; 'minor' is a category which serves to apply a regime of protection.

[149] Directive 2004/38/EC on the right of citizens of the Union and their family members to move and reside freely within the territory of the Member States, OJ 2004 L 158/77, recital 4.

free movement and migration in EU law. The autonomy of free movement law vis-à-vis migration law was questioned, insofar as free movement and migration are structurally and conceptually interdependent. This then begged the question of why, indeed, free movement law is portrayed as an original legal construction. I have argued that progressivism is the key notion that helps to capture the defining features of free movement law: its aim is to support progress in the social condition of EU citizens. When the EU institutions deviate from this ideal, the risk is that free movement law loses its exceptional character and reverts to being a simple branch of economic migration law.

This chapter therefore aims to offer a new perspective. The current key academic debate on this topic tends to oppose two dominant visions. While some hold that the emancipatory potential of free movement advances together with the evolution towards postnational political order within which cross-border solidarity emerges, opponents argue that free movement in its current form has deleterious effects on the capacity of democratic polities to implement collective political will. By emphasizing progressivism as the fuel for free movement law, I certainly do not suggest that the present practice of the EU right to freedom of movement is irreproachable. For example, it is entirely legitimate to reflect on how to reconcile the right to freedom of movement with the rights and needs of sedentary groups. The limited role of the Charter of Fundamental Rights cannot be used to broaden the scope of EU law even when restrictions on freedom of movement under Article 21 TFEU are at stake,[150] or when there is a real risk of harm to the dignity of the person.[151] It is also time to reassess the exclusionary effect of free movement law. Can we view the regression in free movement law as a positive step towards the end of the 'European apartheid' described by Balibar?[152] Or, on the contrary, are we witnessing a generalized regression of the rights of people in movement? By comparing free movement law with migration law, I have attempted to draw attention to the risk inherent in proposals that aim to recalibrate free movement (law). To break with the dominant narrative of free movement law is hardly an uncontroversial operation, and we must insist that it could transform EU free movement law into a modest regime of economic migration.

---

[150] See the contrast between the Opinion of AG Trstenjak (EU:C:2012:296) and the judgment of the Court (EU:C:2012:691) in Case C-40/11, *Lida*.

[151] Case C-638/16 PPU, *X and X* (EU:C:2017:173).

[152] E. Balibar, *We, the People of Europe? Reflections on Transnational Citizenship* (2009).

3

Posted Workers Are Persons Too! Posting and the Constitutional Democratic Question of Fair Mobility in the European Union

Sacha Garben[*]

1. Introduction

Demands for European Union (EU) mobility law to be 'fair' have emerged in the political arena with increasing force over the past years.[1] While in the context of these debates there does not necessarily seem to be a commonly agreed understanding of the notion of 'fairness', such calls appeal to a deeply engrained societal assumption that the law should, indeed, be fair. Despite its specificity and arguably limited practical incidence,[2] the rich and complex area of posted work in EU

---

[*] The author wishes to thank the participants in the EUI Academy of European Law summer school for the valuable exchanges on the topic. The views expressed are entirely personal and do not in any way represent the views of the European Commission.

[1] See for instance the Open Letter of 6 March 2018 from PES Socialists and Democrats to (then) Commission President Juncker asking for 'social fairness' and in particular 'equal treatment and fair mobility' in the context of posted workers (PES, *Beyond words: a package that delivers more social fairness across the EU* (2018) available at https://pes.eu/documents.php?p=6 (last viewed 17 January 2022). Under the Juncker Presidency, the Commission started to often refer to 'fairness' as an objective for its policies, particularly on EU mobility and posting. See for instance: J.-C. Juncker, *Address on the State of the Union* (2017); European Commission, 'Fair Mobility', *Social Agenda No 51* (2018). Recently, the European Trade Union Confederation (ETUC) has reiterated its calls for fairness in EU labour mobility and migration law: ETUC, *Resolution on Fair Labour Mobility and Migration* (2021), available at: https://www.etuc.org/en/document/etuc-resolution-fair-labour-mobility-and-migration (last viewed 17 January 2022). The European Parliament renewed calls for fair mobility in its Resolution of 20 May 2021 'on impacts of EU rules on the free movements of workers and services: intra-EU labour mobility as a tool to match labour market needs and skills' (EP Resolution of 20 May 2021, OJ 2022 C 15/137), stating that 'the protection of mobile workers' working and living conditions based on the principle of equal treatment must cover the free movement of workers as well as the freedom to provide services' and expressing concern 'about the persisting shortcomings in the protection of mobile workers, including cross-border and frontier workers, highlighted by the COVID-19 pandemic', stressing 'that workers must not face any disadvantages as a result of having exercised their right to freedom of movement or because of Union rules on the free provision of services'.

[2] U. Batsaikhan, Z. Darvas, and I. Raposo (eds), *People on the Move: Migration and Mobility in the European Union* (2018). Posting is estimated to amount to about 0.4 per cent of total EU employment, and even in those specific Member States where the incidence is highest, such as Luxembourg, it amounts still only to about 6 per cent. See Pacolet and De Wispelaere, 'The Benefits of Posting – Facts

---

Sacha Garben, *Posted Workers Are Persons Too! Posting and the Constitutional Democratic Question of Fair Mobility in the European Union* In: *Revisiting the Fundamentals of the Free Movement of Persons in EU Law*. First Edition. Edited by: Niamh Nic Shuibhne, Oxford University Press. © Sacha Garben 2023. DOI: 10.1093/oso/9780198886273.003.0003

law has become a proxy for the thorny issue of fair mobility in the EU in general, and in that respect it continues to feed polemic[3] debates. This contribution revisits the well-worn discussion, recounting the saga from *Rush Portuguesa*[4] and *Laval*[5] to the current Revised Posted Workers Directive 2018/957,[6] as recently upheld by the Court of Justice in *Hungary v. Parliament and Council*,[7] and proposes different terms for our legal arguments in relation to this contentious topic. It attempts to operationalize 'fairness' in a meaningful way, by reference to the overarching, basic common values of constitutionalism and democracy,[8] and on that basis critically evaluates the current law.

This analysis reveals that the law on mobility in the EU as interpreted by the Court of Justice fails to convince and persuade as fair. It neither justifies its outcomes by using constitutional democratic language, nor do the outcomes always conform to any of the various options that could reasonably be achieved on the basis of a coherent reasoning within that (still very broad and pluralistic) normative framework. Sometimes, the reasoning and justification are beyond Delphic, or absent entirely. At its worst, the case law lays down crucial legal principles of constitutional value, without meeting the minimum requirements of either democracy or constitutionalism and doing so without meaningful justification. It is arguably precisely this vacuity and the myopic pursuit of further integration that have led to the aberrant exclusion of posted workers from the Treaty provisions on free movement of workers that lies at the root of the swirling controversy on everything posting-related. There is some reason to be hopeful, since the recent judgment of the Court validating the revised Directive has not only brought the legal situation closer to what can be defended as compatible with democratic constitutionalism, but perhaps even more importantly moves methodologically in the

---

and Figures on the Use and Impact of Intra-EU Posting', in J. Arnholtz and N. Lillie (eds), *Posted Work in the European Union – The Political Economy of Free Movement* (2019) 31. Arguing that a broader definition should be adopted to capture a range of related practices and phenomena: Houwerzijl and Bertsen, 'Posting of Workers – From a Blurred Notion Associated with "Cheap Labour" to a Tool for "Fair Labour Mobility"?', in J. Arnholtz and N. Lillie (eds), *Posted Work in the European Union – The Political Economy of Free Movement* (2019) 147.

[3] Feenstra, 'How Can the Viking/Laval Conundrum Be Resolved? Balancing the Economic and the Social: One Bed for Two Dreams?', in F. Vandenbroucke, C. Barnard, and G. De Baere (eds), *A European Social Union after the Crisis* (2017) 309.

[4] Case C-113/89, *Rush Portuguesa* (EU:C:1990:142). See also Cases C-49/98 et seq, *Finalarte* (EU:C:2001:564).

[5] Case C-341/05, *Laval un Partneri Ltd* (EU:C:2007:809).

[6] Directive 2018/957/EU of the European Parliament and of the Council amending Directive 96/71/EC concerning the posting of workers in the framework of the provision of services, OJ 2018 L 173/16.

[7] Case C-620/18, judgment of the Court (Grand Chamber) of 8 December 2020 (EU:C:2020:1001).

[8] Cahill, 'European Integration and European Constitutionalism: Consonances and Dissonances', in D. Augenstein (ed.), *'Integration Through Law' Revisited – The Making of the European Polity* (2012) 11; J.H.H. Weiler, *The Constitution of Europe: "Do the New Clothes Have an Emperor?" and Other Essays on European Integration* (1999).

right direction of 'constitutionally embedding'[9] the internal market. Nevertheless, these are baby steps, and much work remains to be done.

In demonstrating this, the chapter proceeds as follows. Section 2 argues that we should not shy away from the admittedly formidable difficulty in establishing what is fair in our compound constitutional order, but instead seriously and openly engage with it. Only facing this Herculean challenge head-on, it is posited, will allow us to find meaningful and satisfactory answers to the many concrete questions relating to fair mobility. Democratic constitutionalism[10] is proposed as the appropriate method to do so. Section 3 then turns to the specific issue of posted workers in EU law. The analysis will reveal not just *Laval* but as much *Rush Portuguesa*, and *Finalarte* as errors of judgement, from which many other difficulties have ensued. Even if the most recent instalment of the posting saga sees a development in the right direction, the methodology is still unsatisfactory. Section 4 provides an assessment of how the law on posting actually could and should look applying the methodology of democratic constitutionalism. In particular, it argues for the treatment of posted workers under the provisions pertaining to the free movement of persons, as applicable to all other workers in the EU and, most importantly, ensuring their equal treatment compared to national workers. That solution may now appear almost revolutionary from an EU law perspective, but it was arguably the commonly assumed approach until *Rush* and *Finalarte*. Treating posted workers as workers aligns best not only with a doctrinal legal interpretation of the applicable provisions but would moreover lead to a result that could be considered 'fair mobility': a rigorous application of the principle of equal treatment functions as an important social right for the migrant worker and as a bulwark against regulatory competition, protecting all workers, while it still allows the provision of services across borders.

2. What Is Fair Mobility in the EU? A Theoretical Question of Profound Practical Relevance

A. Fairness

Is it fair if a company closes down in Italy, firing all its workers, and relocates to Bulgaria, hiring the same number of new workers there at far lower minimum

---

[9] Schiek, 'Towards More Resilience for a Social EU – the Constitutionally Conditioned Internal Market', 13 *European Constitutional Law Review* (2017) 611.

[10] See further Garben, 'The Principle of Legality and the EU's Legitimacy as a Constitutional Democracy: A Research Agenda', in S. Garben, I. Govaere, and P. Nemitz (eds), *Critical Reflections on Constitutional Democracy in the European Union* (2019) 385 and Garben, 'The "Fundamental Freedoms" and (Other) Fundamental Rights: Towards an Integrated Democratic Interpretation Framework', in S. Garben and I. Govaere (eds), *The Internal Market 2.0* (2020) 335.

wages? Is it fair if the company receives EU subsidies to do so? Is it fair if a Romanian unemployed single father moves to live in Germany with his two young children and receives welfare benefits there? Is it fair if he is not planning to work there, in order to care for his children? Is it fair if a French student who has not been admitted to medical studies in France moves to Belgium to study medicine, only to move back to France to work there as a doctor after her studies? And what if 100,000 other French students do the same? Is it fair to require from a Dutch art teacher seeking to work at a school in Ireland a good command of the Irish language even if the work is carried out exclusively in English? Is it fair if a Polish worker in Sweden who performs the same work as a Swedish worker is paid less and has less favourable employment conditions? Is it fair if a 'high-wage' Member State prevents companies established in 'low-wage' Member States from competing in its labour market on the basis of their lower labour costs by requiring these companies to comply with its labour legislation on its territory? What if the Member State has no minimum wage legislation and instead local workers (try to) prevent companies competing on the basis of lower labour cost through collective action? Is it fair if a foreign company goes bankrupt due to the strike actions of domestic labour unions?

Milton Friedman states that: 'There is no objective standard of "fairness". "Fairness" is strictly in the eye of the beholder ... To a producer or seller, a "fair" price is a high price. To the buyer or consumer, a "fair" price is a low price. How is the conflict to be adjudicated?'[11] While we may reject this relativism and the suggested moral equivalence between the positions of 'seller' and 'buyer' (or 'employer' and 'worker', or 'rich' and 'poor'), for instance by pointing out the power asymmetries between the two parties, or by arguing that the notion of impartiality can introduce a measure of objectivity,[12] it is difficult to deny that there is an inherently subjective element in play, and that there is an inevitable degree of reasonable disagreement about how countervailing values such as equality and freedom should be weighed and applied in this context. Indeed, the questions listed in the previous paragraph, about what is fair mobility in the EU, all pose a familiar and profound problem of legal and political theory and philosophy: what is fairness, who determines it, and how? Do we apply certain substantive, legal standards to establish what is fair in a given situation? But who has the (moral, legal, political) authority to determine those standards, and on what basis? Or do we take a procedural approach that accepts any substantive outcome as fair, as long as it has been reached following a decision-making procedure that we consider to be fair? But on what grounds do we then determine the fairness of that procedure?

---

[11] Friedman, *Newsweek*, 4 July 1977, as cited by Konow, 'Is Fairness in the Eye of the Beholder? An Impartial Spectator Analysis of Justice', 33 *Social Choice and Welfare* (2009) 101.
[12] Ibid.

B. Constitutional Democracy as a Methodology

Difficult as it is, this theoretical problem cannot be avoided in any meaningful treatment of the many practical legal problems of mobility in the EU. We do not need to agree on every substantive question of fairness, but we do need a framework within which we can agree or disagree—we need a common language, a methodology, that we can use to debate and decide these issues, for without it we risk talking past each other in parallel normative echo chambers. The problem is real: without a meaningful answer on how to answer the 'what, who, and how' of fair mobility, this Union cannot thrive and perhaps not even survive. Disagreement on fair mobility has, as Brexit arguably shows to some extent,[13] the capacity to rupture the Union along pre-existing political, geographical, and socio-economic fault lines. Fair mobility is likely always to remain a sensitive topic, as it triggers infinite quandaries relating to social justice, economic competition, and regulatory power that are as inevitable as they are intricate in a diverse, compound legal, and political order such as the EU. But without a legitimate methodology to debate and decide on it, the topic becomes explosive and has the potential to blow up the entire enterprise. Therefore, while the point of this work is not to present a philosophical treatise on the concept of fairness, it argues that it is necessary for EU legal scholars both in academia and in practice to acknowledge this challenge[14] and to openly embed any assessment of these issues in a normative framework[15]—and to actively work on the development of that framework[16] not in the illusion that a perfect consensus will or can ever be reached, but in the conviction that it provides us with the only sustainable (reflexive) forum to reach at least temporary agreement. This method mixes procedural and substantive conceptions of fairness, by having them continuously inform and reinforce one another: the substantive elements of human

---

[13] Barnard and Fraser Butlin, 'Free movement vs. Fair Movement: Brexit and Managed Migration', 55 *Common Market Law Review* (2018) 203.

[14] For the general point that EU legal scholarship needs more clearly to confront its methodological challenges and normative assumptions: van Gestel and Micklitz, 'Why Methods Matter in European Legal Scholarship', 20 *European Law Journal* (2014) 292. For an interesting approach distinguishing different perceptions of fairness in the context of EU tax law, see Burgers and Mosquera Valderrama, 'Fairness: A Dire International Tax Standard with No Meaning?', 45 *Intertax* (2017) 767.

[15] See the seminal work of G. Conway, *The Limits of Legal Reasoning and the European Court of Justice* (2012). Conway puts forward an argument for a normative theory of interpretation for the Court based on the rule of law and democracy. The approach and argument of this contribution concur with that, with as a main difference that human/fundamental rights are formulated alongside the rule of law as the principle of constitutionalism, whereas Conway's approach does not develop a dialectic relationship between constitutionalism and democracy with human rights as an important component, but instead seems to take Waldron's view about the inherently contestable nature of human rights and therefore does not consider them an integral part of the meta-principles of political morality that should dictate judicial interpretation.

[16] Schiek (n. 9).

rights are interpreted to reinforce democratic procedures, and democratic procedures are shaped by substantive ideas of rule of law.[17]

Indeed, in previous work, I have argued that it is possible, pragmatically and approximately, to derive from the common (theoretical and applied) constitutional traditions of the EU Member States and the EU itself,[18] an overarching commitment to the principles of democracy and constitutionalism (the latter comprising the rule of law and fundamental rights).[19] Of course, there is no agreement about the precise desired configuration and practical implementation of these values, with some attaching more weight to the democratic principle[20] and others to constitutionalism and with differing views on the requirements of each,[21] especially in a transnational context.[22] However, I would argue that what matters is that there is broad agreement about the overarching importance of these values and that this actually is already enough to allow us to use them as our method; as the 'common language' in which we can and should debate and decide. Thus, in discussing and determining what fair mobility in the EU is, we need to use the language of constitutional democracy, instead of mere reference to social or economic interest, or implicitly pursuing a single value such as freedom or equality as such. Arguments for one position or the other need to be explicitly situated by reference to this normative framework, so that they can be accepted or rejected in and on those terms. This method is not necessarily expected to produce a single solution to a given legal problem, but instead to theoretically allow multiple answers that can be accepted as 'fair'. Using the language will in turn reflexively nurture and develop it.

The case law of the Court of Justice, and—I would argue—its increased contestation by academics[23] and national courts, shows the necessity of seriously developing and engaging with an explicit normative framework for the interpretation and application of EU law in this way.[24] Adrift on the waves of various competing and conflicting EU norms, values, and interests, and with only 'European integration' as the desired destination without using the available moral compass

---

[17] See, to some extent similarly: Oddvar Eriksen, 'Democratic or Jurist Made Law? On the Claim to Correctness', ARENA Working Papers (2007), https://www.sv.uio.no/arena/english/research/publicati ons/arena-working-papers/2001-2010/2004/wp04_7.pdf (last viewed 17 February 2022).

[18] Garben, The Principle of Legality (n. 10).

[19] Tully, 'The Unfreedom of the Moderns in Comparison to Their Ideals of Constitutional Democracy', 65 *Modern Law Review* (2002) 204, by reference to the work of Habermas and Rawls. See Habermas, 'Constitutional Democracy – A Paradoxical Union of Contradictory Principles?', 29 *Political Theory* (2001) 766, J. Rawls, *A Theory of Justice* (1971).

[20] J. Waldron, *Law and Disagreement* (1999).

[21] Weiler and Trachtmann, 'European Constitutionalism and Its Discontents', 17 *Northwestern Journal of International Law & Business* (1997) 354.

[22] Schaffer, 'The co-originality of human rights and democracy in an international order', 7 *International Theory* (2015) 96.

[23] For a compelling recent account see T. Horsley, *The Court of Justice of the European Union as an Institutional Actor – Judicial Lawmaking and its Limits* (2018).

[24] Conway (n. 15).

(Article 2 Treaty on European Union (TEU)) to reach it, the law on mobility in the EU as interpreted by the Court fails to convince and persuade as fair. At its worst, like in the area of posting, the case law lays down crucial legal principles of constitutional value, without meeting the minimum requirements of either democracy or constitutionalism and doing so without meaningful justification.

C. Posting as a Case Study

As I have argued elsewhere in more detail,[25] the law on mobility in the EU on the whole fails to deliver[26] in respect of both the principles of democracy and constitutionalism, and in the latter context both as regards fundamental rights and the rule of law. As the present contribution shows, the law on posted workers in the EU is a case in point. Posting involves the movement of workers from one Member State to another, yet posted workers are curiously treated by the Court of Justice not as migrant workers but essentially as 'services' (not service providers), as part of a company's (fundamental) right to provide services across the EU territory. Within that framework, the Court has denied posted workers the right to equal treatment, and instead condemns such equal treatment as a *prima facie* restriction (of the provider's Treaty rights) that has to be justified and proportionate. The Court has furthermore given a strict interpretation of what national measures can be accepted in this respect, although it has more recently softened its stance in response to sustained criticism. As this chapter will argue, it has made these consequential and controversial decisions without meaningful reasoning, explanation, or justification—let alone on the basis of a serious engagement (either implicitly or explicitly) with democratic and constitutional norms and values. The Member States and the EU institutions, including the Court itself, have been playing catch-up ever since this original sin, and they continue to do so even under the revised legal framework.

Posting, as interpreted by the Court,[27] gives rise to a range of highly sensitive questions of EU mobility: the rights of local versus foreign workers, the interests of local versus foreign companies, the interests of all workers versus those of all

---

[25] Garben, 'The "Fundamental Freedoms"' (n. 10).

[26] See for a similar argument in slightly different terms: Davies, 'The Competence to Create an Internal Market: Conceptual Poverty and Unbalanced Interests', in S. Garben and I. Govaere (eds), *The Division of Competences between the EU and the Member States – Reflections on the Past, the Present and the Future* (2017) 74.

[27] It is argued that if the Court had decided to treat posted workers the same as all other workers in the EU, this would have resulted in less controversy, even if it would of course not have been in the interest of the companies of low-wage Member States seeking to post workers to high-wage countries. I find it doubtful that low-wage Member States joined the Union in the assumption that their companies would be allowed to directly compete on wages on the territory of the other Member States, and even if they were, I would argue that the approach under EU law traditionally was to avoid such wage competition as reflected in the provisions on equal pay between men and women, and in the equal treatment provisions concerning the free movement of workers—which the Court already in the early days of integration elevated to fundamental principles of EU law.

46   SACHA GARBEN

employers, the position of 'high-wage' countries versus the position of 'low-wage' Member States, the effects of regulatory competition on a common (social) market (economy) and on national (regulatory/social/constitutional) autonomy, the political versus the judicial, the balancing of fundamental rights, and national level versus European-level decision-making. This has turned it into a symbol, a political proxy for the question of fair mobility in the EU in general.[28] Especially in discussions on the over-constitutionalization[29] of EU law and the imbalance between economic and social values in the integration project, the issue of posting punches far above its weight.[30] Arguably, it is not a coincidence that posting has become so emblematic of corrosive political disagreement about European integration, because as the rest of this contribution will show, it is one of the issues where the failure of EU law to legitimize itself—in other words EU law's vacuity[31]—has been most pronounced.

3. The Posted Workers Saga

A. Phase 1: The Rash Exclusion of Posted Workers from the Notion of Worker: *Rush* and *Finalarte*

1. Why Not Workers?
Let us start at the very beginning (a very good place to start), by considering how we have arrived at the peculiar treatment of posted workers in EU law not as workers and thus under the legal framework applicable to the free movement of workers (where EU law rigorously applies the principle of equal treatment which functions both as an important social right for the migrant worker and as a bulwark against regulatory competition, protecting all workers), but instead as their company's assets that it should be free to deploy across borders as it sees fit.[32] This approach, which is at the root of many of the controversies that have since then

---

[28] Costamagna, 'Regulatory Competition in the Social Domain and the Revision of the Posted Workers Directive', in S. Borelli and A. Guazzarotti (eds), *Labour Mobility and Transnational Solidarity in the European Union* (2019) 83.

[29] D. Grimm, *The Constitution of European Democracy* (2017).

[30] Lubow and Schmidt, 'A Hidden Champion? The European Court of Justice as an Agenda-setter in the Case of Posted Workers', *Public Administration* (2019), https://doi.org/10.1111/padm.12643 (last viewed 3 November 2022).

[31] Weiler (n. 8).

[32] See on this issue generally: Verschueren, 'The European Internal Market and the Competition Between Workers', 6 *European Labour Law Journal* (2015) 135; Verschueren, 'Cross-Border Workers in the European Internal Market: Trojan Horses for Member States' Labour and Social Security Law?', *International Journal of Comparative Labour Law and Industrial Relations* (2008) 171–177. For the same supposition that the unfortunate exclusion of posted workers from the provisions on workers and their treatment under the services provision instead (with all aberrant consequences) was borne out of the Court's 'good intent' to find a solution to the transition period applicable to Portuguese workers in *Rush Portuguesa*, see Ales, 'Italy', in M. Freedland and J. Prassl (eds), *Viking, Laval and Beyond* (2014) 187.

plagued this area, seems to have been taken by the Court somewhat rashly. It may even be that the Court did not itself fully contemplate the long-term consequences of a decision it took to solve a short-term problem with the application and effectiveness of EU law. In reading *Rush Portuguesa*, the judgment where it was first decided that the movement of posted workers could be treated as their company's right to provide services across borders for the purposes of EU law, it seems that the Court's decision was not reached on the basis of a conscious interpretation of the Treaty provisions on workers and on services and their respective functions in the EU legal order, but instead out of a concern to limit the effect of the transitional period in relation to the accession of Portugal. The latter acceded in 1986, but the provisions on the free movement of workers did not apply until 1993, while the provisions on services were not covered by this derogation. The Court, in its 1990 judgment, appears to have opted for the services solution in order to enhance the application of EU law in the face of this transition period.

A prior case, although not cited by the Court, may have inspired this solution: in *Seco*, the Court had held that the obligation imposed by a Member State on a company from another Member State to pay employer's insurance in respect of third country nationals temporarily posted on its territory constituted a restriction of the freedom to provide services.[33] This case therefore, like in *Rush Portuguesa*, concerned posted workers that could not avail themselves of the free movement of workers, in this case because they did not have the nationality of a Member State. But very clearly, in both cases, the free movement of workers did not 'apply' because of external factors (the third country nationality of the workers, and the transitional period): there was nothing to suggest that something in the posted nature of their work as such would disqualify them as workers. Indeed, the Opinion of Advocate General van Gerven[34] in *Rush Portuguesa* shows how aberrant the exclusion of posted workers from the free movement of workers was considered to be:

> The most radical viewpoint in favour of the freedom to provide services is to be found in the observations of Rush. Rush submits in particular that the relevant provisions of the Act of Accession contain no single restriction on the recruitment and employment of Portuguese nationals by a supplier of services. It comes to this conclusion on the basis of the following reasoning. The presence in France of Rush employees has nothing to do with the application of Article 48 of the EEC Treaty: they did not look for work in France and have not entered the French labour market, seeing as they have a contract of employment in Portugal and, in

See also Lo Faro, 'Diritti sociali e libertà economiche del mercato interno: considerazioni minime in margine ai casi Viking e Laval', *Lavoro e Diritto* (2008) 63.

[33] Joined Cases 62 and 63/81, *Seco* (EU:C:1982:34).
[34] Opinion of AG Van Gerven delivered on 7 March 1990 (EU:C:1990:107).

the context of that employment, temporarily come to France in order to perform duties in the service of Rush, without however laying claim to the right to establish themselves for an indefinite period as workers in France. Moreover, their respective employment relationships remain strongly Portuguese in nature. They are paid and charged tax in Portugal and remain subject to the Portuguese social security scheme. From all those circumstances Rush concludes that its employees are not to be regarded as 'workers' within the meaning of Regulation No 1612/68, with the result that the provisions contained in the Act of Accession with regard to Portuguese workers do not apply to them.

This argument cannot be accepted. The Court has consistently stressed that the Community concept of a 'worker' is very broad, and covers any national of a Member State who actually and genuinely performs work in another Member State. In that connection it does not matter whether that work is carried out in the service of an undertaking which is active in other Member States or in the service of an undertaking which is established in the Member State where the work is carried out. In accordance therewith the preamble to Regulation No 1612/68 provides that 'the right of all workers in the Member States to pursue the activity of their choice within the Community should be affirmed ... without discrimination (as regards) permanent seasonal and frontier workers and by those who pursue their activities for the purpose of providing services'. The rules laid down in Regulation No 1612/68 thus undoubtedly extend to protect workers of a supplier of services such as Rush. As I have said, however, the rules relating to the right of Portuguese workers to accept or carry on salaried employment in the territory of one of the 'old' Member States have been restricted until 1993 by Article 216 of the Act of Accession.[35]

Indeed, the Commission had also, prior to *Rush Portuguesa*, approached the issue as one of free movement of workers.[36]

In the Court's judgment in *Rush Portuguesa*, there is no serious consideration of the prior case law on workers, or on the relationship between the free movement of workers, the freedom to provide services, and the phenomenon of posting (let alone to higher principles and values). And actually, the Court does *not* explicitly decide that posted workers are not 'workers' in the sense of (then) Article 48 EEC, and that they are not entitled to equal treatment. To achieve its desired result in the specific case before it—namely, to advance the application of EU law in the face of the transitional period applicable to Portuguese workers—the Court

---

[35] Ibid., paras 13 and 14.

[36] COM(75)653 Amended Proposal for a Regulation of the Council on the Provisions of Conflict of Laws on Employment Relationships within the Community (Brussels, 28 April 1976), which dealt with the subject matter referring to the free movement of workers. Feenstra therefore considers that *Rush Portuguesa* can indeed be seen as a 'turning point' rather than the 'starting point' that most of the scholarship treats it as: Feenstra (n. 3), 316.

'merely' had to make sure that posted workers were not workers *for the purposes of the derogation in the Act of Accession*. Indeed, it is only in this context that the Court refers to the temporary nature of posting: not to distinguish or justify the dis-application of the free movement of workers (where indeed no permanency requirement applies and which includes, for instance, seasonal workers and frontier workers who also, allegedly like posted workers, do not seek to be integrated in the host State), but instead in relation to the specific rationale of the derogation in the Act of Accession (which was made to prevent a potential disruption of host labour markets by mass permanent migration, a disruption not caused by mere temporary movement).[37]

Nonetheless, a path dependency is created. If the Court says here that posted workers are not 'workers' for the purpose of limitations on (then) Article 48 EEC, it will be awkward for it to say the next time that posted workers are 'workers' for the purposes of application of that same provision. And although in the bigger scheme of things it is perhaps even more awkward to disqualify posted workers as workers and to deny them equal treatment, it happens incrementally in the course of a few judgments, which together act as something of a smokescreen through which it becomes harder to pinpoint the exact moment that the (r)evolution happened, perhaps even for the Court itself. And so, in the *Finalarte* judgment,[38] that is how it goes: the Court explicitly carves all posted workers (and not just those who cannot rely on (now) Article 45 of the Treaty on the Functioning of the European Union (TFEU)) because of a transitional period or because they are third country nationals out of the scope of 'workers' under EU law, if not dishonestly then incorrectly pointing back to *Rush Portuguesa* as the precedent.[39]

There is no reasoning or justification for this subsequent decision, which could be framed as a departure from the text of the Treaty and Regulation 1612/68 as well as from the Court's own prior case law on the free movement of workers as set out by Advocate General van Gerven, cited above. Why are the very nationals of the Member States who on the basis of Article 45 TFEU have a full right to move freely to another Member State to work there suddenly not considered as doing precisely that when they are 'posted'? The Court merely repeats, completely out of context, the finding from *Rush Portuguesa* that posted workers allegedly do not seek permanent integration in the host State, and states that 'it follows' that the free movement of workers 'does not apply'.[40] With this, the case law conjures up out of thin air a subjective intention and permanency/integration requirement in relation

[37] Opinion of AG Van Gerven, *Rush Portuguesa* (EU:C:1990:107), paras 14 and 15.

[38] Cases C-49/98 et seq, *Finalarte* (EU:C:2001:564), para. 23.

[39] 'The Court has held that workers employed by a business established in one Member State who are temporarily sent to another Member State to provide services do not, in any way, seek access to the labour market in that second State if they return to their country of origin or residence after completion of their work' (Case C-113/89, *Rush Portuguesa* (EU:C:1990:142), para. 15, and Case C-43/93, *Vander Elst* (EU:C:1994:310), para. 21). It follows that Article 48 of the Treaty does not apply in the circumstances of the main proceedings, para. 22 of the judgment in Cases C-49/98 et seq, *Finalarte* (EU:C:2001:564).

[40] Ibid.

to Article 45 TFEU, which is not, however, applied to other workers under that provision (as poignantly illustrated by seasonal and frontier workers[41]), and which is contrary to both the wording and the *telos* of the free movement of persons.[42] There can be limitations on equal treatment as regards State benefits concerning jobseekers when they do not yet have gainful employment,[43] which is of course very different from the situation of posted workers who are gainfully employed and whose equal treatment does not pertain to benefits but to their employment conditions. No other types of EU workers are deprived of equal treatment as regards employment conditions or deprived of 'worker' status because of the allegedly temporary nature of their movement.

As per *Lawrie-Blum*, anyone who 'for a certain period of time' 'performs services for and under the direction of another person in return for ... remuneration' is a worker under Article 45 TFEU.[44] The temporary nature of a posting as such is not incompatible therewith, while very short postings could where appropriate be excluded under the 'certain period of time' or 'not marginal and ancillary' criteria of the *Lawrie-Blum* test. In *Ninni-Orasche*, in relation to the question whether an employment relationship that had lasted two and a half months could confer the status of 'worker', the Court stressed that 'the fact that employment is of short duration cannot, in itself, exclude that employment from the scope of Article [45 TFEU]', and that the only thing that matters in that regard is that the activity is 'effective and genuine'.[45] For the purposes of establishing the latter, 'factors relating to the conduct of the person concerned before and after the period of employment are not relevant' in establishing the status of worker within the meaning of that article'.[46]

Could it be argued that the fact that the posted worker retains an employment contract under the law of the home Member State means that they are not

---

[41] See for instance Case C-830/18, *Landkreis Südliche Weinstraße v. PF and Others* (EU:C:2020:275).

[42] See also, in the different context of the free movement of students, the Court's approach to the particular situation where large numbers of French and German students came to Belgium and Austria respectively to study medicine there after having been rejected access to these studies in their home Member State, and where there was reason to assume that the students in question had no intention of integrating in the host State labour market but instead intended to return to their home countries after their studies. The Court refuses to accept this as an abuse of EU free movement rights and considers that even in the scenario that all those students indeed leave the host State after their studies, this may only justify restrictions on equal treatment as regards access to higher education to the extent that it would credibly lead to a shortage of medical professionals in the host Member State, Case C-73/08, *Bressol* (EU:C:2010:181); Case C-147/03, *Commission v. Austria* (EU:C:2005:427); and Case C-65/03, *Commission v. Belgium* (EU:C:2004:402). In education cases, like with jobseekers, 'integration' in the host State is only taken into account in the context of receiving State benefits (and not the conditions of education itself): Case C-158/07, *Jacqueline Förster* (EU:C:2008:630).

[43] Notably, Member States may deny jobseekers 'social assistance' (benefits that does not intend to facilitate access to the labour market): Case C-333/13, *Dano* (EU:C:2014:2358); Case C-299/14, *Vestische Arbeit Jobcenter Kreis Recklinghausen v. Jovanna García-Nieto* (EU:C:2016:114). For a temporal limitation on the right of residence, see Case C-292/89, *The Queen v. Immigration Appeal Tribunal, ex parte Gustaff Desiderius Antonissen* (EU:C:1991:80).

[44] Case 66/85, *Lawrie-Blum* (EU:C:1986:284).

[45] Case C-413/01, *Ninni-Orasche* (EU:C:2003:600), paras 25 and 26.

[46] Ibid., para. 28.

integrated in the host Member State by contrast to all other categories of migrant workers, who presumably have an employment contract with a local employer, and that such integration is thus an implicit requirement under *Lawrie-Blum*? While having an employment contract with a local employer could certainly be taken as proof of being a part of the host State labour market (like in the case of seasonal and frontier workers), it does not logically seem to have to be *a sine qua non*: posted workers who perform effective and genuine work on the territory of the host State for a certain period of time do take part in that labour market. They work alongside or in competition with local workers. They will often be present on the territory longer than seasonal workers and they will often reside there throughout their posting in contrast to frontier workers. It seems wholly against the texture and spirit of EU law to consider the nationality of the employer, or of the employment contract, as a (non-rebuttable) factor that would deprive a migrant worker of their rights under the Treaties and secondary law.[47] While it could be contemplated that the status of their employment contract could under certain circumstances justify certain instances of differential treatment, that is of course not the same as disqualifying them from the Treaty rights accorded to migrant workers altogether as a matter of principle.

On a related note, in defence of the Court's approach, much has been made of the EU's private international law (PIL) rules,[48] which provide that in the absence of a choice of law the labour legislation of the habitual place of work applies to a worker and thus, in the case of a temporary posting, the legislation not of the host State but of the home State. The implication is that these rules actually oblige the approach taken by the Court. This argument does not hold water—as the Court itself has now confirmed in *Hungary v. Parliament and Council*. Not only do the PIL rules leave scope for the application of host labour standards as mandatory requirements, they actually defer to the choice of law as laid down in EU instruments,[49] and these rules in any event need to comply with the Treaty provisions and should be interpreted in conformity therewith. That means the PIL rules did not oblige the Court in any way to take the aberrant route that it did, and that it

---

[47] The Court of Justice's approach in *Boukhalfa* suggests that the 'nationality' of the employment relationship is only one of a range of factors that are to be taken into account, to determine the relationship of a worker to a Member State, in that case in order to establish the extra-territorial application of the prohibition of discrimination on grounds of nationality in the case of an EU citizen employed in the embassy of another EU Member State in a third country. See Case C-214/94, *Ingrid Boukhalfa v. Bundesrepublik Deutschland* (EU:C:1996:174).

[48] The Rome I Convention of 19 June 1980, now Regulation 593/2008/EC of the European Parliament and of the Council of 17 June 2008 on the law applicable to contractual obligations (Rome I Regulation), OJ 2008 L 177/1.

[49] According to the principle of precedence of Union law laid down in its Article 20, the Convention does not affect the application of provisions which, in relation to a particular matter, lay down choice-of-law rules relating to contractual obligations and which are or will be contained in acts of the institutions of the European Communities or in national laws harmonized in implementation of such acts.

52 SACHA GARBEN

could just as well have considered posted workers to fall under the Treaty provisions on free movement of workers.

If it all seems nonsensical it is because it makes no sense. And that is, I would argue, because it was actually not intended this way. The Court, in a myopic pursuit of *effet utile* and expansion of EU law, devised a mechanism to work around the limitation of free movement of non-EU and just-acceded workers, and it half-accidentally ends up limiting the concept of EU 'worker' in the process. Indeed, it seems that the Court itself is a little uncomfortable with its exclusion of posted workers from the provisions on free movement of workers. In *Kranemann*, the Court held 'temporary civil servants carrying out a traineeship who are posted abroad to a place of their choice' to be workers for the purposes of Article 45 TFEU.[50] Interestingly, it was precisely the posting abroad that brought the otherwise internal situation within the scope of Article 45 TFEU. While this finding served to impose an obligation of equal treatment (to reimburse travel expenses) on the home country rather than on the host country, the application of Article 45 TFEU to the posting seems inconsistent with *Finalarte* and suggests that if *Finalarte* had been a case brought by unequally treated posted workers (like later, as discussed below, in *Elektrobudowa*), things could have turned out very differently.

Moreover, in *Hudziński and Wawrzyniak*,[51] the Court actually does refer to, and treat, a Polish posted worker in Germany as a 'migrant worker', and while it upholds the principle (as laid down in social security coordination Regulation 1408/71) that the home Member State is competent as regards child benefits, it also considers that where the host country provides the granting of the benefit to posted workers it may not apply a rule that excludes that benefit in case of a partial overlap with the benefit provided by the home Member State by application of 'the Treaty rules on the free movement of workers'.[52] The Court notes in that respect that the national rule 'is not designed to avoid the costs and administrative complications which might arise for undertakings from other Member States posting workers in Germany as the result of a change in the applicable national legislation'[53] as 'the benefit at issue in the main proceedings is granted without the undertakings which employ those workers being obliged to contribute to the financing of that benefit or having any administrative formalities imposed on them in that context'.[54]

2. Equality of EU Workers as a Restriction of EU Law?

To the foregoing one may be tempted to reply: as problematic as the case law is from the perspective of the free movement of workers, as logical it is from the perspective of the freedom to provide services. Of course, as had been held since

---

[50] Case C-109/04, *Kranemann* (EU:C:2005:187).
[51] Joined Cases C-611/10 and C-612/10 (EU:C:2012:339).
[52] Ibid., para. 85.
[53] Ibid., para. 83.
[54] Ibid., para. 83.

Webb,[55] limitations and double burdens imposed on service providers from another Member State because they use their staff (also from another Member State) are to be considered as *prima facie* restrictions of the freedom to provide services. The requirements in *Rush Portuguesa* (engagement *in situ* and obligatory work permits) would have qualified as such, and therefore we are in the scope of application of (now) Article 56 TFEU. But this application of Article 56 TFEU does not have to exclude the application of the free movement of workers: the posted worker could be entitled, in principle, to the same rights and advantages as national workers under Article 45 TFEU while their employer should not be subject to double burdens (like licensing, immigration formalities and the like). The application of Article 56 TFEU would quite naturally find its ally, not its enemy, in the application of Article 45 TFEU. This would also be supported by the fact that Article 57 TFEU frames the services provisions as residual to those on the other freedoms: 'services shall be considered to be "services" within the meaning of the Treaties where they are normally provided for remuneration, in so far as they are not governed by the provisions relating to freedom of movement for goods, capital and persons'.

It is thus important to realize that the issue of posted workers does not reveal an inherent conflict between the two freedoms, as there is a very reasonable way to do justice to both—a way that also better respects the wording, context and prior interpretation of these provisions, as well as the higher values of democracy and constitutionalism.[56] It is only if Article 56 TFEU were interpreted (i) not to be residual to the free movement of persons (*contra* Article 57 TFEU), and (ii) to prohibit not just direct and indirect discrimination and market access restrictions, but to constitute a right to challenge any rule that makes economic activity less attractive,[57] that the two freedoms would come to bite each other, and that the protection of the one would become a restriction of the other. Since that latter interpretation would take the freedom to provide services *beyond* its 'greatest possible observance',[58]

---

[55] Case 279/80, *Criminal proceedings against Alfred John Webb* (EU:C:1981:314).

[56] See further Section 4 of this chapter.

[57] As Advocate General Tizzano emphasized in *CaixaBank France* that such an approach 'would be tantamount to bending the Treaty to a purpose for which it was not intended: that is to say, not in order to create an internal market in which conditions are similar to those of a single market and where operators can move freely, but in order to establish a market without rules. Or rather, a market in which rules are prohibited as a matter of principle, except for those necessary and proportionate to meeting imperative requirements in the public interest'. Opinion of Advocate General Tizzano delivered on 25 March 2004, Case C-442/02, *CaixaBank France* (EU:C:2004:187), at point 63. See also Opinion of Advocate General Tesauro in Case C-292/92, *Hünermund and Others* (EU:C:1993:863), points 1 and 28, and Opinion of Advocate General Wahl delivered on 5 September 2013, Joined Cases C-159/12, C-160/12 and C-161/12, *Alessandra Venturini v. ASL Varese and Others, Maria Rosa Gramegna v. ASL Lodi and Others*, and *Anna Muzzio v. ASL Pavia and Others* (EU:C:2013:529). The Advocates General take issue especially with the idea to allow also national operators to challenge national rules, but the argument applies with similar force to the challenging by foreign companies of indistinctly applicable rules that furthermore affect market access in the same way for foreign or domestic operators. The Court of Justice has not, however, heeded these concerns.

[58] Para. 11 of the Opinion of AG van Gerven (n. 34).

while at the same time artificially and unnecessarily restricting the free movement of workers, one could have expected the Court of Justice to prevent such a clash. Instead, by its increasingly broad approach to services in general, and its (implicit) dismissal of Article 57 TFEU as the applicable 'conflict rule', it actively creates an unnecessary conflict between two of the 'four freedoms'. Again, this decision is 'scattered' over the course of several judgments, pretending that all just follows logically from whatever came before, instead of owning up to the dissonance of the new doctrine and explaining it.

In *Rush Portuguesa*, the Court holds: '[t]o impose such conditions on the person providing services established in another Member State discriminates against that person in relation to his competitors established in the host country who are able to use their own staff without restrictions, and moreover affects his ability to provide the service.'[59] The first part of this sentence is a relatively uncontroversial discrimination-based application of the freedom to provide services. The Court clearly refers to the additional burdens placed specifically on foreign service providers making use of foreign staff, concerning immigration formalities, etc. However, the sting is in the tail, where the requirements in question are 'moreover' considered as restrictions because they affect the company's 'ability to provide the service'. This vague wording allows various interpretations, and we are not given any detailed explanations. The Advocate General had referred to the obligation on Member States, in addition to not discriminate, to not 'negate or unnecessarily restrict' the freedom to provide services. While that hints at the idea of a broad *prima facie* notion of restrictions with a proportionality test to assess necessity, such is not clearly decided. The Court of Justice in *Rush Portuguesa* rather unequivocally states that:

> Community law does not preclude Member States from extending their legislation, or collective labour agreements entered into by both sides of industry, to any person who is employed, even temporarily, within their territory, no matter in which country the employer is established; nor does Community law prohibit Member States from enforcing those rules by appropriate means.[60]

This leaves vague whether home labour rules are not to be considered 'restrictions' in the first place, or whether they are instead regarded as a (justified) restriction. Even in the latter interpretation, *Rush Portuguesa* furthermore suggests that it is unlikely that the application and enforcement of such rules would be precluded by EU law.

It is in *Finalarte* that the Court moves to the more extreme interpretation: it seems to decide that a requirement of equal treatment as regards labour conditions (which, paradoxically, would precisely be required by EU law under the application

---

[59] *Rush Portuguesa*, para. 12.
[60] *Rush Portuguesa*, para. 18.

of the provisions relating to the free movement of persons) constitutes a *prima facie* restriction of the freedom to provide services, and will have to pass a proportionality assessment. *Finalarte* is still not completely clear-cut, because the requirement *in casu* on the posting company to respect the national labour law on paid annual leave comes in the form of a rather complex system applicable to the construction sector where the company is required to pay into a holiday fund and to provide the fund with all sorts of information (more information than national companies have to provide), as a consequence of a national law that itself states openly that it has been adopted 'to protect German businesses in the construction industry from the increasing pressure of competition in the European internal market, and thus from foreign providers of services',[61] meaning that there is an argument that the rules did not apply without distinction. Nevertheless, the judgment reflects the Court's new zeal on services following *Arblade* and *Mazzoleni*,[62] where it moves to the 'render less advantageous' interpretation of a *prima facie* restriction.[63] One of the reasons why *Finalarte* did not cause the controversy that *Laval* did is that the bitter pill was sugar-coated by the accepted justification: the Court held that as long as the application of the national rules genuinely benefited posted workers, they could be accepted as justified. In *Laval*, the Court performs an only slightly more intrusive operation, but without the anaesthesia of justification. It is *Finalarte* that explicitly lays down the two controversial principles on posting: exclusion of posted workers from the category and rights of 'workers' and framing their equal treatment through application of the home State labour protections as a restriction on the freedom to provide services. The Court pretends that this automatically follows from *Rush Portuguesa*, but it does not; and in any event, it does not bother to defend these legal revolutions further.

B. Phase 2: Directive 96/71/EC on Posted Workers (PWD), *Laval*, and its Discontents

1. The PWD

The Court's ruling in *Rush Portuguesa* had, on the one hand, brought posting within the scope of the freedom to provide services but, at the same time, had stated that Member States were 'free' to apply their labour rules to any person who is employed, even temporarily, within their territory, no matter in which country the employer is established, and to enforce these rules.[64] That, then, was also the

---

[61] Cases C-49/98 et seq, *Finalarte* (EU:C:2001:564), para. 38.
[62] Joined Cases C-369/96 and C-376/96, *Arblade and Others* (EU:C:1999:575), para. 33 and Case C-165/98, *Mazzoleni and ISA* (EU:C:2001:162), para. 22.
[63] Cases C-49/98 et seq, *Finalarte* (EU:C:2001:564), para. 28.
[64] *Rush Portuguesa*, para. 18.

56 SACHA GARBEN

spirit in which the Posted Workers Directive (PWD)[65] had been adopted—in fact, it appeared to go a little further, by not so much *allowing* as *requiring* host Member States to apply a hard core of labour standards to posted workers, out of a concern to prevent social dumping and to achieve equal treatment. As the Commission indicated in relation to the PWD as eventually adopted:

> To guarantee that the rights and working conditions of a posted worker are protected throughout the European Union, and to avoid 'social dumping' where foreign service providers can undercut local service providers because their labour standards are lower, the European Community law has established a core of mandatory rules regarding the terms and conditions of employment to be applied to an employee posted to work in another Member State. These rules will reflect the standards of local workers in the host Member State (that is, where the employee is sent to work).[66]

Article 3 is the heart of the PWD. Its first six paragraphs provided that Member States 'shall' ensure the application of a range of labour standards laid down by law or universally applicable collective agreement, including minimum rates of pay, and listed the circumstances (basically, where the posting is very short or insignificant) in which Member States were allowed to derogate from this obligation to apply their legislation. Paragraph 7 stated that the foregoing paragraphs did 'not prevent application of terms and conditions of employment which are more favourable to workers'. Paragraph 8 provided an alternative to universally applicable collective agreements in the absence of a system for declaring collective agreements to be of universal application. All this coincided with the above-stated intention of the Commission, to ensure a core of mandatory rules regarding the terms and conditions of employment to be applied to a posted worker, reflecting the standards of local workers in the host Member State. The Directive showed a clear preference for these standards to be applied by means of legislation, and not by means of collective agreement, but that in itself did not cast a doubt on the protective content of the rules.

At the same time, a careful analysis of paragraphs 9 and 10 may have alerted a (highly) circumspect reader to the possibility of a different approach, where these provisions indicate that Member States 'may' apply their provisions concerning temporary workers in the case the posting takes place via an agency and that the Directive would not preclude the application by Member States, 'in compliance with the Treaty, to national undertakings and to the undertakings of other States,

---

[65] Directive 96/71/EC of the European Parliament and of the Council of 16 December 1996 concerning the posting of workers in the framework of the provision of services, OJ 1996 L 18/1.

[66] As cited by House of Commons Standard Note, SNB/BT/301, 2009, https://researchbriefings.files.parliament.uk/documents/SN00301/SN00301.pdf (last viewed 17 February 2022).

on a basis of equality of treatment' of other terms and conditions of employment 'in the case of public policy provisions'. While paragraphs 1 to 8 suggest the Directive is about obliging Member States to impose their laws, the final two paragraphs are formulated in such a way that by providing a derogation for Member States to apply their laws, they make it seem that the rule is that they generally may not: and that what is listed in Article 3 is exhaustive with the exception of public policy provisions. While paragraphs 1 to 8, as well as the rest of the Directive including its preamble, seem to indicate that its provisions are 'minimum harmonisation' laying down a floor of host labour law protection, paragraphs 9 and 10 hint at the possibility that it may be maximum harmonization, where the floor is also the ceiling.

Despite this slight contradiction in the text of the Directive, the general impression was that the Directive was a floor of host labour law protection, and that it therefore was a 'social' Directive intended to protect workers and not aimed at liberalizing or facilitating the provision of services. In the words of its preamble: 'promotion of the transnational provision of services requires a climate of fair competition and measures guaranteeing respect for the rights of workers'.[67] Yet, is was adopted on the legal basis relating to services, strategically, 'to avoid the unanimity requirements applying to worker protection issues'.[68] The UK government, believing that the proposal was 'anti-competitive and would impede the operation of the Single Market',[69] considered this legal basis inappropriate, but ultimately did not challenge the PWD. It is not entirely clear what exactly the PWD's 'social' improvement to the status quo was considered to be. At that time, the Court had not yet ruled as it did in *Finalarte* that the equal treatment of posted and local workers was a *prima facie* restriction of the freedom to provide services. *Rush Portuguesa* instead had suggested a very wide freedom for the Member States to apply their standards of labour protection to posted workers—perhaps even not so much as a derogation from the freedom to provide services, but as not even being a restriction of it. It thus seems likely that the social aspect of the PWD that was opposed by Portugal and the UK that, as sending countries, benefited from a more liberal regime, lay more in the mandatory nature of the application of the host State's rules than in the firm belief that without the adoption of the PWD, the application of these national labour laws could effectively be challenged under direct application of the Treaty's services provisions.

---

[67] Recital 5 of the preamble.

[68] Dølvik and Visser, 'Free movement, Equal Treatment and Workers' Rights: Can the European Union Solve its Trilemma of Fundamental Principles?', 40 *Industrial Relations Journal* (2009) 513, at 518.

[69] Letter from Ann Widdecombe to Jimmy Hood, MP, 29 November 1994, cited in V. Keter, 'Posted Workers' House of Commons Library, Standard Note SNB/BT/301 2 February 2009, 2.

58 SACHA GARBEN

2. *Laval*

Still, some argued that the PWD as finally adopted gave 'rise to a puzzle',[70] with its provisions considered (by some too) protective of national labour standards, while at the same time based on the services provisions, and—as discussed above—at times ambiguously formulated. The Court was invited to solve this puzzle in the *Laval* case.[71] *Laval* concerned a Latvian construction firm that won a government contract to renovate a school in Sweden, where it posted some of its Latvian workers. The Swedish construction union started negotiations with Laval's Swedish subsidiary to extend the sectoral collective agreement to the posted workers and to negotiate their wages. Laval refused to agree to some of the conditions in the agreement, and so the negotiations failed, and the union called a blockade of Laval's building sites, assisted by the electricians' union, leading to the subsidiary's bankruptcy. The Court faced three important questions: (1) did the collective action by the workers—an exercise of their fundamental right to strike—constitute a *prima facie* 'restriction' on Laval's freedom to provide services, and if so, (2) were the labour conditions that the unions tried to procure covered by the PWD, and therefore mandated, or (3) if the labour conditions that the unions tried to procure were not covered by the PWD, could they be justified under the rule of reason, especially by reference to the fundamental right to strike and bargain collectively?

The Court ruled that the freedom to provide services applied to the actions of the workers, despite the fact that they were exercising their fundamental right to strike.[72] That finding is highly problematic in terms of fundamental rights protection and with regard to the horizontal application of the freedom to provide services,[73] but those questions lie outside the scope of our inquiry. Relevant for

---

[70] Davies, 'Posted Workers: Single Market or Protection of National Labour Law Systems?', 34 *Common Market Law Review* (1997) 571, at 572.

[71] Case C-341/05, *Laval un Partneri* (EU:C:2007:809). Libraries have been filled with case comments and critical commentary. See, inter alia, Hinarejos, 'Laval and Viking: The Right to Collective Action versus EU Fundamental Freedoms', 8 *Human Rights Law Review* (2008) 714, Freedland and Prassl (n. 32), de Schutter, 'Transborder provision of Services and 'Social dumping': Rights-Based Mutual Trust in the Establishment of the Internal Market', in I. Lianos and O. Odudud (eds), *Regulating Trade in Services in the EU and the WTO. Trust, Distrust and Economic Integration* (2011) 346, A. Bücker and W. Warnek, *Reconciling Fundamental Social Rights and Economic Freedoms after Viking, Laval and Rüffert* (2011), Joerges and Rodl, 'Informal Politics, Formalised Law and the "Social Deficit" of European integration: Reflections after the Judgments of the ECJ in Viking and Laval', 15 *European Law Journal* (2009) 18, Davies, 'One Step Forward, Two Steps Back? The Viking and Laval Cases in the ECJ', 37 *Industrial Law Journal* (2008); Barnard, 'Viking and Laval: an Introduction', 10 *Cambridge Yearbook of European Legal Studies* (2008) 463.

[72] Case C-341/05, *Laval un Partneri* (EU:C:2007:809), para. 95.

[73] For one, from the perspective of democratic constitutionalism there is much to say against the *Schmidberger* approach that considers the State's permission of individuals' exercise of their fundamental rights as a *prima facie* restriction (see Case C-112/00, *Schmidberger* (EU:C:2003:333)): the Court in *Laval* treats the internal market provisions as fundamental rights without any justification as to why (and to what extent) this should be the case, and does not engage in fair balancing (the rule-exception framework places the fundamental right to collective action in the position where it needs to be proportionate, while this is not required in turn from the internal market fundamental right). Secondly, we are not in the *Schmidberger* scenario where the State is held liable for the individuals' restriction, but instead the trade union in question is held directly liable, facing heavy fines. The Court in *Laval* applies the

our purposes is the fact that the judgment, curiously without explicitly referring to *Finalarte*, consolidates the radical approach that was piloted in that case, deciding that the equal treatment of posted workers and national workers is a restriction on 'one of the fundamental principles of the Community', as it is 'liable to make it less attractive, or more difficult'[74] for foreign companies to work in the Member State. This is not just a complete abandonment of the discrimination and even market access approach, but actually requires *advantageous* treatment of foreign service providers.[75] Primary law now apparently requires that these are given a competitive advantage over local companies, on the back of workers—who remain mysteriously carved out of the provisions on free movement of persons. There is no meaningful reasoning or explanation justifying this extreme interpretation, and the judgment does not address the paradoxical result that the very equal treatment held up as the central duty of Member States in the context of the free movement of workers is now a restriction of EU law that needs to be justified and proportionate.[76] This is all the more peculiar in light of the Court's reference to the general importance of the principle of equal treatment in EU law[77] and phrasing of the freedom to provide services as a 'specific expression' thereof[78]—a principle that is violated by its dis-application concerning posted workers and its abandonment with the deregulatory interpretation of *prima facie* restrictions.

freedom to provide services horizontally, against individuals, and it spends one meagre paragraph (95) on this revolution, simply invoking the judgments in Case 36/74, *Walrave* (EU:C:1974:140), Case C-415/93, *Bosman* (EU:C:1995:463) and Case C-309/99, *Wouters* (EU:C:2002:98) as precedents without any meaningful reasoning. While actually, it's apples and oranges. Most importantly, in those cases the private bodies in question had the actual, unilateral power to determine rules that regulated economic activities. Collective agreements are concluded between trade unions and employers—trade unions do not have a unilateral regulatory power. There was no actual regulation taking place, only attempts at arriving at such regulation. Furthermore, in *Walrave* and *Bosman*, there was a clear 'emphasis on attributing such (a horizontal) effect to the principle of non-discrimination on grounds of nationality' (Opinion of AG Mengozzi in *Laval* (EU:C:2007:291), para. 223), while in *Wouters* the Court actually refrains from explicitly ruling on the possibility of horizontal direct effect of the freedom to provide services beyond a focus on nationality-discrimination by stating that in any even the restriction in question was justified (*Wouters*, paras 121 and 122). An extension of the direct application of the freedom to provide services warrants an explanation, which is not given. The Opinion of AG Mengozzi does spend a little more time on the issue of horizontal direct effect, however, it basically amounts to an analysis of the Court's own previous case law on the issue (paras 223–227). The only actual argument that is put forward is a pure '*effet utile*' one: it will be difficult clearly to demarcate situations that include clear nationality discrimination from all others that the Court is prone to include as 'restrictions' (problematic as that in itself is), so it is easiest and most effective just to apply it to all scenarios.

[74] Case C-341/05, *Laval un Partneri* (EU:C:2007:809), para. 99.
[75] Or, if the argument is that there is somehow a disadvantage for the foreign provider compared to local companies, perhaps in the lack of transparency inherent in the Swedish system that affects foreign providers more, this argument is not made let alone substantiated anywhere.
[76] In fact, not just regarding 'workers' but as regards the free movement of 'persons' more generally. See Case 157/84, *Maria Frascogna v. Caisse des dépôts et consignations* (EU:C:1985:243), para. 23, where the Court referred to 'the fundamental principle of non-discrimination in the sphere of the free movement of persons' in reference to Article 7 of Regulation 1612/68.
[77] Case C-341/05, *Laval un Partneri* (EU:C:2007:809), para. 54.
[78] Ibid., para. 55.

60 SACHA GARBEN

As to the second question concerning the PWD more specifically, the Court considered that minimum rates of pay constitute a term of employment which, in Sweden, is not laid down in accordance with one of the means provided for in the PWD (either legislation or universally applicable collective agreements) and that therefore Sweden was not allowed 'to impose on undertakings established in other Member States, in the framework of the transnational provision of services, negotiation at the place of work, on a case-by-case basis, having regard to the qualifications and tasks of the employees, so that the undertakings concerned may ascertain the wages which they are to pay their posted workers'.[79] This is a crucial evolution in the law on posting. As Kilpatrick notes, this is the 'most visible step in the new approach in relation to host State standard-setting' as it makes 'the minimum floor in the Directive a ceiling'[80] and Article 3(1) an 'exhaustive list'.[81] As mentioned above, Article 3 is arguably something of a mixed bag, with some elements pointing in the direction of minimum harmonization, and others in the direction of maximum harmonization. One of the strongest textual elements supporting the former reading, is the seventh paragraph of the Article, which, the Court admitted, 'provides that paragraphs 1 to 6 are not to prevent application of terms and conditions of employment which are more favourable to workers'.[82] The Court essentially disapplies this provision, stating that it 'cannot be applied' as such, with the rather tone-deaf addition that this is, however, 'without prejudice to the right of undertakings established in other Member States to sign of their own accord a collective labour agreement in the host Member State, in particular in the context of a commitment made to their own posted staff, the terms of which might be more favourable'.[83] This interpretation of Article 3(7) PWD has been called *contra legem*,[84] and although the drafting history reveals that the provision may actually have been intended to refer to more favourable *home* State provisions,[85] the actual wording of the provision indeed strongly suggests a different approach—a departure from

[79] Ibid., para. 71.
[80] Kilpatrick, 'Laval's Regulatory Conundrum: Collective Standard-setting and the Court's New Approach to Posted Workers', 6 *European Law Review* (2009) 844, at 848.
[81] Ibid. See also M. Rocca, *Posting of Workers and Collective Labour Law: There and Back Again. Between Internal Markets and Fundamental Rights* (2015).
[82] In addition, according to recital 17, the mandatory rules for minimum protection in force in the host country must not prevent the application of such terms and conditions.
[83] Case C-341/05, *Laval un Partneri* (EU:C:2007:809), para. 81.
[84] Costamagna (n. 28), 86.
[85] Many thanks to Niall Coghlan for referring me to this drafting history: the European Parliament had proposed to insert 'Article 3d - This Directive shall be without prejudice to the right of Member States to apply or lay down laws, Regulations or administrative provisions which are more advantageous to workers posted to work temporarily in another Member State' ([1993] OJ C 72/83). The revised Commission proposal then stated '3. Paragraph 1 shall not prevent application of the terms and conditions of employment provided for by the law applicable which are more favourable to workers' with the explanation that this paragraph was inserted 'to reflect the opinion of Parliament and is designed to guarantee the application of the more favourable working conditions provided for by the law applicable, usually the law of the home country' (COM(93) 225 final, 3). See also Feenstra (n. 3) 321.

which would have needed a more elaborate justification than just saying that 'it cannot be interpreted' as what it literally says.

Finally, the Court held that the union's attempt to make Laval accept working conditions (other than pay) of a standard over and above the minimum set out in the PWD could not be justified with regard to the objective of protection of workers, since the Directive already served this purpose sufficiently. As regards the negotiations on pay, the Court reasoned that if a Member State wanted to protect workers, all it had to do was impose a minimum rate of pay through legislation or universal collective agreement. The strike action was thus unlawful, exposing the trade union to punitive damages.

When it rains, it pours. *Laval* has, of course, to be seen in conjunction with the equally infamous *Viking* ruling, which did not concern posting but instead a conflict between the freedom of establishment of a ferry company and the rights of its workers to prevent a re-flagging for the purposes of lowering labour costs;[86] and with *Rüffert*, in which it was held that EU law precluded Member States from requiring in public procurement that contractors pay their employees the remuneration prescribed by the collective agreement in force at the place where those services are performed.[87] Especially striking in that latter judgment was the reasoning of the Court as regards the possible justification on grounds of worker protection: requiring a level of remuneration that exceeds the minimum rate of pay applicable pursuant to national legislation cannot be necessary for the protection of workers—otherwise the same rate of pay would be required nationally and/ or for the whole sector. Completing the quartet is *Commission v. Luxembourg*, in which the Commission sought to push the new doctrine even further, an invitation accepted by the Court.[88] While *Laval* departed from the previously held assumption that the host State standards listed in Article 3(1) PWD were minimum standards, it did not explicitly exclude the possibility of higher standards being imposed on public policy grounds based on Article 3(10) PWD. The Commission actively sought to limit this possibility, opening infringement proceedings against Luxembourg for imposing a range of social standards in reference to public policy grounds, which the Court upheld with a restrictive reading of Article 3(10) PWD.

3. Discontents

The rulings were heavily criticized in academia,[89] and the political fall-out was significant, especially in the 'old' Member States that feared the systematic undercutting of their labour standards by companies established in 'new' Member States.[90] The issue played an important role in the 2014 European Parliament

---

[86] Case C-438/05, *Viking Line* (EU:C:2007:772).
[87] Case C-346/06, *Rüffert* (EU:C:2008:189).
[88] Case C-319/06, *Commission v. Luxembourg* (EU:C:2008:350).
[89] See literature n. 71.
[90] On 18 June 2015, Ministers of seven EU Member States (the 'higher wage' group made up of Austria, Belgium, France, Germany, Luxembourg, the Netherlands, and Sweden) sent a letter to the

elections, and has cropped up in national elections as well. Perhaps most prominently, the Court's approach furthermore led to a clash with the Council of Europe and the International Labour Organization.[91] *Laval* specifically was condemned for infringing the European Social Charter (hereafter ESC)—an international Treaty of the Council of Europe that occupies a special constitutional position in the EU legal order.[92] The Swedish Government had adopted the so-called *Lex Laval*, a package of measures to bring Swedish law into compliance the *Laval* judgment. In response to the ensuing complaint lodged with the European Committee of Social Rights, the enforcement body of the ESC, it was held that:

> the facilitation of free cross-border movement of services and the promotion of the freedom of an employer or undertaking to provide services in the territory of other States – which constitute important and valuable economic freedoms within the framework of EU law – cannot be treated, from the point of view of the system of values, principles and fundamental rights embodied in the Charter, as having a greater a priori value than core labour rights, including the right to make use of collective action to demand further and better protection of the economic and social rights and interests of workers.[93]

The Committee upheld the complaint and while only directly condemning the Swedish measures and not the judgment of the Court of Justice, it cast another shadow over that controversial case law.[94] Poignantly, the Committee took issue not just with the subordination of strike action to economic freedom,[95] but also with the exclusion of posted workers from the right to equal treatment: in other words, with the Court of Justice's decision to carve posted workers out of the EU notion of 'worker'. The Committee considered the *Lex Laval* to infringe Article

---

EU Employment Commissioner demanding a substantive change in the regulation of posting along the principle of 'equal pay for equal work in the same place' as the only way to re-balance economic and social principles in a fair way, and to avoid social dumping. Reported in European Parliament, *Posting of Workers Directive – current situation and challenges* (2016), https://www.europarl.europa.eu/RegData/etudes/STUD/2016/579001/IPOL_STU%282016%29579001_EN.pdf (last viewed 24 April 2023).

[91] See further Garben, 'A Balloon Dynamic in the Area of Social Rights', in I. Govaere and S. Garben (eds), *The Interface Between EU and International Law* (2019) 125.

[92] Ibid.

[93] European Committee of Social Rights, *Swedish Trade Union Confederation (LO) and Swedish Confederation of Professional Employees (TCO) v. Sweden*, No 85/2012 (3 July 2013), para. 122.

[94] Report by the Secretary General of the Council of Europe, 'State of Democracy, Human Rights and Rule of Law in Europe' (2014) SG (2014)1-Final, 41.

[95] Recently, the European Court of Human Rights (also) held that the EU economic freedoms are not to be considered as counter-balancing fundamental rights to the freedom of association and the right to take collective action in Art. 11 ECHR, but rather as elements to be taken into consideration in the assessment of proportionality of the restriction of a right included in the ECHR. See ECtHR, *Norwegian Confederation of Trade Unions (LO) and Norwegian Transport Workers' Union (NTF) v. Norway*, Application no. 45487/17, Judgment of 10 June 2021. Decision available online at http://hudoc.echr.coe.int/ (last viewed 13 April 2023).

19§4 ESC, which is the ESC's equivalent to Article 45 TFEU, on the right of migrant workers and their families to protection and assistance by the host State, and in particular to 'treatment not less favourable than that of their own nationals in respect of ... remuneration and other employment and working conditions'. Notably, the Committee considered that while in terms of length and stability of presence in the territory of the host State, and in terms of their relationship with the host State, the situation of posted workers is different from those migrant workers who go to another State to seek work and be permanently embedded there, this does not change the fact that 'for the period of stay and work in the territory of the host State, posted workers are workers coming from another State and lawfully within the territory of the host State' and thus 'fall within the scope of application of Article 19 of the Charter and they have the right, for the period of their stay and work in the host State to receive treatment not less favourable than that of the national workers of the host State in respect of remuneration, other employment and working conditions, and enjoyment of the benefits of collective bargaining.'[96]

C. Phase 3: Readjustment and its Limits

1. A Readjusted Case Law

Perhaps in response to the criticism, the Court of Justice readjusted its position to the benefit of national social regulatory autonomy in two subsequent rulings. In *Elektrobudowa*, the Court was again asked to interpret the PWD.[97] The case concerned 186 Polish workers posted to Finland who considered that they had not received sufficient wages. They assigned their claims to a Finnish trade union, which seized a national court, which in turn asked the Court for guidance on what the employer could be obliged to pay the workers under host State rules. The Court, in a remarkably different tone from the *Laval* quartet, sided with the trade union, confirming the possibility of workers to assign their wage claims to unions if the host Member State law so provides, regardless of whether home State law permits this. Even more importantly, the Court gave a broad interpretation of what host States could consider as part of the mandatory 'minimum rates of pay' under Article 3(1) of the Directive. Contrary to the Advocate General, the Court held that the minimum wage could be calculated by categorizing workers into pay groups based on criteria such as qualifications, training, experience and type of work (as long done transparently), and that it could include a posting-specific flat-rate daily allowance applicable for the entire duration of the posting. Similarly, it could include a reimbursement for daily travelling time. The Court also considered that the

---

[96] European Committee of Social Rights (n. 93), para. 134.
[97] Case C-396/13, *Sähköalojen ammattiliitto ry v. Elektrobudowa Spółka Akcyjna* (EU:C:2015:86).

cost of the accommodation provided by the employer and meal vouchers could not be deducted from the minimum rates of pay payable to the workers.

This important shift was followed in the highly anticipated *Regiopost* ruling.[98] Contrary to the position of the Commission, the Court held that the award of public contracts may be made subject by law to a minimum wage. In particular, the Court accepted the requirement of *Stadt Landau* for tenderers to commit to paying (sub-)contractors the wage of EUR 8.50 as stipulated in the regional public procurement law. Regiopost, one of the three German tenderers to provide municipal postal services, had argued that this requirement was incompatible with Article 56 TFEU and could not be authorized under the PWD or the Public Procurement Directive 2004/18, in reference to the *Rüffert* and *Bundesdruckerei* judgments.[99] While in *Rüffert* the collective agreement in question had not been declared universally applicable as required under Article 3(8) PWD, and the Public Procurement Directive (which allows the imposition of special social conditions) was not yet applicable, and while the *Bundesdruckerei* case involved the rather specific situation where the work was to be carried out in the home State, Regiopost appealed to the underlying reasoning of the Court in these two cases, where it subjected both Directives to the interpretation of Article 56 TFEU as primary law and held that wage requirements could only be justified in the name of worker protection if constituting the absolute minimum applicable in the most general terms, and so not including higher levels of protection set by public procurement.

The Court disagreed, considering the regional provision a 'law' that lays down a 'minimum rate of pay' under Article 3(1) PWD. The fact that the law only applied to public contracts did not make any difference, since the Directive makes the criterion of 'universal application' only applicable to collective agreements. This interpretation was 'confirmed ... by a reading ... in light of Article 56 TFEU'.[100] The Court reiterated that while wage requirements can constitute a restriction of the freedom to provide services, they may be justified by the objective of protecting workers. The fact that the requirement only applies in the context of public contracts again did not matter. While thereby departing from the *Rüffert* approach, the Court does not explicitly reverse its stance but instead goes to great length to distinguish it, stating that its ruling was based 'on certain characteristics specific to th[e] measure [in question]'.[101] The measure in *Rüffert* was a collective agreement applying solely to the construction sector, which did not cover private contracts and had not been declared universally applicable, and the pay set by that collective agreement exceeded the minimum pay applicable to that sector under the German

---

[98] Case C-115/14, *RegioPost GmbH & Co. KG v. Stadt Landau* (EU:C:2015:760).

[99] Directive 2004/18/EC of 31 March 2004 on the coordination of procedures for the award of public works contracts, public supply contracts and public service contracts, OJ 2004 L 134/114. Case C-549/13, *Bundesdruckerei GmbH v. Stadt Dortmund* (EU:C:2014:2235).

[100] *Regiopost*, para. 67.

[101] *Regiopost*, para. 73.

Posted Workers Law. By contrast, the minimum pay imposed in *Regiopost* is laid down in a legislative provision, which applies generally to the award of public contracts in the Land Rhineland-Palatinate, irrespective of the sector, and (at the time of the facts) no other minimum wage provisions applied.

2. Equal Pay for Equal Work: the Revised PWD

To avoid an explicit and principled reversal of its case law, the Court confined the rulings in *Elektrobudowa* and *Regiopost* to the specific facts, thereby leaving a number of burning questions unanswered.[102] But even if the extent to which *Laval*, *Rüffert*, *Luxembourg*, and *Bundesdruckerei* were overturned is open for discussion, the more permissive signal was a strong one. The judgments thereby arguably went quite some way to address the political concerns about social dumping since the *Laval* quartet that had led to calls for the revision of the PWD. In his election campaign, Commission President Jean-Claude Juncker had prominently committed to bolster the right of host States to enforce their labour standards through revision of the PWD following an 'equal pay for equal work' principle.[103] This approach thus promised a (limited) return of some kind to what appears to have been the better interpretation of EU law all along, namely to simply apply the principle of equality to posted workers as it does to all other workers in the EU. While the revised stance of the Court of Justice in *Elektrobudowa* and *Regiopost* is still a very long way from reintegrating posted workers into the Treaty provisions concerning the free movement of persons, it did boost the labour standards that host States were allowed to apply by means of legislation. That may have provided a crucial change in the bargaining positions of the Member States in the Council, to the favour of the Member States receiving posted workers.[104] Before the Court's change of direction, under application of the *Laval* quartet, the only legislative adjustment that had proven possible (and that, barely) was the adoption of an Enforcement Directive, allowing host States more effective methods of policing their legitimately imposed labour standards, rather than broadening the scope of these standards themselves.[105]

---

[102] First, it is not clear whether in the event of a generally applicable minimum wage, Member States can impose higher minimum standards by law in the specific context of public procurement. Secondly, the difficult relationship between the PWD and Article 56 TFEU is not fully clarified. Finally, it is unclear whether the same outcome can be expected in situations of cross-border service provision that imply the use of home State workers in a host State, but that for one reason or another do not fall under the PWD.

[103] See European Parliament, 'Parliament elects new European Commission', 22 October 2014 http://www.europarl.europa.eu/news/en/news-room/content/20141016IPR74259/html/Parliament-elects-new-European-Commission (last viewed 24 April 2023); Euractiv.com, 'Juncker defines 10 priorities for EU, seeks inter-institutional support', 14 November 2014 http://www.euractiv.com/sections/eu-priorities-2020/juncker-defines-10-priorities-eu-seeks-inter-institutional-support (last viewed 24 April 2023).

[104] Lubow and Schmidt (n. 30).

[105] Directive 2014/67/EU of the European Parliament and of the Council of 15 May 2014 on the enforcement of Directive 96/71/EC concerning the posting of workers in the framework of the provision of services and amending Regulation 1024/2012/EU on administrative cooperation through the Internal Market Information System, OJ 2014 L 159/11.

After *Elektrobudowa* and *Regiopost*, it was possible to adopt the Revised Posted Workers Directive (2018/957, hereafter RPWD).[106]

Most notably, the RPWD replaced the notion of 'minimum rates of pay' of Article 3(1)(c) PWD with 'remuneration'. There is a strong focus on equality in the RPWD, which mentions it 10 times and states, in the preamble, that:

> the principle of equal treatment and the prohibition of any discrimination on grounds of nationality have been enshrined in Union law since the founding Treaties. The principle of equal pay has been implemented through secondary law not only between women and men, but also between workers with fixed term contracts and comparable permanent workers, between part-time and full-time workers and between temporary agency workers and comparable workers of the user undertaking. Those principles include the prohibition of any measures which directly or indirectly discriminate on grounds of nationality.[107]

Crucially, the revision has guaranteed that, on the basis of equal treatment, posted workers will be entitled to all the constituent elements of remuneration rendered mandatory in the host Member State, so that those workers should receive remuneration based on the same binding rules as are applicable to the workers employed by undertakings established in the host Member State. The revision has furthermore established that where the effective duration of a posting exceeds 12 months, Member States shall ensure, 'irrespective of which law applies to the employment relationship', that undertakings guarantee, on the basis of equality of treatment, workers who are posted to their territory, in addition to the terms and conditions of employment referred to in Article 3(1), all the applicable terms and conditions of employment which are laid down in the Member State where the work is carried out.

Still, the RPWD, more than its predecessor, also engages with the freedom to provide services, and the preamble states that:

---

[106] Directive 2018/957/EU of the European Parliament and of the Council of 28 June 2018 amending Directive 96/71/EC concerning the posting of workers in the framework of the provision of services, OJ 2018 L 173/16. The Commission had proposed the revision on 8 March 2016 (COM(2016) 128 final). On the basis of the Protocol on the application of the principles of subsidiarity and proportionality, annexed to the TEU, 11 Member States' parliaments or chambers submitted a reasoned opinion (Bulgaria, Czech Republic, Denmark, Estonia, Croatia, Latvia, Lithuania, Hungary, Poland, Romania, and Slovakia). As the threshold of at least one third of the votes was reached, the so-called 'yellow card' procedure was triggered. On 20 June 2016 the European Commission concluded that the proposal did not constitute a breach of the subsidiarity principle and decided to maintain it. The text was adopted by the European Parliament in Plenary on 29 May 2018 and by the Council on 21 June 2018. The final act was signed on 28 June 2018. Member States had to adopt and publish, by 30 July 2020 at the latest, the laws, regulations, and administrative provisions necessary to comply with the RPWD.

[107] Recital 6 of the preamble.

ensuring greater protection for workers is necessary to safeguard the freedom to provide, in both the short and the long term, services on a fair basis, in particular by preventing abuse of the rights guaranteed by the Treaties. However, the rules ensuring such protection for workers cannot affect the right of undertakings posting workers to the territory of another Member State to invoke the freedom to provide services, including in cases where a posting exceeds 12 or, where applicable, 18 months. Any provision applicable to posted workers in the context of a posting exceeding 12 or, where applicable, 18 months must thus be compatible with that freedom. In accordance with settled case law, restrictions to the freedom to provide services are permissible only if they are justified by overriding reasons in the public interest and if they are proportionate and necessary.[108]

This demonstrates how the EU legislator remains caught in the web spun by the Court of Justice's case law.[109] Whether or not there was a political desire explicitly to reintegrate posted workers in Treaty provisions on the free movement of persons and/or to rescind the qualification of equal treatment as a *prima facie* restriction on the freedom to provide services, the EU legislator would not have been permitted to do so, as secondary legislation has to comply with the Court's interpretation of primary law. Indeed, the Court has held that 'the prohibition on restrictions on freedom to provide services applies not only to national measures, but also to measures adopted by the European Union institutions'.[110] It is only the Court itself that is allowed fundamentally to amend the approach on posted workers under the Treaty provisions on persons and services.

3. The RPWD Upheld by the Court of Justice: 'OK, as Long as They Are Not Fully Equal'

Precisely that relationship between primary and secondary law was at issue in the challenge by Hungary to the RPWD.[111] Hungary argued that the Directive could not have been based on the Treaty's services provisions, because it does not promote the freedom to provide services, and that—in fact—it should not have been adopted at all because it contravenes that freedom as interpreted by the Court and because it concerns the issue of pay which under the social policy legal basis of Article 153 TFEU (which Hungary argued was the appropriate provision) is excluded as per Article 153(5) TFEU. The Court disagreed on all counts and upheld the validity of the RPWD. That, in itself, is an important outcome, as it serves to protect at least a minimum degree of democratic input into the governance of the

---

[108] Recital 10 of the preamble.
[109] Gareth Davies has described the EU legislator as an 'agent' of the Court, also referring to the area of posting albeit before this revision: Davies, 'The European Union Legislature as an Agent of the European Court of Justice', 54 *Journal of Common Market Studies* (2016) 846.
[110] Case C-97/09, *Schmelz* (EU:C:2010:632), para. 50 and the case law cited.
[111] Case C-620/18, *Hungary v. Parliament and Council* (EU:C:2020:1001).

68 SACHA GARBEN

issue of posting in the EU, even if—as noted above, and further discussed below—the decision-making power of the democratic institutions is still dramatically circumscribed by the Court's legal configuration of the area.[112] Apart from that, for the purposes of our discussion, three important legal findings emanate from the judgment: (1) the scope of the services legal basis in the context of pursuit of the general interest; (2) the extent to which full equal treatment may be imposed in the context of posted workers; and (3) the application of Article 153 TFEU in the area of posting.

Re (1): In what is methodologically the strongest aspect of the judgment, the Court of Justice takes a step towards a 'constitutional embedding' of the internal market.[113] It builds on its *Tobacco Advertising* case law[114] in the context of the free movement of goods, to consider that as long as the conditions for use of an internal market legal basis are fulfilled, the legislator can rely on this legal basis to adopt measures pursuing other public interests. In a strong statement to this effect, the Court rules that:

> in relation to the free movement of goods, persons, services and capital the measures adopted by the EU legislature, whether measures for the harmonisation of legislation of the Member States or measures for the coordination of that legislation, not only have the objective of facilitating the exercise of one of those freedoms, but also seek to ensure, when necessary, the protection of other fundamental interests recognised by the Union which may be affected by that freedom.[115]

Especially where the EU has already legislated, the Court of Justice finds that there should be the possibility of amending this legislation in light of changed circumstances or advances in knowledge, to improve the protection of a public interest affected by the freedom that was facilitated by the adoption of the prior act.[116] In such a situation, 'the EU legislature can properly carry out its task of safeguarding those general interests and those overarching objectives of the European Union recognised by the Treaty only if it is open to it to adapt the relevant EU legislation to take account of such changes or advances.'[117] This holistic, constitutional approach

---

[112] Davies (n. 109); Lubow and Schmidt (n. 30).

[113] Schiek (n. 9).

[114] Case C-380/03, *Federal Republic of Germany v. European Parliament and Council of the European Union* (EU:C:2006:772).

[115] Case C-620/18, *Hungary v. Parliament and Council* (EU:C:2020:1001), para. 105.

[116] 'Where a legislative act has already coordinated the legislation of the Member States in a given EU policy area, the EU legislature cannot be denied the possibility of adapting that act to any change in circumstances or advances in knowledge, having regard to its task of safeguarding the general interests recognised by the FEU Treaty and of taking into account the overarching objectives of the European Union laid down in Article 9 of that Treaty, including the requirements pertaining to the promotion of a high level of employment and the guarantee of adequate social protection': Case C-620/18, *Hungary v. Parliament and Council* (EU:C:2020:1001), para. 41.

[117] Ibid., para. 42.

is consistent with the TFEU's various mainstreaming clauses[118] and the contextualization of the internal market in Article 3(3) TEU, and boosts the capacity of the EU legislative process as a forum of transnational democratic decision-making.

Re (2): As to the possibility to require the full equal treatment of posted workers, the ruling is not unequivocal, but seems to suggest that the Court prohibits the EU legislator from doing so. Hungary had argued that it was disproportionate for the RPWD to require almost full application of the host Member State's employment laws in relation to postings exceeding 12 months, in response to which the Court states (para. 156) that:

> Such rules in relation to a posting for a long period appear necessary, appropriate and proportionate, in order to ensure greater protection in relation to terms and conditions of employment for workers posted for a long period to a host Member State, while distinguishing the situation of those workers from that of workers who have exercised their right to freedom of movement or, more generally, that of workers who reside in that Member State and are employed by undertakings that are established there.

Similarly, in relation to Hungary's argument that, having regard to the fact that posting is temporary, 'the provisions of the contested directive, since their effect is to ensure posted workers equal treatment with workers employed by undertakings established in the host Member State, go beyond what is necessary to achieve the objective of protection of those posted workers',[119] the Court considers that the RPWD's amendments do not 'have the consequence that those workers are placed in a situation that is identical to or analogous to the situation of workers who are employed by undertakings established in the host Member State'[120] and 'do not entail the application of all the terms and conditions of employment of the host Member State, since only some of those terms and conditions are, in any event, applicable to those workers under Article 3(1) of the amended Directive 96/71'.[121]

While these statements could be interpreted as simply debunking Hungary's assertions without making any final judgement on what would happen if instead the full 'identical or analogous' treatment were required by a hypothetical directive, they do give the impression that the Court will not allow the EU legislator to 'correct' the Court's fundamental decision to exclude posted workers from the free

---

[118] Article 7 TFEU provides that: 'The Union shall ensure consistency between its policies and activities, taking all of its objectives into account and in accordance with the principle of conferral of powers', and in Articles 8 to 13 TEU, the Union is required to take account in its policies of equality and non-discrimination, 'a high level of employment, the guarantee of adequate social protection, the fight against social exclusion, and a high level of education, training and protection of human health, environmental protection and sustainable development and consumer protection'.

[119] Case C-620/18, *Hungary v. Parliament and Council* (EU:C:2020:1001), para. 147.

[120] Ibid., para. 148.

[121] Ibid., para. 149.

movement of persons in EU law. I would posit that the only leeway there could be is if the EU legislator would (in a hypothetical future measure) present changed circumstances or advances in knowledge that would justify an amended legal framework—more specifically, if it could produce evidence that the alleged reasons for the exclusion of posted workers from equal treatment and worker status have been superseded. And they have. Empirical studies now show that:

> firms see posting as a way to engage a highly flexible and exploitable workforce. Firm posting practices centre around reducing labour costs and increasing flexibility, if necessary by evading local labour laws and norms, as a way of gaining a competitive edge. Posting is not so much a discrete form of employment as it is one of several parallel recruitment modalities used to establish a flexible European labour market governed by neither host nor sending country. This contrasts with the underlying assumptions behind the European legislation and CJEU case law, which insist that posted workers are embedded in their home country labour markets and never enter into the host country labour market.[122]

In particular, the EU legislator could make an appealing argument to the Court that its exclusion of posted workers from the free movement provisions is based on a now outdated distinction between, on the one hand, those migrant workers who would choose one other Member State to emigrate to, and where they would stay for the rest of their lives, they and their families ultimately fully assimilating to nationals of that State; and, on the other hand, the posted workers who would for a short period in their life fulfil a specific work mission in another Member State, all the while remaining fully attached to and integrated in their home state, where they would return and stay for the rest of their lives—neither category corresponding to the dynamic reality of the lives of EU transnational workers who may very well study/train, work and live in various Member States, never fully attaching to any one Member State but instead embodying what it is to be a European worker. To deprive such 'Eurostars'[123] of the status of EU worker can, on the basis of these 'changed' circumstances and insights (or so one could argue), no longer be defended, as EU workers is what they are par excellence.

Re (3): The Court's approach to Article 153 TFEU seems problematic. As this legal basis allows the EU to adopt, 'by means of directives, minimum requirements' in the field of 'working conditions', it is difficult to follow the Court in its decision that it 'could not constitute the legal basis of the contested directive'.[124] The Court arrives at this conclusion with the somewhat bewildering argument that 'it is clear' that the RPWD 'does not in any way constitute a harmonisation directive, since it

---

[122] Houwerzijl and Berntsen (n. 2).
[123] A. Favell, *Eurostars and Eurocities. Free Movement and Mobility in an Integrating Europe* (2008).
[124] Case C-620/18, *Hungary v. Parliament and Council* (EU:C:2020:1001), para. 69.

does no more than prescribe as obligatory certain rules of the host Member State in the event of a posting of workers by undertakings established in another Member State, while respecting, as is stated in recital 24 of the contested directive, the diversity of national industrial relations'.[125] This is a *non sequitur* in various ways. First, it seems to indicate that the EU may only use Article 153(2)(b) to 'harmonize', but this does not follow from the text of that provision at all, which does not refer to harmonization but to 'minimum requirements'. No definition of harmonization that requires the imposition of substantive uniform norms, nor a requirement to 'harmonize' and not to 'coordinate' when using a particular legal basis, has ever been applied before. Furthermore, while it is true that the RPWD does not substantively harmonize the working conditions that it mandates/requires host States to apply, the same goes for a number of social policy measures. Notably, the directives on non-standard forms of employment such as temporary agency work (adopted on the basis of Article 153 TFEU), fixed-term and part-time work (adopted as directives implementing EU social partner agreements on the basis of Article 155 TFEU, which refers back to the conditions of Article 153 TFEU) all provide for equal treatment as regards working conditions for these types of workers without substantively harmonizing these working conditions. Is the validity of these measures suddenly in question? The Court appears to make a highly consequential distinction between the 'coordination' and 'harmonization' of national laws, without further explanation. Does this now mean that Article 114 TFEU, which refers to 'harmonization', may not be used to adopt 'coordination' measures? And that Article 53 TFEU which refers to directives 'for the coordination of the provisions laid down by law, regulation or administrative action in Member States' excludes the adoption of substantive harmonization?

A new distinction in EU law between coordination and harmonization and the prohibition to use legislative legal bases in relation to one or the other, depending on whether they refer to 'requirements by means of directives', 'approximation', 'coordination', or 'harmonization': all of this would be revolutionary if taken seriously. But in fact, the better view is that we should not take this too literally. The Court's main concern is, quite evidently, to validate the use of Articles 53 and 62 TFEU as the legal basis of the RPWD. In its case law on the choice of legal basis, it has held that if there are two legal bases that could be used for a measure, the choice must be made by reference to the measure's aims: if there is a main one, then the more specific legal basis relating to the dominant aim has to be used; if the aim is genuinely dual, then both legal bases must be used. Worker protection is clearly either the main aim of the RPWD or equally as important as the promotion of services, not less, so that would mean that if Article 153 TFEU were available as a legal basis, the current RPWD would be wrongly based and have to be annulled. It would thus

---

[125] Ibid., para. 68.

72 SACHA GARBEN

seem that it is for that specific purpose that the Court declares that Article 153 TFEU cannot be used as the legal basis, and the 'harmonization versus coordination' argument is a (rather poor) improvization to forge that result.

While this realization may mitigate the above-mentioned concerns about these new distinctions, it is such case-specific constitutional gymnastics that landed us in the posting quandary to begin with. Such shenanigans are not just inadvisable in terms of unforeseen long-term consequences but go to the heart of a central legitimacy problem facing EU law, where—as further explored in Section 4 below—the end (i.e. to promote deeper integration) appears to justifies all means (of legal interpretation). And it is unnecessary: credible alternative solutions were available that would still have maintained the end result. For instance, it is now clear that the PWD and, assumingly, its revision, constitute both the minimum *and maximum* standards that host Member States must apply. Since Article 153 TFEU only allows the adoption of 'minimum standards', it would not have been able to constitute the legal basis for the RPWD.[126] Indeed, that apparently constituted the main argument of the Legal Services of the Parliament and the Council to oppose the Parliament and Council's desire to adopt the RPWD on the dual legal bases of Articles 53/62 TFEU and Article 153 TFEU.[127] The Court could thus have referred to its interpretation of the PWD as both minimum and maximum harmonization in *Laval*, and have concluded that Article 153 TFEU was therefore not available as a legal basis for the RPWD, thereby rejecting Hungary's argument without having to make any unhelpful distinctions between 'coordination' and 'harmonization'.

4. Posting Assessed on the Basis of Democracy and Constitutionalism

A. The (Over)Constitutionalization of the Internal Market Provisions: the Free Movement Provisions as Fundamental Rights

Who determines what is fair mobility in the EU, and on what basis? To a very large degree, as testified by the above discussion in the specific area of posting, it is the Court of Justice, and it does so without any real methodology apart from a concern for expanding European integration. The Court has placed itself in this position, constitutionalizing[128] the free movement provisions, according them direct effect

[126] Alternatively, the Court could consider that the centre of gravity test does not apply in the same way when revising an existing measure, where there may be an interest in being able to maintain the original legal basis.

[127] Lubow and Schmidt (n. 30).

[128] On the term, see Loughlin, 'What Is Constitutionalisation?', in P. Dobner and M. Loughlin (eds), *The Twilight of Constitutionalism: Demise or Transmutation?* (2010) 47. On EU constitutionalism: M. Poiares Maduro, *We The Court. The European Court of Justice and the European Economic Constitution* (1998); Hatje, 'The Economic Constitution within the Internal Market', in A. Bogdandy and J. Bast (eds), *Principles of European Constitutional Law* (2010) 589; Schiek (n. 9); Davies (n. 109). It should be

and primacy including over national constitutional law, and giving them an enormous scope of application and normative position in the EU legal order, without ever really clarifying the normative reasons or justifications for treating them as such. These provisions benefit from a constitutional protection against majoritarian decision-making at national and EU levels that stands in a tense relationship to the principle of democracy and that on an application of constitutionalism can only be justified in the case of fundamental rights. In other work I have concluded that, in the EU legal order, the free movement provisions are indeed interpreted and applied as fundamental rights, even if this is not openly acknowledged, and that they are treated by the Court in that context as *primuses inter pares*: as the *most fundamental* fundamental rights.[129] Such a fundamentalized treatment of the free movement provisions does not necessarily follow from the text of the Treaties, nor—at face value—does it seem justified by human dignity[130] (or entailed by 'what it means to be a person'[131]) or to ensure a well-functioning democracy.[132]

Some prominent scholars have questioned this degree of constitutionalization,[133] and the *Laval* quartet has certainly played its role in their critique.[134] Should the application and interpretation of the freedom to provide services and freedom of establishment, and the free movement of persons, goods and services, as well as their interrelation, be determined by the legislative process (only)? What is the appropriate degree of constitutional value that should be given to (some aspects of) the free movement provisions (alongside more conventional fundamental rights)? And, as a meta-question, how are we to tackle these difficult questions? Here we return to our methodology of democratic constitutionalism. If we consider the

---

noted that 'constitutionalization' in itself does not have to equate the free movement provisions to 'real' fundamental rights as such. This touches on the related, yet distinct, question of hierarchy or 'balance' between the free movement provisions and fundamental rights such as protected national constitutions, the EU Charter and the ECHR. It is one thing for the free movement provisions to have primacy and direct effect in relation to national legislation, another for them to circumscribe the EU legislative process, yet another for them to condition fundamental rights protected at national, at EU and/or at the international level.

[129] Garben, 'The "Fundamental Freedoms"' (n. 10).

[130] Human dignity is considered the source of all human rights.

[131] For Hoffman, there are three factors to weigh in the question of whether a right is fundamental: (i) is the right specifically identified as fundamental by a controlling text or authority or logically entailed by a right to be recognized; (ii) is the right empirically necessary to the realization of a recognized fundamental right; (iii) is possession of the right entailed by what it means to be a person, so that no person devoted to human dignity could reasonably prefer to live in a society where the right was not recognized: Hoffman, 'What Makes a Right Fundamental', in D. Hoffman (ed.), *Our Elusive Constitution – Silences, Paradoxes, Priorities* (1942) 191.

[132] It is argued that fundamental rights should not be conceptualized to constrain democracy (*contra* Waldron) but instead as necessary to ensure the well-functioning of an inclusive and robust democracy in the long term. See also C. Gearty, *Principles of Human Rights Adjudication* (2004), at 88.

[133] Grimm (n. 29); Davies (n. 109); Scharpf, 'The Asymmetry of European Integration, or Why the EU Cannot Be a "Social Market Economy"', 8 *Socio-Economic Review* (2010) 211; S. Schmidt, *The European Court of Justice and the Policy Process: The Shadow of Case Law* (2018).

[134] Scharpf (n. 133), Lubow and Schmidt (n. 30).

common ground of contemporary constitutional democracy to be the commitment to the triptych of democracy, the rule of law and fundamental rights,[135] and within that context the latter to be concerned with upholding human dignity and guaranteeing a robust and inclusive democracy,[136] then we can identify three justifications for the treatment of the free movement provisions as fundamental rights that can be applied directly to the Member States to supersede their democratically enacted laws, and that similarly bind the EU legislator. As we will come to see, however, that treatment can only be defended to a narrower extent than the current interpretation applied by the Court of Justice.

1. Individual Agency and Dignity

The first defence of the constitutional treatment of the Treaty's free movement provisions is what de Witte has called 'the argument from aspirational justice': that the free movement provisions expand 'individual agency beyond the parameters of permissive behaviour in the citizens' own Member State, and as such provides a trampoline for the attainment of the individual's aspirations'.[137] This is an individualistic approach that considers the right to move freely between Member States as a way to foster individual dignity through enhanced agency and self-determination. It could furthermore be considered an essential part of what it means to be a member of a political order: that one has the possibility to pursue one's life in every territorial part of it, on an equal basis as other members. That idea would therefore also provide the normative ground for the right to equal treatment in relation to the economic opportunities offered in different parts of the federal territory and ties this argument to citizenship and the general principle of equality and the fundamental right to non-discrimination. A less 'aspirational' and more basic dimension of the argument, but all the more relevant for fairness, is that free movement provides an exit from fundamental rights abuses and oppressive regimes within the federal territory—which in turn may act as a disincentive for rulers to oppress and thereby act as a federal bulwark against autocracies.[138]

All this provides a strong normative justification for treating free movement provisions as fundamental rights, but only when it comes to the actual movement of individuals in their capacity as citizen, worker, or self-employed person and their equal treatment, in a way that enhances their dignity—which is the dimension of the 'fundamental freedoms' that is indeed already captured in Article 15(2) of the EU Charter of Fundamental Rights. It is certainly less convincing in relation

---

[135] Garben, Govaere, and Nemitz (n. 10).

[136] Gearty (n. 132).

[137] De Witte, 'Sex, Drugs & EU Law: The Recognition of Moral and Ethical Diversity in EU Law', 50 *Common Market Law Review* (2013) 1545, at 1552.

[138] For the general argument that federalism acts as a protection against autocracies, see D. Halberstam, 'Federalism: A Critical Guide' (2011) *University of Michigan Public Law Working Paper* No. 251.

to business' economic rights to 'market access' in relation to services (or goods, capital, and establishment for that matter). It would furthermore not be an absolute right, and open to some counterbalancing against other fundamental rights and interests.

2. Transnational Democracy

A second defence of the constitutionalization of the free movement provisions is an argument of transnational democracy,[139] also referred to as the argument from 'transnational effects'.[140] Market integration is, to the extent that it de-nationalizes decision-making to ensure that affected interests from other Member States are taken into account, 'desirable on account of democracy itself'.[141] This transnational democracy argument is strong in relation to positive market integration through the adoption of EU-level rules regulating the internal market. This is an important counterbalance to the often-heard argument that the EU legislative process is not as democratically legitimate as national decision-making. Here, however, we are concerned with the 'negative' integration dimension of the internal market, through the application of the free movement provisions, and the constitutionalization thereof—which actually circumscribes positive integration through legislation. It is in this context that the transnational democracy argument has been most widely used, becoming 'a shibboleth for the European pro-attitude'[142] even if its validity is much less obvious than in relation to positive market integration. The idea is that the fact that individual actors can confront the rules of other Member States that disadvantage (or inconvenience?) them but in which they have had no representation, and to have these rules subjected to a judicial balancing test, is democracy-enhancing because it takes account of those excluded from the decision-making process. Maduro rendered the first comprehensive account of this argument in relation to the free movement provisions, considering that 'the representation of the interests of nationals of other Member States within national political processes'[143] argues in favour of a 'fundamental rights conception of the free movement rules'.[144]

The normative basis for the right to have one's interest taken into account that underlies this argument could be that the democratic principle demands that the interests of those that are affected by a decision need to be weighed in that decision

---

[139] Joerges, 'European Law as Conflict of Laws', in C. Joerges and J. Neyer (eds), *Deliberative Supranationalism Revisited* 20 *EUI Working Paper Law* (2006) 22.

[140] Somek, 'The Argument from Transnational Effects I: Representing Outsiders through Freedom of Movement', 16 *European Law Journal* (2010).

[141] Ibid., 315.

[142] Ibid.

[143] Maduro, 'Article 30 and the European Economic Constitution: Reforming the Market or the State?', in M. Maduro (ed.), *We The Court: The European Court of Justice and The European Economic Constitution* (1998) 167.

[144] Ibid., 168.

somehow.[145] But there needs to be some qualification as to what it means to be 'affected' to the extent that it triggers the right to be 'represented' or have one's interest weighed. If any theoretical and elusive effect were to be counted, with the inclusion of opportunity costs, everyone should always be represented everywhere, leading to theoretically and practically absurd outcomes. The original democratic idea of 'no representation without taxation' would suggest a much higher threshold: an actual, direct cost needs to be incurred. That it very different from the opportunity cost of potentially having made more money if the rules on economic activity would have been more lenient. Somewhat tongue in cheek, it may be noted that the free movement provisions seem to have been given an interpretation closer to 'representation without taxation' rather than the other way around. It would thus have to be determined which foreign 'affected interests' are so important that they need to be judicially enforced in national democracies.

Additionally, for the democratic argument to make sense, it needs to be ensured that all relevant interests are balanced proportionately. But what does that entail? It would seem to necessitate some weighing of interest by reference to the number of people, as is done in democratic procedures. *Note bene*: that is a very different exercise from a judicial proportionality test, where interests are weighed in the abstract, detached from the actual democratic weight given in numbers of citizens attached to these interests. And whose excluded interests are we to weigh exactly? Are we speaking of the individual interest of the foreign company that has to comply with product composition rules when wanting to sell on the host State market? If so, the free movement rules are a rather disproportionate 'counterbalance': they put the interest of, say, some foreign alcohol producers on par[146] with those of potentially millions of citizens who may favour their specific rules on the production of beer. Giving priority to this foreign minority interest through judicial imposition of 'mutual' recognition amounts to a decisively non-democratic way to 'enhance transnational democracy'. Moreover, this foreign private interest is very difficult to separate from the more general private interest, shared by all alcohol producers both within and outside the host State, of having a laxer regulatory regime. That particular interest has already been weighed in the national democratic process and has therefore not been really excluded,[147] and thus does not deserve to be enforced by the supranational constitution.

Are we instead speaking of the 'economic benefit' of other Member States more generally and abstractly? Perhaps as a collective extension of the idea of improved individual dignity through economic opportunity and upward social mobility?

---

[145] For a critical account of this 'all-affected principle' more generally, see Lagerspetz, 'Democracy and the All-Affected Principle', 10 *Res Cogitans* (2015) 6.

[146] Not to speak of the fact that the free movement provisions in their current interpretation are the rule and all other interests the exception, arguably thereby weighing the former more heavily than the latter. See Garben, 'The "Fundamental Freedoms"' (n. 10).

[147] Somek (n. 140).

Aside from the fact that it is very difficult to determine the due weight that should be attached to such an abstract interest, it is also not entirely true that other Member States are without any representation in national decisions of market-regulation: to the extent that this falls within the EU's legislative competence under the internal market, common rules can be adopted to supersede national ones. That means that there is a genuinely democratic avenue to have all relevant federal interests taken into account. Objections that this decision-making process is arduous and prone to deadlock do not deny that what matters most for the transnational effects argument is the *existence of a forum* of transnational democratic decision-making in which the relevant interests can be brought to the table, regardless of the result. Finally, it should be noted that to the extent that mutual recognition implies that market actors should be able to export their 'home' regulatory regimes to other Member States, it does not resolve but instead 'flips' the democracy-failure: the people of the host State are forced to accept the rules decided on in another Member State in which they have had no say. That can hardly be a satisfactory solution from the very democratic perspective that lies at the heart of the justification.

All in all, the democratic argument seems to be able to justify the constitutionalization of the free movement provisions only to the limited extent that it concerns the adoption by a Member State of a rule that *specifically and directly* harms the economic interest of foreign economic actors, i.e. a rule that discriminates. It is only that interest that is really excluded from the national democratic process (as general economic interests are not) and may not sufficiently be protected by the EU legislative process. This interest may, however, still be counterbalanced by other interests: the democratic principle merely provides an argument for the weighing of the foreign actor's interest in due proportion alongside the (many!) other interests that make up the decision-making process. This suggests a rather broad scope for possible 'justification' of even overtly protectionist measures. As to the argument that we are only able to effectively enforce that rule if we adopt an obstacle-approach rather than an intention-approach, and thereby include also indistinctly applicable measures to trigger the judicial weighting exercise (since Member States will simply cover up their protectionism behind a veneer or impartiality), we need to insist again that there is always[148] an even more transnationally democratic remedy available: the adoption of common EU-level rules.

Since the negative application of the Treaty's free movement provisions is the much less refined, less effective and more contentious method of market integration from a democratic perspective, the democratic argument itself requires that precedence is given to positive market integration. This is a crucial point, because the constitutionalization of the free movement provisions does not only mean that they trump national legislation, but in some ways more importantly also that

---

[148] The EU's competences are, ostensibly, limited by the principle of conferral but its internal market competence is broad and cross-cutting.

they trump EU-level legislation. After all, the free movement provisions are primary law and in the EU's hierarchy of norms they outrank ordinary legislation. That means we should be especially careful not to let the far less democratic transnational forum of negative integration limit the far more democratic transnational forum of positive integration. Such would, in any event, undermine the extent to which negative integration can lay claim to the argument of transnational democracy to justify itself. Far from sustaining the current sweeping reach and application of the free movement provisions, the democratic argument can thus only support a narrow version of their constitutionalization, limited to protectionist measures, and does not allow the limitation of the far more democratic transnational forum of positive integration. Not respecting these limits will mean that the democratic argument collapses in on itself, having the free movement provisions create a democratic deficit not only in relation to national democracy but also in relation specifically to transnational democracy.

3. The Protection of Individual Economic Autonomy

Finally, one could consider the protection of individual economic autonomy as a normative justification for the treatment of the free movement provisions as fundamental rights. Babayev has considered that there is an overlap between the freedom to conduct a business, as laid down in Article 16 of the Charter of Fundamental Rights (CFR), and the free movement provisions.[149] He argues that Article 16 CFR 'reflects the customary liberal meaning of individual economic autonomy and protects it as an end in itself. On the other hand, a more specific form of such autonomy appears to be manifested through free movement rights'.[150] Seen as such, the free movement provisions are still 'not aimed to ensure the freedom to carry out an economic activity *per se*', but they would 'confer the freedom to access the market in a Member State'[151] in a way that potentially exceeds the justifications under the transnational democracy and aspirational justice arguments. For our purposes, the relevant idea is that the protection of economic entrepreneurship is already part of the fundamental rights catalogue of the EU, and the free movement provisions can therefore legitimately be seen as specific manifestations of that fundamental right in a federal, cross-border context. But that does not yet provide us with the underlying normative justification, from a perspective of democratic constitutionalism, of such a fundamental right to economic autonomy in the first place, and what that underlying value means for the interpretation of that right in general and the specific manifestations in a free movement context.[152]

---

[149] Babayev, 'Private autonomy at Union level: On Article 16 CFREU and free movement rights', 53(4) *Common Market Law Review* (2016) 979.

[150] Ibid.

[151] Ibid., 981.

[152] In this regard, it may be relevant to consider the meaning of Article 52(2) CFR, which provides that 'Rights recognised by this Charter which are based on the Community Treaties or the Treaty on European Union shall be exercised under the conditions and within the limits defined by those Treaties'.

Article 16 CFR provides that '[t]he freedom to conduct a business in accordance with Union law and national laws and practices is recognised'. The wording indicates that this freedom is inherently relative and can be limited by both regulations and practices, suggesting it is one of the 'weaker'[153] rights in the EU Charter.[154] It is widely considered to be 'one of the less traditional rights',[155] not generally protected in international human rights instruments. The freedom to conduct a business under Article 16 CFR is drawn from the Court's case law[156] and the constitutional traditions common to Member States. To what end and extent does national constitutional law protect this individual autonomy against majoritarian decision-making? It is not traditionally or universally present in the national constitutional law of the Member States, with many having only recognized versions of this right very recently and some not as a(n enforceable) constitutional right at all.[157] Where the freedom to conduct a business is recognized in national constitutional law, it tends to allow a relatively wide scope of limitation in the public interest and it is generally conceived as a right of individuals to set up an economic activity or join a profession rather than concerning the general exercise of economic activity.[158]

The EU Fundamental Rights Agency considers that the 'freedom to conduct a business is about enabling individual aspirations and expression to flourish, about encouraging entrepreneurship and innovation, and about social and economic development'.[159] Applying the principles of democracy and constitutionalism, the freedom to conduct a business has a certain role in ensuring a robust democracy, to the extent that it helps to empower individuals—especially those who are disadvantaged—through economic activity to prevent concentrations of (economic) power and equalize societal asymmetries. This would suggest a reading where the right is about fostering the possibility of individual entrepreneurship, in the sense of enabling citizens to set up an economic activity or join a profession, within a broader picture of creating more socio-economic progress and equality

---

That could be taken to mean that Article 16 CFR should not be applied so as to expand the scope of the internal market provisions, which speaks against the approach by the Court of Justice in Case C-201/15, *Anonymi Geniki Etairia Tsimenton Iraklis (AGET Iraklis) v. Ypourgos Ergasias, Koinonikis Asfalisis kai Koinonikis Allilengyis* (EU:C:2016:972), where the freedom to conduct a business laid down in Article 16 CFR was used to broaden the application of the freedom of establishment notably by requiring a *prima facie* restriction to comply with Article 16 CFR in order for it to be justified.

[153] Groussot et al., 'Weak Right, Strong Court – The Freedom to Conduct Business and the EU Charter of Fundamental Rights', in S. Douglas-Scott and N. Hatzis (eds), *Research Handbook on EU Law and Human Rights* (2017) 326.
[154] Ibid.
[155] European Union Agency for Fundamental Rights, 'Freedom to conduct a business: exploring the dimensions of a fundamental right' (2015) Luxembourg, Publications Office of the European Union.
[156] Cases 4/73, *Nold* (EU:C:1974:51) and 230/78, *SpA Eridiana and others* (EU:C:1979:216) (freedom to exercise an economic or commercial activity); Case 151/78, *Sukkerfabriken Nykøbing* (EU:C:1979:4); Case C-240/97, *Spain v. Commission* (EU:C:1999:479) (freedom of contract).
[157] For an overview, European Union Agency for Fundamental Rights (n. 155)
[158] Ibid.
[159] Ibid.

in society. The free movement provision would serve this interest specifically in a transnational setting. This fundamental right would not, upon such a constitutional democratic reading, provide a 'sword' for companies in the operation of their business against workers, citizens, and general public interest standards—that would be a perverse result. This brings us very close to the reading of the fundamental rights dimension of the free movement provisions already contained in Article 15(2) CFR: that of individual empowerment and agency in a federal context. Especially the idea that the free movement provisions (in their constitutional form) are not only about territorial mobility as an end in itself, but also about creating the possibility for upward *social* mobility, brings us quite firmly within justified fundamental rights territory. But that would reject a reading of Article 16 CFR and the Treaty's free movement provisions as being about businesses' right to contractual freedom or the running of a business (across borders) without any interference.

4. Intermediate Conclusion: A Re-constructed Scope of Constitutional Protection of Free Movement

Thus, taken together, the arguments from aspirational justice, transnational democracy, and individual economic autonomy support the constitutionalization of the free movement provisions to a degree: a strong right to actual physical movement and equal treatment of individuals (not so much companies) in their capacity as citizen, worker, or self-employed person, and some degree of economic autonomy/entrepreneurship—which is the dimension of the 'fundamental freedoms' that is already captured in Articles 15(2), 16, and 17 CFR. In addition, we may include a right to challenge (but not necessarily see disapplied) protectionist restrictions on the cross-border activities of companies. Any constitutionalization beyond this important, but—compared to the status quo deeply internalized by EU law and its community—rather limited dimension cannot benefit from the arguments for aspirational justice, individual autonomy, and transnational democracy even cumulatively applied,[160] regardless of whether this is provided for in the Treaties.

The free movement provisions should thus be re-interpreted as focused specifically on reviewing direct and, possibly, clear indirect discrimination and not on the general economic freedom of companies; moreover, leaving significant scope for counterbalancing with other fundamental rights and public interests (such as the right to fair and just working conditions of not just the posted workers, but also the local workers). Internal market rights, on this logic, should not be interpreted as forcing national democracies to take decisions applicable on their own territory that are detrimental to their own interests for the benefit of other jurisdictions'

---

[160] *Contra* de Witte, who considers that the arguments from aspirational justice, transnational effects, and a more general argument of constraining democracy to combat minority-rights abuses, can justify the current approach in EU free movement law. See de Witte (n. 137).

interests, unless this is necessary for the dignity of EU citizens from other Member States. And importantly, they should be interpreted so as to leave maximum scope for transnational democratic decision-making through the EU legislative process, and thus be very careful not to circumscribe this process apart from for what is necessary to respect Articles 15(2), 16, and 17 CFR.[161]

This interpretation is, indeed, a fundamental departure from the settled case law of the Court of Justice. In that sense, this chapter joins other calls from various scholars to revisit some of the basic EU law doctrines,[162] especially those concerning the place of the market freedoms in society,[163] in light of progressive insight as well as a changed (constitutional) context of the post-Lisbon EU legal order.[164] The current expansive approach to the free movement provisions was perhaps appropriate for an ambitious and dynamic supranational trade organization, but—it is argued—is not befitting the constitutional order that the EU has now become (somewhat ironically, arguably in part thanks to those free movement provisions), and the constitutional democracy that it should aim to be in the future. In such a constitutional democracy, the only substantive norms that should be upheld by the judiciary against democratic decision-making are fundamental rights. The foregoing analysis has shown that only a limited part of the free movement provisions can be legitimately treated as fundamental rights in this way. The rest, therefore, is 'over-constitutionalized'.[165]

B. Posting Assessed from a Perspective of Democratic Constitutionalism

Where does that leave us in relation to the specific issue under discussion in this contribution: the transnational posting of workers in the EU? The above normative framework suggests that the judiciary should only constitutionalize the question—thereby limiting the scope of democratic decision-making at national and EU levels—to the extent that this is necessary to protect the constitutional right to

---

[161] As noted above, Article 52(2) CFR provides that: 'Rights recognised by this Charter which are based on the Community Treaties or the Treaty on European Union shall be exercised under the conditions and within the limits defined by those Treaties'. This supports the fact that there may be a partial overlap between the CFR rights and the Treaty provisions on free movement, and suggests that in terms of their scope and conditions of application of these rights to the extent that they overlap, one should refer to the Treaties and not the CFR. That does not, in my view, mean that we cannot and should not consider the appropriate scope of application, and interpretation, of the Treaty provisions in light of fundamental rights theory. It should be stressed that nothing in the Treaties as such prevents the interpretation of the internal market provisions as proposed in this chapter, and it is instead the case law interpreting these provisions that is invited to change.

[162] For instance, C. Barnard, 'Restricting Restrictions: Lessons for the EU from the US?', 68 *The Cambridge Law Journal* (2009) 575.

[163] See, for instance, Davies (n. 26).

[164] Such as Schiek (n. 9).

[165] Grimm (n. 29); Scharpf (n. 133); Schmidt (n. 133).

82   SACHA GARBEN

actual physical movement and the equal treatment of posted workers in order to enhance their agency and dignity, and, in the name of transnational democracy, to allow posting companies to (rebuttably) challenge directly (and possibly very clear cases of indirectly) discriminatory measures. The reality is a far cry from this.

1. The Dignity of Posted Workers

The case law serves the possibility of posted workers' actual physical movement across borders, even if this is presently on the basis of an indirect right via their posting company. Most problematically, as we have seen, the case law has denied the posted worker the rights conferred by the Treaty provisions concerning the free movement of workers. At the same time, they are not 'service providers' with attendant rights either—rather, they are treated as 'services' with no actionable right under either the provisions on services or workers (except, as we have seen as per *Kranemann* and *Hudziński and Wawrzyniak*, where such application of the provisions on workers does not entail a cost for the employer). By treating the posted worker as a mere production factor in their companies' cross-border activities and depriving them of their status and rights as EU 'worker', the case law actively disempowers and disowns posted workers, arbitrarily denying them the rights accorded to all other permanently—or temporarily—mobile workers. How undignified not to treat them as persons under the free movement provisions in the Treaties, and how discriminatory.

Some will argue that it is not actually in the interest of posted workers to be treated equally to local workers: that it is in their socio-economic interest to be able to work under 'home' wages in 'host' countries, since this provides employment opportunities, and that if they really want to benefit from host State conditions, they should apply for a permanent job with an employer established there. First of all, even if this implausible and far-fetched argument that less favourable treatment benefits posted workers were accepted, it would still not justify the outcomes achieved by the Court of Justice's case law: it cannot justify that they are constitutionally deprived, by the judiciary, of the right to equal treatment. Furthermore, this rather cynical approach over-estimates the agency of the (posted) worker that it in turn undermines (and underestimates the corrosive effects that wage/regulatory competition has on the labour market and the posted worker's opportunities thereon). Yes, it has been empirically reported that posted workers even where subject to precarious and exploitative employment relationships that bordered on human trafficking and forced labour and featured wage theft, excessive working hours, employer intimidation, and substandard accommodation, still did not protest because '(1) "a bad employer was at least better than no employer at all", that (2) pay in the home country was less than in the host country, even when the employer was cheating, and that they (3) fear employer intimidation and financial sanctions'.[166] But these are 'choices' made out of disempowerment and not

---

[166] Houwerzijl and Berntsen (n. 2), referring to Berntsen, 'Reworking Labour Practices: on the Agency of Unorganized Mobile Migrant Construction Workers', 30 *Work, Employment and Society*

empowerment. Study after study documents the dystopian reality of exploitative posting practices.[167] Most studies also 'document that mobile EU workers prefer to be employed by a host country-based firm'.[168] This is not to say that all posting amounts to exploitation. But it seems hard to argue that by way of constitutional decree, posted workers should receive lower standards of labour protection because this befits them.

If only anecdotally, then still symbolically, a case like *Elektrobudowa* sees a group of posted workers indeed fighting for equal treatment, in solidarity with local workers. The Court ultimately responds with sympathy, but it can only be too little too late, since the case law now merely plays within the rules it itself has created and cannot apparently make the principled reversal on equal treatment that it should. Under the readjusted case law, consolidated now in the RPWD, the situation is brought closer to the one where posted workers would be treated as all other EU workers but their position remains less favourable (as the Court itself stresses in defence of the validity of the RPWD); they remain deprived of direct rights and are thus vulnerable to the whims of interpretation of acceptable justifications and *prima facie* restrictions under the services provisions. Indeed, the defence of their interest is structurally placed in the hands of others and thus only pursued where it so happens to coincide with those others' interests: to the extent that local trade unions will stand up for these foreign workers because it is also in the interest of their own members, or to the extent that the host Member State decides to 'fight' for the application of its rules because this is in the interest of its own labour market, or—ostensibly—to the extent that the posting employer's interest is also that of the worker. And moreover, the treatment of the posted worker as a 'service' and not a 'worker' is offensive as a matter of principle.

One is left to wonder if things would have turned out very differently had the *Finalarte* case featured not the complaint of a company under the services provisions but instead posted workers who received less favourable employment conditions from their posting employer. Or, as said above, if the Act of Accession of Portugal had not happened to limit the free movement of Portuguese workers for a transitional period. Judgments such as *Kranemann* and *Hudziński and Wawrzyniak* indeed suggest that the Court would not have denied posted workers their fundamental rights, and that it has ultimately all been a bit of a methodological mistake rather than a deliberate decision. A more mistrustful view is, however, also available: perhaps the posting case law shows that for the Court, equal treatment or the well-being of mobile EU workers is not, ultimately, the concern, and that it is only

---

(2016) 472, and Thörnqvist and Bernhardsson, 'Their Own Stories – How Polish Construction Workers Posted to Sweden Experience Their Job Situation, or Resistance Versus Life Projects', 21 *European Review of Labour and Research* (2015) 23.

[167] See the various studies discussed in Houwerzijl and Berntsen (n. 2).
[168] Ibid.

84   SACHA GARBEN

'championing' these (for which it has often been credited) *as an instrument* to further integration. Indeed, the only thing that can explain the exclusion of posted workers from the free movement of persons, and their (poor) treatment as assets of their employers as a rational decision of the Court rather than an inadvertent mistake, is that this maximizes the mobility under both freedoms (services and workers) even if it is at the cost of the actual well-being and rights of the moving worker. Equality, then, is not really a goal or value in itself. It is easily sacrificed on the altar of (market-) expansionism.[169]

2. Transnational Constitutional Democracy and the (R)PWD

This means that from a constitutional democratic perspective, the only acceptable solution is and remains to treat posted workers as EU workers, to include them in the free movement provisions and thus to apply the principle of non-discrimination. Not doing so is a fatal mistake that renders the law on posting decidedly unfair. But the transgression does not stop here. Apart from this, we need also to address the problematic approach in *Laval* to transnational democratic decision-making. To be clear, on the basis of the foregoing discussion, if the case law had correctly treated posted workers as EU workers, the EU legislator would not have needed to adopt the PWD. In fact, it would not have had the right to do so: even if it were interpreted as minimum harmonization, the PWD would have been at odds with the idea that by way of the constitutional commitment to equality *all* labour protections of the host State would have to be applied. Such would have circumscribed the legislative process, but as discussed in the previous section, that constitutional conditioning of democracy would have been justified in the name of posted workers' fundamental rights. In *Laval*, the Court circumscribes the legislative process in the opposite direction: it limits the capacity of the political process to procure equal treatment for posted workers, and to protect local workers from the corrosive effects of downward wage competition.

The area of posted work is, indeed, a perfect case study to demonstrate the profound democratic deficit implied by the over-constitutionalization of the freedom to provide services.[170] All the EU legislator can do is play within the fundamental rules of the game designed by the Court, and perhaps try to tinker in the

---

[169] While the effects of Court of Justice's expansive approach to EU law generally, and the internal market provisions in particular, have arguably favored a free-market or ordo-liberal approach to political economy (as argued prominently by Scharpf), this would seem to be the consequence of the Court's commitment to furthering European integration rather than an ideological commitment of the Court itself. For a comprehensive analysis of the case law of the Court on the free movement and competition provisions in relation to the opposing Ordo-Liberal and Service Public schools of thought, and the conclusion that what drives the case law is functionalism and neither of these theories: W. Sauter and H. Schepel, '"State" and "Market" in the Competition and Free Movement Case Law of the EU Courts', TILEC Discussion Paper (2007) 24. See also, for further discussion of this issue, Garben, 'The "Fundamental Freedoms"' (n. 10).

[170] Davies (n. 109).

margins.[171] Whether or not modifications of the case law are accepted depends entirely, and unpredictably, on the mood of the Court. At all times, the legislator's approach can be overturned by reference to the Court's (re)interpretation of primary law. As Lobow and Schmidt have found on the basis of a detailed qualitative assessment of the RPWD's negotiation and adoption process:

> The constraining case law of the ECJ and the far-reaching rights under the free provision of services has marked the negotiation over the reform of the PWD. Following the politically contentious case law of the Laval ruling, there was mounting pressure to revise the status quo on posted workers and further prevent opportunities for social dumping. The Court played the role of a procedural agenda-setter. Moreover, it acted as a gate-keeper, restricting the available policy options on the agenda.[172]

There is no justification in democratic constitutionalism for this approach. We have seen that the Court's far-reaching interpretation of the freedom to provide services that renders the legislator as a disempowered agent[173] of the judiciary is not mandated by the protection of fundamental rights or transnational democracy: on the contrary, it infringes both. It is not even mandated by the text of the respective provisions in the Treaties, which (1) position the application of the freedom to provide services as secondary to the application of the free movement of persons (Article 57 TFEU); (2) as regards the freedom to provide services, speak consistently of the rights of 'persons' and 'nationals' (Articles 56 and 57 TFEU) and not 'companies' or 'firms' (as in the provisions on establishment); (3) furthermore suggest that restrictions on services need to be actively abolished by the legislator (Article 61 TFEU); and (4) in any event need to be interpreted in conformity with Article 3(3) TEU, which contextualizes the aims of the internal market by reference to a competitive 'social market economy' aiming at 'social progress', the combating of 'social exclusion and discrimination', and the promotion of 'social justice and protection', as well as 'economic, social and territorial cohesion, and solidarity among Member States'[174]—thereby squarely precluding an application of the freedom to provide services as a right to structurally undermine social protection and to induce wage competition.

---

[171] See on the complex dynamics between primary and secondary law including in the area of posting Syrpis, 'The Relationship between Primary and Secondary Law in the EU', 52 *Common Market Law Review* (2015) 461, commenting on the somewhat unusual methodology in *Rüffert* where the Court is limiting the freedom to act under the Treaties by its controversial interpretation of secondary law (the PWD), at 479.

[172] Lubow and Schmidt (n. 30).

[173] Davies (n. 109).

[174] See also the Court of Justice's judgment in Case C-620/18, *Hungary v. Parliament and Council* (EU:C:2020:1001), paras 41, 48, 105, and 106.

5. Conclusion

All is not well that ends well. While the RPWD, as upheld by the Court, will be considered a victory by most critics of the case law on posted workers, and has indeed brought the situation closer to one that can be accepted as compatible with democratic constitutionalism, it has resolved neither the unfairness of excluding posted workers from the Treaty provisions on persons and the right to non-discrimination nor the unfairness of the procedure through which these decisions have been and continue to be made. This needs to change. Fortunately, some tentative signs of a different approach are visible in the Court's ruling in *Hungary v. Parliament and Council*, where it constitutionally embeds the legal basis on services, giving a holistic, public interest reading that bolsters the capacity of the EU legislative process to act as a genuinely effective forum of transnational democracy. This approach needs to be pursued further, not just in relation to positive integration but far more importantly with regards to the negative reach of the internal market provisions. Their direct application needs to be scaled back to the point where their judicial enforcement is necessary only in light of the protection of the fundamental free movement rights of persons. The precise implications thereof are open for debate, but the central argument of this contribution is that that debate needs to take place in terms of democratic constitutionalism and not vacuous integrationism.

4

Economic Activity and EU Citizenship Law: Seeding Means-based Logic in a Status-based Freedom

Niamh Nic Shuibhne[*]

1. Introduction

Alongside the political rights conferred by Articles 22–24 of the Treaty on the Functioning of the European Union (TFEU), two of the most active areas of European Union (EU) citizenship law illustrate the potential significance of Union citizenship from a legal perspective. First, the limits of the right to move and reside protected by Article 21 TFEU are extensively litigated and debated in the context of eligibility for social assistance (and social security more generally) when Union citizens are not economically active within the meaning of Article 7(1)(a) of Directive 2004/38[1] in a host Member State.[2] Second, Article 20 TFEU extends

---

[*] I am very grateful to the participants in the Authors' Workshop for their comments and especially to Marc Steiert for reading an earlier draft of this chapter.

[1] Directive 2004/38/EC on the right of citizens of the Union and their family members to move and reside freely within the territory of the Member States, OJ 2004 L 158/77.

[2] See in particular, Case C-85/96, *Martínez Sala* (EU:C:1998:217); Case C-184/99, *Grzelczyk* (EU:C:2001:458); Case C-413/99, *Baumbast* (EU:C:2002:493); Case C-456/02, *Trojani* (EU:C:2004:488); Joined Cases C-22/08 and C-23/08, *Vatsouras and Koupatantze* (EU:C:2009:344); Case C-140/12, *Brey* (EU:C:2013:565); Case C-333/13, *Dano* (EU:C:2014:2358); Case C-67/14, *Alimanovic* (EU:C:2015:597); Case C-299/14 *García-Nieto* (EU:C:2016:114); Case C-308/14 *Commission v. UK* (EU:C:2016:436); Case C-181/19, *Jobcenter Krefeld* (EU:C:2020:794); Case C-710/19, *G.M.A. (Demandeur d'emploi)* (EU:C:2020:1037); Case C-535/19, *A (Soins de santé publics)* (EU:C:2021:595); Case C-709/20, *CG* (EU:C:2021:602); Case C-247/20, *VI v. Commissioners for Her Majesty's Revenue and Customs (Assurance maladie complète)* (EU:C:2022:177). From a wide literature, e.g. Davies, 'Has the Court Changed or Have the Cases? The Deservingness of Litigants as an Element in Court of Justice Citizenship Adjudication', 5 *Journal of European Public Policy* (2018) 1442; Dougan, 'The Constitutional Dimension to the Case Law on Union Citizenship', 31 *European Law Review* (2006) 613 and 'The Bubble that Burst: Exploring the Legitimacy of the Case Law on the Free Movement of Union Citizens', in M. Adams, H. de Waele, J. Meeusen, and G. Straetmans (eds), *Judging Europe's Judges: The Legitimacy of the Case Law of the European Court of Justice* (2013) 127; Editorial comments, 'The Free Movement of Persons in the European Union: Salvaging the Dream While Explaining the Nightmare', 51 *Common Market Law Review* (2014) 729; Hailbronner, 'Union Citizenship and Access to Social Benefits', 42 *Common Market Law Review* (2005) 1245; Iliopoulou-Penot, 'Deconstructing the Former Edifice of Union Citizenship? The *Alimanovic* Judgment', 5 *Common Market Law Review* (2016) 1007; Kramer, 'Earning Social Citizenship in the European Union: Free Movement and Access to Social Assistance Benefits Reconstructed', 18 *Cambridge Yearbook of European Legal Studies* (2016) 270; Nic Shuibhne, 'Limits Rising, Duties Ascending: the Changing Legal Shape of Union Citizenship', 52 *Common Market*

Niamh Nic Shuibhne, *Economic Activity and EU Citizenship Law: Seeding Means-based Logic in a Status-based Freedom*
In: *Revisiting the Fundamentals of the Free Movement of Persons in EU Law*. First Edition. Edited by: Niamh Nic Shuibhne,
Oxford University Press. © Niamh Nic Shuibhne 2023. DOI: 10.1093/oso/9780198886273.003.0004

protection to Union citizens that does not depend on the exercise of free movement at all, notably through residence rights in the Union citizen's home State for third country national family members on whom the Union citizen is dependant.[3] Why do these examples represent the distinctive legal qualities of Union citizenship? Because Articles 20 and 21 TFEU have been used by the Court of Justice to determine the questions that they raise: more specifically, neither the claims to equal treatment of citizens who are not economically active in a host State nor the residence status of third country national family members in a static Union citizen's home State can be based on the Treaty's economic freedoms.

Conversely, Member State nationals who work or are self-employed in a host State[4] are not usually categorized or thought about as 'citizens' since it is assumed

---

Law Review (2015) 889; O'Brien, 'Civis Capitalist Sum: Class as the New Guiding Principle of EU Free Movement Rights', 53 *Common Market Law Review* (2016) 937, and 'The Great EU Citizenship Illusion Exposed: Equal Treatment Rights Evaporate for the Vulnerable (*CG v The Department for Communities in Northern Ireland*) (Case Comment)', 46 *European Law Review* (2021) 801; Rennuy, 'The Trilemma of EU Social Benefits Law: Seeing the Wood and the Trees', 56 *Common Market Law Review* (2019) 1549; Tecqmenne, 'Migrant Jobseekers, Right of Residence and Access to Welfare Benefits: One Step Forward, Two Steps Backwards?', 46 *European Law Review* (2021) 765; Thym, 'The Elusive Limits of Solidarity: Residence Rights of and Social Benefits for Economically Inactive Union Citizens', 52 *Common Market Law Review* (2015) 17; and Verschueren, 'Preventing "Benefit Tourism" in the EU: a Narrow or Broad Interpretation of the Possibilities Offered by the ECJ in *Dano?*', 52 *Common Market Law Review* (2015) 363.

[3] See in particular, Case C-34/09, *Ruiz Zambrano* (EU:C:2011:124); Case C-434/09, *McCarthy* (EU:C:2011:277); Case C-256/11, *Dereci and Others* (EU:C:2011:734); Case C-456/12, *O and B* (EU:C:2014:135); Case C-165/14, *Rendón Marín* (EU:C:2016:675); Case C-115/15, *NA* (EU:C:2016:487); Case C-133/15, *Chavez-Vilchez* (EU:C:2017:354); Case C-82/16, *KA and Others* (EU:C:2018:308); Case C-836/18, *Subdelegación del Gobierno en Ciudad Real* (EU:C:2020:119); and Case C-451/19, *Subdelegación del Gobierno en Toledo (Séjour d'un membre de la famille – Ressources insuffisantes)* (EU:C:2022:354). See further, Azoulai, 'Transfiguring European Citizenship: from Member State Territory to Union Territory', in D. Kochenov (ed.), *EU Citizenship and Federalism: The Role of Rights* (2017) 178; Coutts, 'The Shifting Geometry of Union Citizenship: a Supranational Status from Transnational Rights', 21 *Cambridge Yearbook of European Legal Studies* (2019) 318; Kalaitzaki, 'The Application of EU Fundamental Rights during the Financial Crisis: EU Citizenship to the Rescue?', 27 *European Public Law* (2021) 331; Kroeze, 'The Substance of Rights: New Pieces of the *Ruiz Zambrano* Puzzle', 44 *European Law Review* (2019) 238; Nic Shuibhne, '(Some of) the Kids Are All Right: Comment on *McCarthy* and *Dereci*', 49 *Common Market Law Review* (2012) 349, and 'The "Territory of the Union" in EU Citizenship Law: Charting a Route from Parallel to Integrated Narratives', 38 *Yearbook of European Law* (2019) 267; Reynolds, 'Exploring the "Intrinsic Connection" between Free Movement and the Genuine Enjoyment Test: Reflections on EU Citizenship after *Iida*', 38 *European Law Review* (2013) 376; and van Eijken and Phoa, 'The Scope of Article 20 TFEU Clarified in *Chavez-Vilchez*: Are the Fundamental Rights of Minor EU Citizens Coming of Age? (Case Comment)', 43 *European Law Review* (2018) 949.

[4] Work and self-employment for the purposes of this chapter reflect the understanding of economic activity in Article 7(1) of Directive 2004/38/EC, which establishes that '[a]ll Union citizens shall have the right of residence on the territory of another Member State for a period of longer than three months if they: (a) are workers or self-employed persons in the host Member State.' Freedom to provide or receive services is not mentioned in Directive 2004/38/EC and is presumed to be connected to Article 6(1), which provides a right to reside 'on the territory of another Member State for a period of up to three months without any conditions or any formalities other than the requirement to hold a valid identity card or passport'; and Article 7(1)(b), which establishes a right of residence for longer than three months where Union citizens 'have sufficient resources for themselves and their family members not to become a burden on the social assistance system of the host Member State during their period of residence and have comprehensive sickness insurance cover in the host Member State. Work is defined

that Articles 45 and 49 TFEU will provide all the legal protection that might be needed. More than this, also considering the rights conferred on workers by Regulation 492/2011,[5] it is normally taken for granted that freedom of movement for workers and freedom of establishment produce *deeper* legal privilege. While, in many respects, that is undoubtedly true,[6] the aim of this chapter is to probe the relationship between Union citizenship and economic activity further. More specifically, in what ways does Union citizenship matter in economic free movement law?

The right to move and reside conferred by Article 21(1) TFEU is formally characterized as a residual right that applies only when one of the Treaty's economic freedoms does not. But that conception does not properly capture the more meshed nature of free movement rights in reality. However, while the influence of economic free movement rights on citizenship rights has been largely constitutive and rights-deepening, the influence of citizenship rights on economic free movement rights has become—in some respects—more deconstructive and rights-thinning. For the purposes of this chapter, a distinction between status and means is invoked both to explain and evaluate the implications of that claim in more detail. In economic free movement law, once the definition of worker or self-employed person is satisfied, equal treatment on the grounds of nationality then flows from the holding of that status. In EU citizenship law, for economically inactive citizens, holding the nationality of a Member State—and thus the status of Union citizenship[7]—is necessary but not sufficient: access to equal treatment is conditioned further by the citizen's economic means[8] or otherwise, in some situations, navigated through requirements that measure the extent of the citizen's integration in the host State.

---

in the case law of the Court of Justice as 'activities which are real and genuine, to the exclusion of activities on such a small scale as to be purely marginal and ancillary' while, distinguishing work from self-employment (and therefore from freedom of establishment), '[t]he essential feature of an employment relationship is, according to the case-law of the Court, that for a certain period of time a person performs services for and under the direction of another person in return for which he receives remuneration' (Case C-542/09, *Commission v. Netherlands* (EU:C:2012:346), para. 68).

[5] Regulation 492/2011/EU on freedom of movement for workers within the Union, OJ 2011 L 141/1.

[6] A debate often framed around the theme of EU law and personhood: see e.g. O'Brien, 'I Trade Therefore I Am: Legal Personhood in the European Union', 50 *Common Market Law Review* (2013) 1643; L. Azoulai, S. Barbou des Places, and E. Pataut (eds), *Constructing the Person in EU Law: Rights, Roles, Identities* (2016); and Kramer, 'From Worker to Self-entrepreneur: The Transformation of *Homo economicus* and the Freedom of Movement in the European Union', 23 *European Law Journal* (2017) 172.

[7] As the Court has expressed it, '[b]y Article 9 TEU and Article 20 TFEU, the authors of the Treaties thus established an inseparable and exclusive link between possession of the nationality of a Member State and not only the acquisition, but also the retention, of the status of citizen of the Union' (Case C-673/20, *Préfet du Gers* (EU:C:2022:449), para. 48).

[8] These conditions are mainly captured by the requirement of lawful residence, which, for citizens not economically active in the host State, is mainly (though not exclusively) fulfilled by satisfying the conditions on sufficient resources and comprehensive sickness insurance in Article 7 of Directive 2004/38/EC (see again, n. 4; and outlining the 'gradual system' of residence rights that the Directive establishes over time, see Joined Cases C-316/16 and C-424/16, *B and Vomero* (EU:C:2018:256), paras 51–54).

90 NIAMH NIC SHUIBHNE

Fundamentally, this chapter shows that the conventional emphasis on status in economic free movement law[9] yields increasingly to the emphasis on means and/ or integration in EU citizenship law.[10] But it cautions that conflating different free movement ecologies represents a darker side of the idea that Union citizenship is 'destined to be the *fundamental* status of Member State nationals'[11] and of Directive 2004/38's ambition of 'remedying th[e] sector-by-sector, piecemeal approach to the right of free movement and residence' (recital 4).

The chapter is structured as follows. Section 2 introduces the relationship between economic activity, citizenship, and the free movement of persons in a formal sense, explaining the intended residual nature of the right to move and reside conferred by Article 21 TFEU. The actual legal significance of citizenship for economic activity is then investigated in more detail through the lens of equal treatment with host State nationals. Section 3 looks at integration requirements and considers, more particularly, the extent to which economic activity establishes *sufficient* integration in a host State for the purposes of claiming equal treatment there. Section 4 then interrogates anomalies produced by the interplay of relevant legal sources, addressing the interaction of primary law and secondary law, on the one hand, and of Directive 2004/38 and Regulation 492/2011, on the other.

Across these examples, it is argued that efforts to recalibrate economic free movement rights have not yet been systemically worked through. It is acknowledged that the questions raised by this chapter sit in the thorny wider domain of debates about the shape and purpose of freedom of movement and Union citizenship. In that light, defending the historical disconnect between status and means in economic free movement law has, unsurprisingly, come under strain. An admitted difficulty with pursuing or even contemplating more comprehensive reform is that, in the current political and economic climate, confronting status and means mismatches might aggravate more than relieve the vulnerability of economically active citizens—vulnerability created in part, ironically, by the application of concepts and definitions designed for EU citizenship law. We should think very carefully before essential features of economic free movement are recast: importantly—in large part, because the evidence base that is presumed to support more restrictive free movement rights would have to be more robust, beyond an intuitive sense of relevant factors or preferences;[12] but also, because the freedoms long protected by EU internal market law really matter on their own terms.

---

[9] Though also acknowledging anomalies: see in this volume, for example, the argument advanced by Sacha Garben (Chapter 3), which proposes reframing the scope of Article 45 TFEU to address the exclusion of posted workers from 'worker' status within the meaning of EU law.

[10] For the purposes of this chapter, 'EU citizenship law' refers to the rights and duties that find their legal basis in Articles 20–24 TFEU.

[11] Case C-184/99, *Grzelczyk* (EU:C:2001:458), para. 31 (emphasis added).

[12] See e.g. Šadl and Sankari, 'Why Did the Citizenship Jurisprudence Change?', in D. Thym (ed.), *Questioning EU Citizenship: Judges and Limits of Free Movement and Solidarity in the EU* (2017) 89; Davies (n. 2); and Blauberger, Heindlmaier, Kramer, Sindbjerg Martinsen, Sampson Thierry, Schenk, and Werner, 'ECJ Judges Read the Morning Papers: Explaining the Turnaround of European Citizenship

2. Economic Activity, Citizenship, and the Free Movement of Persons in EU Law

The free movement rights conferred by Union citizenship have deep roots in the Treaty's economic freedoms.[13] This is true with respect to both recognizing the human dimensions of economic free movement, on the one hand,[14] and dissociating free movement rights from economic activity, on the other.[15] In that light, it is arguable that free movement law was always at least as concerned with protecting Member State nationals who found themselves in cross-border situations as it was with advancing or promoting cross-border economic activity more abstractly. Additionally, holding the status of worker, self-employed person, or service provider/recipient enabled more extensive EU legal protection than the status itself might suggest.

The extent of the equal treatment granted to workers by Article 7(2) of Regulation 1612/68 (now 492/2011) provides a good example. Article 7(2) establishes that workers who are nationals of other Member States 'shall enjoy the same social and tax advantages as national workers'. Importantly, though, the Court's interpretation of 'social and tax advantages' extended its reach well beyond the context of work: 'in view of the equality of treatment which the provision seeks to achieve, the substantive area of application must be delineated so as to include all social and tax advantages, *whether or not attached to the contract of employment*'.[16] As the Court later clarified, 'the advantages which [Article 7(2)] extends to workers who are nationals of other Member States are all those which, whether or not linked to a contract of employment, are generally granted to national workers primarily

---

Jurisprudence', 25 *Journal of European Public Policy* (2018) 1422; Nic Shuibhne, 'Reconnecting Free Movement of Workers and Equal Treatment in an Unequal Europe', 43 *European Law Review* (2018) 477.

[13] See generally, S. O'Leary, *The Evolving Concept of Community Citizenship: From the Free Movement of Persons to Union Citizenship* (1996).

[14] The protection of certain family members provides a significant example: see in particular, Regulation 1612/68/EEC on freedom of movement for workers within the Community, OJ 1968 Sp. Ed. L 257/2, p. 475, Articles 10 and 11 (the only two provisions of the Regulation repealed by Directive 2004/38/EC—see especially Articles 2 and 3 of the Directive, setting out the family members who are 'beneficiaries' of EU legal protection). See also, Directive 68/360/EEC on the abolition of restrictions on movement and residence within the Community for workers of Member States and their families, OJ 1968 Sp. Ed. L 257/13, p. 485, and Directive 73/148/EEC on the abolition of restrictions on movement and residence within the Community for nationals of Member States with regard to establishment and the provision of services, OJ 1973 L 172/14 (both measures fully repealed and replaced by Directive 2004/38/EC). Work for the purposes of EU free movement law was defined in Case 66/85, *Lawrie-Blum* (EU:C:1986:284).

[15] Examples include the rights created by case law for Member State nationals who studied in another Member State (e.g. Case 293/83, *Gravier* (EU:C:1985:69)) and the (conditional) free movement and residence rights, detached from economic activity, that were created by legislation (Directive 90/364/EEC on the right of residence, OJ 1990 L180/26; Directive 90/365/EEC on the right of residence for employees and self-employed persons who have ceased their occupational activity, OJ 1990 L 180/28; and Directive 93/96/EEC on the right of residence for students, OJ 1993 L 317/59).

[16] Case 32/75, *Cristini* (EU:C:1975:120), para. 13 (emphasis added).

because of their objective status as workers *or by virtue of the mere fact of their residence on the national territory* and the extension of which to workers who are nationals of other Member States therefore seems suitable to facilitate their mobility within the Community.[17] Importantly for present purposes, and drawing from the preamble to the Regulation, the Court also indicated that social and tax advantages connect to 'promoting [the] social advancement' of workers in a host State.[18] That idea establishes a link between the worker and the *society*—and not just the labour market—of the host State, which is examined further in Section 3 below.

It is therefore not surprising that economic free movement law has always been deeply entangled with EU citizenship law, provoking debate about the 'true' nature of Union citizenship—about whether it has ever progressed beyond a suboptimal market citizenship, for example;[19] or about the constraining connection between Member State nationality, Union citizenship, and free movement rights.[20] For present purposes, returning to non-discrimination on the grounds of nationality, claiming equal treatment under Article 18 TFEU depends on the Union citizen being lawfully resident in the host State.[21] However, according to the Court of Justice, 'the principle of non-discrimination, laid down generally in Article 18 TFEU, is given more specific expression in Article 24 of Directive 2004/38 in relation to Union citizens who ... exercise their right to move and reside within the territory of the Member States.'[22] This means that 'a Union citizen can claim equal treatment with nationals of the host Member State under Article 24(1) of Directive 2004/38 only if his residence in the territory of the host Member State complies with the conditions of Directive 2004/38'.[23] For economically inactive citizens and

---

[17] Case 65/81, *Reina* (EU:C:1982:6), para. 12 (emphasis added).

[18] Case 39/86 *Lair* (EU :C :1988 :322), para. 22. See also, recital 3 of Regulation 1612/68/EEC (now reflected in recital 4 of Regulation 492/2011/EU): '[w]hereas freedom of movement constitutes a fundamental right of workers and their families; whereas mobility of labour within the Community must be one of the means by which the worker is guaranteed the possibility of improving his living and working conditions and promoting his social advancement, while helping to satisfy the requirements of the economies of the Member States; whereas the right of all workers in the Member States to pursue the activity of their choice within the Community should be affirmed.'

[19] E.g. Everson, 'The Legacy of the Market Citizen', in J. Shaw and G. More (eds), *New Legal Dynamics of European Union* (1995) 73; Nic Shuibhne, 'The Resilience of EU Market Citizenship', 47 *Common Market Law Review* (2010) 1597; and P.J. Neuvonen, *Equal Citizenship and Its Limits in EU Law: We The Burden?* (2016).

[20] Most obviously, in the context of Brexit: e.g. Coutts, 'Citizens of Elsewhere, Everywhere and ... Nowhere? Rethinking Union Citizenship in Light of Brexit', *Northern Ireland Legal Quarterly* (2018) 231; Łazowski, 'When *Cives Europae* Became Bargaining Chips: Free Movement of Persons in the Brexit Negotiations', 18 *ERA Forum* (2018) 469; O'Brien, 'Between the Devil and the Deep Blue Sea: Vulnerable EU Citizens Cast Adrift in the UK Post-Brexit', 58 *Common Market Law Review* (2021) 431; Roeben, Minnerop, Telles, and Snell, 'Revisiting Union Citizenship from a Fundamental Rights Perspective in the Time of Brexit', 5 *European Human Rights Law Review* (2018) 450; and Spaventa, 'Mice or Horses? British Citizens in the EU27 after Brexit as "Former EU Citizens"', 44 *European Law Review* (2019) 589, and Chapter 6 of this volume ('Brexit and the Free Movement of Persons: What Is EU Citizenship Really About?').

[21] Case C-85/96, *Martínez Sala* (EU:C:1998:217), para. 63.

[22] Case C-333/13, *Dano* (EU:C:2014:2358), para. 61.

[23] Case C-67/14, *Alimanovic* (EU:C:2015:597), para. 49. Locating the precise boundaries of 'lawful residence' is an evolving question in EU citizenship law; see Haag, 'The *coup de grâce* to the Union

citizens who are students, this means compliance with the sufficient resources and sickness insurance conditions in Articles 7(1)(b) and 7(1)(c) respectively. A host State is also entitled to impose proportionate integration requirements before equal treatment is extended in situations that are not expressly determined by Directive 2004/38.[24]

The relevance of integration requirements for economically active citizens is examined in Section 3.A below. But more generally, legal privilege for economic activity is built into the Directive in several ways, reflecting Kramer's idea that the Directive is 'mostly imbued with an "integration through work" philosophy'.[25] Most importantly, for residence rights beyond three months, Article 7(1)(a) confers unconditional rights on Member State nationals who either work or are self-employed in the host State. In other words, once the *status* of worker or self-employed person is held, the Directive imposes no other requirements, including with respect to having sufficient resources—there are therefore no requirements as to *means*.[26] Article 7(3) ensures that, in certain circumstances, Member State nationals retain the status of worker or self-employed person after economic activity has actually ceased.[27] Other instances of special protection for workers and self-employed persons in the Directive include Article 14(4)(a), which limits grounds for expulsion from the host State;[28] Article 17, which creates faster pathways to permanent residence rights for former workers and formerly self-employed persons in certain circumstances; and Article 24(2), which preserves entitlement to 'maintenance aid for studies' for 'workers, self-employed persons, persons who retain such status and members of their families' before permanent residence rights are acquired in the host State.

Citizen's Right to Equal Treatment: *CG v. The Department for Communities in Northern Ireland*', 59 *Common Market Law Review* (2022) 1081.

[24] E.g. Joined Cases C-523/11 and C-585/11, *Prinz and Seeberger* (EU:C:2013:90), para. 36; Case C-247/17, *Raugevicius* (EU:C:2018:898), para. 46.

[25] Kramer (n. 6), 185.

[26] The case law basis for this approach is outlined in Section 3.A below.

[27] I.e. 'For the purposes of paragraph 1(a), a Union citizen who is no longer a worker or self-employed person shall retain the status of worker or self-employed person in the following circumstances: (a) he/she is temporarily unable to work as the result of an illness or accident; (b) he/she is in duly recorded involuntary unemployment after having been employed for more than one year and has registered as a job-seeker with the relevant employment office; (c) he/she is in duly recorded involuntary unemployment after completing a fixed-term employment contract of less than a year or after having become involuntarily unemployed during the first twelve months and has registered as a job-seeker with the relevant employment office. In this case, the status of worker shall be retained for no less than six months; (d) he/she embarks on vocational training. Unless he/she is involuntarily unemployed, the retention of the status of worker shall require the training to be related to the previous employment.'

[28] I.e. 'By way of derogation from paragraphs 1 and 2 and without prejudice to the provisions of Chapter VI, an expulsion measure may in no case be adopted against Union citizens or their family members if: (a) the Union citizens are workers or self-employed persons.' Article 14(4)(b), which concerns jobseekers, is returned to in more detail in Section 4.A below.

94   NIAMH NIC SHUIBHNE

Since different considerations apply to both residence rights and equal treatment for economically active and economically inactive Union citizens, it makes sense that the structural relationship between free movement rights linked to the Treaty's economic freedoms and to the Treaty's provisions on Union citizenship respectively needs to be prescribed by EU law. For the Court, that structural relationship is residual in nature: in other words, 'Article 21(1) TFEU, which sets out in general terms the right of every citizen of the Union to move and reside freely within the territory of the Member States, finds specific expression in Article 45 TFEU concerning freedom of movement for workers, in Article 49 TFEU concerning freedom of establishment and in Article 56 TFEU concerning the freedom to provide services.'[29] As a result, 'if the national legislation at issue falls within the scope of Article 45 TFEU, of Article 49 TFEU or of Article 56 TFEU, it will not be necessary for the Court to rule on the interpretation of Article 21 TFEU.'[30] In that understanding, free movement rights are either based on the economic freedoms or, otherwise, based on Union citizenship.

However, things are not so neatly separable in reality—especially because, for some purposes, the Court has explicitly blended elements of Union citizenship and the economic freedoms. The main example is provided by the fusion of Articles 21 and 45 TFEU to overcome the pre-citizenship exclusion of jobseekers from equal treatment with respect to social and tax advantages in the host State. In *Collins*, the Court first acknowledged that, according to its previous case law on the basis of Article 45 TFEU alone, 'Member State nationals who move in search for work benefit from the principle of equal treatment *only as regards access to employment*', as compared to 'those who have already entered the employment market [who] may, on the basis of Article 7(2) of Regulation No 1612/68, claim the same social and tax advantages as national worker.'[31] However, the Court then departed from that case law, ruling that '[i]n view of the establishment of citizenship of the Union ... it is no longer possible to exclude from the scope of Article [45](2) of the Treaty – which expresses the fundamental principle of equal treatment ... a benefit of a financial nature intended to facilitate access to employment in the labour market of a Member State.'[32] This fusion enabled equal treatment for jobseekers that was not possible on the basis of either Article 45 or Article 21[33] TFEU alone, which is far from an abstract question when it is remembered that the added legal

---

[29] Case C-168/20, *BJ and OV* (EU:C:2021:907), para. 61.
[30] Ibid.
[31] Case C-138/02, *Collins* (EU:C:2004:172), para. 31 (emphasis added); referring to Case 316/85, *Lebon* (EU:C:1987:302), para. 26 and Case C-278/94, *Commission v. Belgium* (EU:C:1996:321), paras 39–40.
[32] Case C-138/02, *Collins* (EU:C:2004:172), para. 63; confirmed in Joined Cases C-22/08 and C-23/08, *Vatsouras and Koupatantze* (EU:C:2009:344), para. 37.
[33] Noting that Article 24(2) in conjunction with Article 14(4)(b) of Directive 2004/38/EC expressly precludes jobseekers from entitlement to social assistance in the host State.

value methodologically supplied by Article 21 TFEU cannot be used for jobseekers under the EEA Agreement, for example.[34]

The *Collins* case law did not endure over time with respect to claims for host State support that can be defined as social assistance.[35] But the point for present purposes is that citizenship-based and economic free movement rights are sometimes legally entangled; that both frameworks are drawn from to create hybrid legal statuses (here, the 'citizen-worker') to deliver outcomes that could not be reached on the basis of either status on its own. However, as the examples in the following sections will illustrate in more detail, fusing the two spheres of rights together glosses over a key distinction between them: that rights based on Articles 45 and 49 TFEU alone are—in principle at least—only *status*-dependent; whereas rights based on Article 21 TFEU alone are also *means*-dependent.[36] As emphasized previously, workers and self-employed persons who reside in a host State on the basis of Article 7(1)(a) of Directive 2004/38 are not required to have sufficient financial resources to avoid becoming a burden on the host State's social assistance system (or comprehensive sickness insurance) in order to reside there lawfully. At one level, then, the strict separation of economically active and economically inactive citizens through the differing requirements of Articles 7(1)(a) and 7(1)(b)/7(1)(c) of the Directive respectively reflects the formal conception outlined above: that free movement rights are designed to occupy, in structural terms, two parallel legal worlds under the broader umbrella of EU free movement law. The historical construction of citizenship-based free movement rights shows that this was never really the case. More recently, it is the crossing of legal worlds from citizenship law *back to* economic free movement law that calls for greater attention. Interrogating both integration requirements (Section 3) and the interplay of legal sources (Section 4) in economic free movement law takes up that challenge.

3. Equal Treatment I: Economic Activity as an Indicator of (Sufficient?) Integration in the Host State

In Section 2, the expansive definition of social and tax advantages applied to Article 7(2) of Regulation 492/2011 was introduced. To justify its scope, the Court has emphasized the importance of integration in the host State, stating, first, that

---

[34] Franklin and Fredriksen, 'Of Pragmatism and Principles: The EEA Agreement 20 Years on', 52 *Common Market Law Review* (2015) 629, at 640.

[35] Case C-67/14, *Alimanovic* (EU:C:2015:597); Case C-299/14, *García-Nieto* (EU:C:2016:114).

[36] Building on note 4, freedom to provide and receive services, based on Article 56 TFEU, is the outlier here again: it entails economic activity by definition, but it is not mentioned in Article 7(1)(a) of Directive 2004/38/EC in the context of otherwise unconditional rights to reside in a host State for more than three months, which means that Union citizens providing or receiving services in a host State for more than three months must meet the conditions that Article 7(1)(b) of the Directive prescribes for economically *inactive* citizens.

freedom of movement for workers under Article 45 TFEU 'entails *the right of in-tegration* into the host State, especially for the worker's family, in order to avoid the adverse consequences for freedom of movement which would otherwise arise'; and, second, that 'equal treatment, particularly in the field of social advantages, provided for in Article 7(2) of [Regulation 492/2011] ... pursues the same objective and constitutes an important factor affecting integration into the host State'.[37] In *Baumbast*, the Court linked the objective of integration to 'compliance with the principles of liberty and dignity'.[38]

In that understanding, integration was the aim of—rather than a precondition for—the equal treatment of workers. However, the influence of EU citizenship law has more recently provoked questions about integration as a precondition for the equal treatment of economically active citizens, with respect to both claim-making on the part of workers and self-employed persons (Section 3.A) and restriction-defending on the part of the Member States (Section 3.B).

A. Integration and Claim-making

As noted in Section 2, a host State can impose proportionate integration require-ments on Union citizens before equal treatment is extended in situations not expressly covered by Directive 2004/38.[39] Two main forms of integration require-ment evolved in citizenship case law: in a general sense, demonstrating a certain degree of integration into host State society, which materialized in pre-Directive 2004/38 case law on student maintenance grants;[40] and more specifically, for citi-zens seeking work, demonstrating a real link to the host State's geographic employ-ment market.[41] Article 24(2) of the Directive now establishes express exclusions from equal treatment in three situations: as regards social assistance, during the first three months of residence or where citizens reside as jobseekers for a longer period on the basis of Article 14(4)(b); and for maintenance aid for studies, where claimants do not have the right of permanent residence unless they are 'workers, self-employed persons, persons who retain such status and members of their fam-ilies'. More extensive equal treatment for the latter group connects to Article 45 TFEU and Article 7(2) of Regulation 492/2011, returned to below. However, as also

---

[37] Case C-308/93, *Cabanis-Issarte* (EU:C:1996:169), para. 38 (emphasis added).

[38] Case C-413/99, *Baumbast and R* (EU:C:2002:493), para. 50.

[39] E.g. Joined Cases C-523/11 and C-585/11, *Prinz and Seeberger* (EU:C:2013:90), para. 36; Case C-247/17, *Raugèvicius* (EU:C:2018:898), para. 46. Kramer's idea of 'a mutual responsibility between the Union citizen and his/her host Member State towards social and economic activity, self-sufficiency and integration' reflects the essence of such requirements in EU free movement law in a holistic sense (Kramer, n. 6, 188).

[40] Case C-209/03, *Bidar* (EU:C:2005:169), para. 57.

[41] Case C-224/98, *D'Hoop* (EU:C:2002:432), para. 38. See generally, O'Brien, 'Real Links, Abstract Rights and False Alarms: the Relationship between the ECJ's "Real Link" Case Law and National Solidarity', 33 *European Law Review* (2008) 643.

noted in Section 2 above, equal treatment claims for social assistance not excluded by Article 24(2) of the Directive and based only on Article 21 TFEU depend on lawful residence in the host State. Controversially, as the ruling in *CG* now appears to confirm, lawful residence on the basis of national law alone no longer enables protection under Article 18 TFEU and, instead, residing lawfully on the basis of EU law seems non-negotiable.[42] For economically inactive citizens, this normally means residence that complies with the conditions in Article 7(1)(b) (or 7(1)(c) for students) of the Directive, which realistically means that most claims will fail: if the economically inactive citizen complies with these conditions in the first place, there would most likely be no need to claim social assistance, underlining once again the idea that rights based on EU citizenship law are fundamentally means-based.

However, another basis for lawful residence under EU law concerns the retention of status-based residence rights for citizens who were *previously* economically active. In *Jobcenter Krefeld*, the Court confirmed that a former worker who is no longer economically active yet resides lawfully in the host State as the primary carer of children completing their education there—i.e. on the basis of Article 10 of Regulation 492/2011—may claim equal treatment as regards entitlement to social assistance.[43] Such claimants share with Article 21 TFEU claimants that they do not currently exercise economic activity in the host State, yet EU law distinguishes their situations: for those residing in the host State on the basis of the Regulation, the 'particular expression' of their right to equal treatment is not Article 24 of Directive 2004/38 but, instead, Article 7(2) of the Regulation.[44] And importantly, it has long been established that 'a benefit guaranteeing a minimum means of subsistence constitutes a social advantage, within the meaning of [Article 7(2) of] Regulation [492/2011], which may not be denied to a migrant worker who is a national of another Member State and is resident within the territory of the State paying the benefit, nor to his family'.[45]

Just as importantly, in general terms, receiving social assistance in a host State does not undermine the claimant's status as a worker.[46] However, stretching the scope of Article 7(2) of the Regulation from previous employment across potentially several years of continuing host State residence linked to the education of the former worker's child(ren),[47] without any further economic

---

[42] Case C-709/20, *CG* (EU:C:2021:602); compare earlier, Case C-85/96, *Martínez Sala* (EU:C:1998:217) and Case C-456/02, *Trojani* (EU:C:2004:488). This question is returned to in Section 4 below.

[43] Case C-181/19, *Jobcenter Krefeld* (EU:C:2020:794), paras 72–78.

[44] Ibid., paras 77 and 78.

[45] Case 249/83, *Hoeckx* (EU:C:1985:139), para. 22.

[46] Case 139/85, *Kempf* (EU:C:1986:223).

[47] The Court has confirmed that a primary carer's derived right of residence in such circumstances will continue at least until the child concerned reaches the 'age of majority' and 'may nevertheless extend beyond that age, if the child continues to need the presence and the care of that parent in order to be able to pursue and complete his or her education' (Case C-480/08, *Teixeira* (EU:C:2010:83), para. 86).

activity,[48] raises two different paradoxes. First, the Court enables equal treatment as regards social and tax advantages in the absence of any (continuing) work as defined by EU law.[49] Second, in so doing, it dilutes the requirement of economic activity—which, in turn, renders the exclusion from equal treatment of citizens who are economically inactive but do not meet the criteria for residence based on Article 10 of the Regulation harder to digest.[50] It deepens the legal significance of status over means, even where the connective thread to economic activity is empirically thin.

1. Economic Activity as 'in Principle, a Sufficient Link of Integration'

Lawful residence constructs a *formal* bridge between the two paradoxes outlined above. For equal treatment claims linked to Union citizenship, the Court consistently refers to 'persons *lawfully* resident in the territory of [the host] State'.[51] In contrast, it is rare to find explicit references to lawful residence in economic free movement case law; though in *Mutcsh*, for example, having noted the prohibition on nationality discrimination in Article 18 TFEU, the Court did observe that 'Article [45 TFEU] is *likewise* based on the principle that nationals of any Member State *lawfully established* in another Member State for the purpose of employment must be treated in the same way as nationals of that State'.[52] Now, Article 7(1)(a) of the Directive confirms, in effect, that anyone who works or is self-employed in the host State is lawfully resident there, without needing to fulfil any further conditions.

However, a more *substantive* bridge is provided by the additional requirement of integration. For situations connected to Article 45 TFEU, it was noted in Section 2 above that social and tax advantages are extended to workers in a host State '*by virtue of the mere fact of their residence* on the national territory'.[53] At a deeper level,

---

[48] Compare the expectation that economic activity will be resumed in case law on retaining the status of worker when economic activity is temporarily ceased to accommodate pregnancy and childbirth: see Section 4 below.

[49] This is a feature of EU citizenship law too: the benefit claimed in *Martínez Sala* was categorized as a social and tax advantage under Article 7(2) of the Regulation in the early part of the judgment, based on Article 45 TFEU and the Regulation; and then more briefly and generally referred to as a benefit within the material scope of EU law in the later part of the judgment, based on Articles 18 and 21 TFEU yet reflecting the Article 7(2) understanding of benefits paid purely because of residence in the host State (Case C-85/96, *Martínez Sala* (EU:C:1998:217), paras 25–26 and 63). As O'Leary described it at the time, 'Union citizenship explodes the "linkages" which EC law previously required for the principle of non-discrimination to apply, namely performance or involvement in an economic activity as workers, established persons or providers and recipients of services, preparation for a future economic activity as a student or stagiaire or some sort of relationship with an economic actor as a family member or dependant' (O'Leary, 'Putting Flesh on the Bones of European Union Citizenship', 24 *European Law Review* (1999) 68, at 77–78).

[50] As expressed by Iliopoulou-Penot, 'the lines that separate different categories within the circle of Union citizens who do not considerably contribute to the economy of the host State becomes more difficult to draw; the distinction between those deserving support and those excluded is hard to explain' (Iliopoulou-Penot, n. 2, 1021).

[51] Case C-85/96, *Martínez Sala* (EU:C:1998:217), para. 63 (emphasis added).

[52] Case 137/84, *Mutsch* (EU:C:1985:335), para. 12 (emphasis added).

[53] Case 65/81, *Reina* (EU:C:1982:6), para. 12 (emphasis added).

this is so because participating in the host State labour market 'establishes, in principle, *a sufficient link of integration* with the society of that Member State, allowing [workers] to benefit from the principle of equal treatment, as compared with national workers, as regards social advantages'.[54] More specifically, '[t]he link of integration arises from, *inter alia*, the fact that, through the taxes which he pays in the host Member State by virtue of his employment, the migrant worker also contributes to the financing of the social policies of that State and should profit from them under the same conditions as national workers'.[55] If the Member States had intended to do things differently, the Court suggests, then adding further categories of exclusion to Article 24(2) of the Directive represents an opportunity not taken.[56]

The latter point raises the question of whether the EU legislator has similar limiting powers under Articles 21 and 45/49 TFEU respectively, which will be returned to in Section 3.B below. For now, the key point is that, as noted just above with reference to *Commission v. Netherlands*, economic activity establishes '*in principle*, a sufficient link of integration with the society of [the host] State' (emphasis added). However, in contrast to earlier case law that characterized integration as an *objective*, the 'in principle' qualifier highlights integration as a *precondition* for enjoying equal treatment.

To date, it is generously interpreted. In *Jobcenter Krefeld*, for example, considering the personal scope of Article 7(2) of the Regulation, the Court referred back to Article 7(1)'s guarantee that '[a] worker who is a national of a Member State may not, in the territory of another Member State, be treated differently from national workers by reason of his nationality in respect of any conditions of employment and work, in particular as regards remuneration, dismissal, *and, should he become unemployed,* reinstatement or re-employment'. The equal treatment extended here to workers who 'become unemployed' is arguably rather clearly connected to their 'reinstatement or re-employment'. Yet the Court extracted equal treatment guarantees from Article 7(1) in a much more generalized way, conceiving 'a protection that extends *beyond just the period of employment* of those workers'.[57] Since, as noted above, the Court had already established that Article 7(2) of the Regulation is the 'particular expression' of the principle of equal treatment in Article 45(2) TFEU, it then reasoned that 'the fact that JD had become economically inactive ... cannot lead to the result that the principle of equal treatment laid down in Article 7(2) of [the] Regulation ... becomes inapplicable. Moreover, ... the rights enjoyed *by the worker who is a Union citizen* and his or her family members under Regulation No 492/2011 may, in certain circumstances, persist even after the termination of the employment relationship'.[58]

---

[54] Case C-542/09, *Commission v. Netherlands* (EU:C:2012:346), para. 65 (emphasis added).
[55] Ibid., para. 66.
[56] Ibid., para. 64.
[57] Case C-181/19, *Jobcenter Krefeld* (EU:C:2020:794), para. 43 (emphasis added).
[58] Ibid., paras 47–48 (emphasis added).

One such set of 'certain circumstances' concerns residence based on Article 10 of the Regulation. In fact, 'the right of residence of the parent who cares for those children becomes, once acquired, *independent of the original right of residence that is based on the status of the parent concerned as a worker, and may continue to exist beyond the loss of that status*, in order to provide enhanced legal protection to those children, thereby ensuring that their right to equal treatment as regards access to education is not deprived of any practical effect'.[59] The extent of this protective shield is remarkable on its own terms, but all the more when account is taken of JD's very limited employment history in the host State.[60] The Advocate General in *Alimanovic* had drawn attention to the possible relevance of Article 10 in his Opinion,[61] but the Court did not consider it at all—too soon, perhaps, to go there after *Dano*.[62] More generally, for the purposes of this chapter, is interrogation of the *sufficiency* of the integration represented by economic activity more evident in economic free movement law now; and is this because of the centrality of integration conditionality in EU citizenship law?

Arguably, integration conditionality was always implicitly present in economic free movement law too. The definition of work in *Lawrie-Blum*, for example, can be read as an expectation that activities should be 'real and genuine, to the exclusion of activities on such a small scale as to be regarded as purely marginal and ancillary' in order to trigger equal treatment with host State nationals. Conversely, work that fails to meet that definition does not establish, 'in principle, a *sufficient* link of integration with the society of the host State'. Criticism of the exclusion of voluntary and care-related work from the definition of work in EU law strongly contests the conflation of remunerated economic value to the host State and integration to its society more broadly.[63] However, the case law on residence and equal treatment based on Article 10 of the Regulation does suggest bias towards (previously) satisfying worker status more than integration into society: having once been a worker for the purposes of EU law is legally more significant, in other words, than other integrative factors—such as, in *Dano*, living in the host State with family members already settled or giving birth to children there.

---

[59] Ibid., para. 49 (emphasis added). It is not clear whether a primary carer of children who resides on the basis of Article 10 yet who has never been an EU worker can claim equal treatment in the same way; see further, Ristuccia, 'The Right to Social Assistance of Children in Education and Their Primary Carers: *Jobcenter Krefeld*', 58 *Common Market Law Review* (2021) 877, at 889–890.

[60] Case C-181/19, *Jobcenter Krefeld* (EU:C:2020:794), para. 20.

[61] AG Wathelet in Case C-67/14, *Alimanovic* (EU:C:2015:210), paras 117–122 of the Opinion.

[62] Compare the alternatives set out in Ristuccia (n. 59), 886–887 and 893ff. See generally, Hyltén-Cavallius, 'Who Cares? Caregivers' Derived Residence Rights from Children in EU Free Movement Law', 57 *Common Market Law Review* (2020) 399.

[63] See e.g. S. Currie, *Migration, Work and Citizenship in the Enlarged European Union* (2008); O'Brien, 'Social Blind Spots and Monocular Policy Making: the ECJ's Migrant Worker Model', 46 *Common Market Law Review* (2009) 1120; and Carter, 'Inclusion and Exclusion of Migrant Workers in the EU', in J. Moritz (ed.), *European Societies, Migration and the Law* (2020) 301.

ECONOMIC ACTIVITY AND EU CITIZENSHIP LAW   101

At a general level, then, the status of worker does indeed seem to establish a sufficient link to host State society 'in principle'—it provides a shortcut to meeting integration conditionality requirements; to establishing the *sufficiency* of the integrative link. Early case law on retaining worker status for the purposes of being supported to undertake vocational training reflected the same logic: the Court needed to find a way to progress the social advancement objective of free movement—but it needed also to find a way to connect that aim *sufficiently* to economic activity.[64] That is why, in *Brown*, the Court held that 'it cannot be inferred ... that a national of a Member State will be entitled to a grant for studies in another Member State by virtue of his status as a worker where it is established *that he acquired that status exclusively as a result of his being accepted for admission to university* to undertake the studies in question' because, in that situation, 'the employment relationship, *which is the only basis for the rights deriving from Regulation No 1612/68, is merely ancillary* to the studies to be financed by the grant'.[65] It is why, in *Förster*, previous work was not enough to sustain a connection to Article 45 TFEU for the purposes of eligibility for a student maintenance grant.[66] It is also why, in *Givane*, a connection to work that fell just short of the legislative conditions set for retaining that status (and associated residence rights for family members) did not override factors suggesting the substantive integration of a deceased worker's family in host State society.[67] According to the Court, Article 3(2) of Regulation 1251/70 'envisages that the worker must, on the date of his decease, have resided continuously in the territory of the host Member State for at least two years', a condition that was 'intended *to establish a significant connection between, on the one hand, that Member State, and on the other hand, that worker and his family, and to ensure a certain level of their integration in the society of that State*'.[68] Providing an interesting

---

[64] See e.g. Case 39/86 *Lair* (EU:C:1988:322), para. 37: 'In the field of grants for university education, such a link between the status of worker and a grant awarded for maintenance and training with a view to the pursuit of university studies does, however, presuppose *some continuity between the previous occupational activity and the course of study; there must be a relationship between the purpose of the studies and the previous occupational activity*' (emphasis added). In contrast, in formative case law on tuition fees and non-discrimination, the Court had more general recourse to Article 128 EEC in conjunction with the prohibition on nationality discrimination in Article 7 EEC, finding in *Forcheri* that 'if a Member State organizes educational courses relating in particular to vocational training, to require of a national of another Member State *lawfully established* in the first Member State an enrolment fee which is not required of its own nationals in order to take part in such courses constitutes discrimination by reason of nationality' (Case 152/82, *Forcheri* (EU:C:1983:205), para. 18 (emphasis added))—as Marc Steiert observed at the Authors' Workshop for this volume, the Court's language here, requiring *lawful* establishment in the host State, presages *Martínez Sala*. For further discussion, see AG Cosmas in Case C-411/98, *Ferlini* (EU:C:1999:442), paras 66–70 of the Opinion.

[65] Case 197/86, *Brown* (EU:C:1988:323), para. 27 (emphasis added).

[66] Case C-158/07, *Förster* (EU:C:2008:630). The Court's position on retaining worker status in this case is returned to in Section 4 below; more generally, the Court also held that the claim could not be made on the basis of EU citizenship law, considering the contested five-year residence requirement, just before the entry into force of (Article 24(2) of) Directive 2004/38/EC, to be proportionate.

[67] Case C-257/99, *Givane and Others* (EU:C:2003:8). Commission Regulation 1251/70/EEC on the right of workers to remain in the territory of a Member State after having been employed in that State, OJ 1970 L 142/24.

[68] Case C-257/99, *Givane and Others* (EU:C:2003:8), para. 46 (emphasis added).

point of contrast to the later ruling in *Jobcenter Krefeld*, the Court considered that '[t]he existence of a significant connection between the host Member State and the worker concerned could not be ensured if the right of residence in the territory of a Member State provided for by ... Article 3(2) of [the] Regulation ... were to be acquired as soon as a worker had resided for at least two years in that State at some stage of his life, even in the distant past.'[69] In contrast, AG Alber emphasized substantive integrative factors, observing that '[t]he subsequent arrival of family members generally entails considerable changes for that family, such as, for example, leaving their homeland and social environment, giving up the home to which they have become accustomed, a possible transfer of school-age children to another school, establishment of a reasonable standard of accommodation and living in the host State.'[70]

2. Integration as an Activator of Limits in Economic Free Movement Law

For claims based on Article 21 TFEU, the Court in *Bidar* could replace the required connection to economic activity with reference to 'developments' in EU law and notably the creation of Union citizenship;[71] enabling precisely the qualitative assessment of the claimant's circumstances and degree of integration that was ruled out by the Court but undertaken by AG Alber in *Givane*. Thus, two opposing things seem true at the same time. On the one hand, integration conditionality was, to some extent, always built into economic free movement law. On the other hand, the intuition that a rights-curbing trend is more evident in economic free movement law since the institution of Union citizenship can also be shown to be correct.[72] With respect to the role of integration and equal treatment claim-making, limiting concepts have travelled in both directions, as demonstrated by the idea of *sufficient* integration applied in some strands of case law based on Article 45 TFEU becoming even more important for claims based on Article 21 TFEU. However, the influence of citizenship law on economic free movement law has been mainly about *activating* those limits—about exposing connections to economic activity that are *not* sufficient to justify legal protection.[73]

For example, note how the Court later confined the scope of its *Carpenter* ruling on residence permits for the third country national family members of

---

[69] Ibid., para. 47.

[70] AG Alber in Case C-257/99, *Givane and Others* (EU:C:2002:297), para. 64 of the Opinion.

[71] Case C-209/03, *Bidar* (EU:C:2005:169), paras 38–42.

[72] See further, Verschueren, 'Being Economically Active: How it Still Matters', in H. Verschueren (ed.), *Residence, Employment and Social Rights of Mobile Persons: On How EU Law Defines Where They Belong* (2016) 187, at 210–212, showing how the Court 'seems to have introduced the "integration model" it adopts in its case-law on economically inactive EU citizens into its judgments on migrant workers, thus giving up the "assimilation" model it previously accepted' (211). See further, Barbou des Places, 'The Integrated Person in EU Law', in Azoulai, Barbou des Places, and Pataut (eds.), (n. 6), 179.

[73] See similarly, Verschueren (n. 72) 212: '[i]t remains to be seen if the C[ourt] will continue in this vein in its future case-law. However, we can predict that Member States will use the opportunities offered by this kind of case-law to limit the rights of EU migrant workers'.

economically active Union citizens in cross-border situations. In *S and G*, the Court ruled that 'the fact ... that the third-country national in question takes care of the Union citizens' child may, as is apparent from the judgment in *Carpenter*, be a relevant factor to be taken into account by the referring court when examining whether the refusal to grant a right of residence to that third-country national may discourage the Union citizen from effectively exercising his rights under Article 45 TFEU'.[74] However, this was qualified immediately afterwards: 'although in the judgment in *Carpenter* the fact that the child in question was being taken care of by the third-country national who is a family member of a Union citizen was considered to be decisive, that child was, in that case, taken care of by the Union citizen's spouse. *The mere fact that it might appear desirable* that the child be cared for by the third-country national who is the direct relative in the ascending line of the Union citizen's spouse is not therefore sufficient in itself to constitute such a dissuasive effect'.[75] Significantly for present purposes, the 'mere fact that it might appear desirable' language appears otherwise *only* in case law on family member residence rights based on Article 20 TFEU and Union citizenship.[76]

The contention that citizenship law incites the activation of limits in economic free movement law is perhaps most powerfully demonstrated through considering the much-criticized application of integration reasoning in case law on study finance and frontier workers. In principle, Article 7(2) of Regulation 492/ 2011 'equally benefits both migrant workers resident in a host Member State and frontier workers employed in that Member State while residing in another Member State'.[77] However, for 'the grant of State financial aid for higher education studies to the non-resident children of migrant and cross-border workers, ... the fact that the parents of the student concerned have been employed, for a significant period, in the Member State providing the aid applied for might be appropriate for the purposes of showing *the actual degree of attachment with the society or labour market* of that State'.[78] Furthermore, was the Court's agreement in *Bragança Linares Verruga and Others* that requiring a minimum period of five years of employment

---

[74] Case C-457/12, *S and G* (EU:C:2014:36), para. 43. See previously, Case C-60/00, *Carpenter* (EU:C:2002:434).

[75] *S and G* (emphasis added).

[76] Case C-256/11, *Dereci and Others* (EU:C:2011:734), para. 68 ('the mere fact that it might appear desirable to a national of a Member State, for economic reasons or in order to keep his family together in the territory of the Union, for the members of his family who do not have the nationality of a Member State to be able to reside with him in the territory of the Union, is not sufficient in itself to support the view that the Union citizen will be forced to leave Union territory if such a right is not granted'); confirmed in e.g. Case C-82/16, *KA and Others* (EU:C:2018:308), para. 57.

[77] Case C-410/18, *Aubriet* (EU:C:2019:582), para. 24.

[78] Ibid., para. 35 (emphasis added); confirming e.g. Case C-20/12, *Giersch and Others* (EU:C:2013:411), para. 7. Moreover, 'indirectly discriminatory national legislation restricting the grant to frontier workers of social advantages within the meaning of Article 7(2) of [the] Regulation ... where there is not *a sufficient connection to the society in which they are pursuing their activities* without residing there may be objectively justified' (Case C-410/18, *Aubriet* (EU:C:2019:582), para. 34 (emphasis added); confirming e.g. Case C-213/05, *Geven* (EU:C:2007:438), para. 26).

104 NIAMH NIC SHUIBHNE

in 'the Member State granting the aid on the part of the frontier worker parent, in order for the children of frontier workers to be able claim financial aid from the State for higher education studies' represents 'such a connection on the part of those workers to the society of that Member State and a reasonable probability that the student will return to that granting Member State after completing his studies' really a coincidence,[79] noting the exclusion of entitlement to maintenance grants for the same period—for economically inactive citizens—in Article 24(2) of Directive 2004/38?[80]

National conditions requiring continuous employment for the previous five years or for five years within the previous seven failed the necessity element of the Court's proportionality test when challenged in *Bragança Linares Verruga and Others* and *Aubriet*, respectively. Nevertheless, the important point for present purposes is that undertaking a qualitative assessment of *sufficiency* of connection to the host State—beyond the fact of work on its own terms—was found to be justifiable in principle. That conclusion finds support in earlier frontier worker case law. Recital 8 of Regulation 883/2004 affirms that '[t]he general principle of equal treatment is of particular importance for workers who do not reside in the Member State of their employment, including frontier workers.'[81] At a general level, the Court upholds that commitment—for example, it considers that 'compulsory membership of the [host State] social security system, which ensures that workers pay social contributions to that system, *constitutes a sufficiently close* connection *with [host State] society* to enable cross-border workers to benefit from ... social advantage[s]'.[82] However, that 'sufficiently close connection' remains a precondition for equal treatment. The Court also considers that '[a]lthough the Member States' power ... to require nationals of other Member States to show a certain degree of integration in their societies in order to receive social advantages, such as financial assistance for education, *is not limited to situations in which the applicants for assistance are economically inactive citizens*, the existence of a residence requirement ... to prove the required degree of integration *is, in principle, inappropriate* when the persons concerned are migrant workers or frontier workers.'[83] Again, though, the Court's use of 'in principle' here leaves a door open to residence conditions being accepted in certain cases.

In *Hartmann*, a residence condition was attached to a child-raising allowance on the basis that it was 'an instrument of national family policy intended to encourage

---

[79] Case C-238/15, *Bragança Linares Verruga and Others* (EU:C:2016:949), para. 58.
[80] An alignment in the case law on study finance and frontier workers that Vershueren characterizes as 'particularly disquieting' since the Court 'almost literally took over the wording of this provision, but omitted to quote the final wording thereof, which says that it only applies to "persons other than workers, self-employed persons, persons who retain such status and members of their families"' (Vershueren, n. 72, 211; discussing Case C-20/12, *Giersch* (EU:C:2013:411), para. 80).
[81] Regulation 883/2004/EC on the coordination of social security systems, OJ 2011 L 166/1.
[82] Case C-269/07, *Commission v. Germany* (EU:C:2009:527), para. 60 (emphasis added).
[83] Case C-542/09, *Commission v. Netherlands* (EU:C:2012:346), para. 63 (emphasis added).

the birth-rate' in Germany and was granted 'to benefit persons who, by their choice of residence, have established a real link with German society'.[84] The applicant did not come within the personal scope of Regulation 883/2004, but the Court looked at the benefit as a social advantage under Regulation 492/2011 and observed that 'under the German legislation in force at the material time, residence *was not regarded as the only connecting link* with the Member State concerned [since] a *substantial* contribution to the national labour market also constituted *a valid factor of integration into the society* of that Member State. *In those circumstances*, the allowance at issue ... could not be refused to a couple ... who do not live in Germany, but one of whom works full-time in that State'.[85] The implications of the Court's focus on integration for the purposes of equal treatment unfolded further in *Giersch*, where it was notoriously stated that 'the frontier worker is not always integrated in the Member State of employment in the same way as a worker who is resident in that State'.[86] The Court then suggested that 'to ensure that the frontier worker who is a taxpayer and who makes social security contributions in [the host State] has a *sufficient* link with [that] society, the financial aid could be made conditional on the frontier worker ... having worked in that Member State *for a certain minimum period of time*' and it drew attention to the five-year requirement (for permanent residence) in Article 16 of Directive 2004/38 in 'another context'.[87]

Yet as noted above, national legislation taking the Court's guidance very literally—i.e. applying a five-year residence condition before financial aid was granted to frontier workers—was rejected by the Court because of the 'significant period of time' the applicants had worked in the host State.[88] AG Wathelet has therefore been critical of the confusion generated by the case law on frontier workers, contrasting it with clearer equal treatment reasoning in earlier rulings: clarity that he explicitly described as 'blurred' by EU citizenship law, i.e. by 'introducing the concept of sufficient integration or genuine link with the host Member State into ... case law relating to workers'.[89] He acknowledged the cross-flow of integration reasoning from EU citizenship law to economic free movement law, but was 'reticent about that development'.[90] He framed the frontier worker case

---

[84] Case C-212/05, *Hartmann* (EU:C:2007:437), paras 32–33.

[85] Ibid., paras 36–37 (emphasis added); compare the narrower approach taken by AG Geelhoed (EU:C:2006:615).

[86] Case C-20/12, *Giersch* (EU:C:2013:411), para. 65. Note, too, the implicit reflection on future economic contributions to the host State labour market in paras 66–68.

[87] Ibid., para. 80 (emphasis added).

[88] Case C-238/15, *Bragança Linares Verruga and Others* (EU:C:2016:949), paras 63–69. See further, Jacqueson, 'Any News from Luxembourg? On Student Aid, Frontier Workers and Stepchildren: *Bragança Linares Verruga* and *Depesme*', 54 *Common Market Law Review* (2018) 901; and Silga, 'Luxembourg Financial Aid for Higher Studies and Children of Frontier Workers: Evolution and Challenges in Light of the Case-law of the Court of Justice', 19 *European Public Law* (2019) 13.

[89] AG Wathelet in Case C-238/15, *Bragança Linares Verruga and Others* (EU:C:2016:389), para. 36 of the Opinion.

[90] Ibid., paras 67–68 of the Opinion; see similarly, paras 75–76 of the Opinion.

law outlined above as an 'exception' to the general rule that 'as regards migrant workers and frontier workers, the fact that they have participated in the employment market of a Member State establishes, in principle, a sufficient link of integration with the society of that Member State, allowing them to benefit from the principle of equal treatment ... as regards social advantages' and considered that, as an exception, it should be 'applied restrictively'.[91] Similarly, AG Mengozzi observed in *Giersch* that '[w]hen interpreting Article 7(2) of Regulation [492/2011], the Court has made no distinction between the concepts of migrant worker and frontier worker precisely because [the] Regulation ... does not treat those two categories of worker differently'.[92]

A final example to consider is that integration can also be signalled through an intention to return to the host State labour market following a break in employment. This idea was originally developed in the finding that Turkish workers 'already duly integrated into the labour force of the host Member State' could continue to be registered as belonging to that labour force and continue to enjoy the right to reside there when a 'temporary break' from work was taken.[93] More specifically, 'the temporary break in the period of active employment of a Turkish worker ... while he is detained pending trial is not in itself capable of causing him to forfeit the rights which he derives directly from the third indent of Article 6(1) of Decision No 1/80, provided that he finds a new job within a reasonable period after his release'.[94] The latter condition was later transposed to the context of imprisoned EU workers in *Orfanopoulos and Oliveri*,[95] and extended subsequently to cover temporary breaks in economic activity for the purposes of childbirth in *Saint Prix*.[96] Importantly, this case law sustains a protective EU legal status based directly on Article 45 TFEU and beyond the circumstances expressly provided for in Article 7(3) of Directive 2004/38. Moreover, retaining the status of worker not only ensures shorter-term equal treatment in the host State but also continued *lawful* residence there, with implications into the longer term for acquiring permanent residence rights.[97] These questions are returned to in Section 4 below, with particular focus on the interplay of Article 7(3) of Directive 2004/38 and rights drawn from primary law.

---

[91] Ibid., para. 68 of the Opinion.

[92] Cf. AG Mengozzi in Case C-20/12, *Giersch* (EU:C:2013:70), para. 30 of the Opinion.

[93] Case C-340/97, *Nazli* (EU:C:2000:77), para. 40.

[94] Ibid., para. 41.

[95] Joined Cases C-482/01 and C-493/01, *Orfanopoulos and Oliveri* (EU:C:2004:262), para. 50.

[96] Case C-507/12, *Saint Prix* (EU:C:2014:2007), para. 41.

[97] E.g. Joined Cases C-424/10 and C-425/10 *Ziolkowski and Szeja* (EU:C:2011:866), para. 47: 'a period of residence which complies with the law of a Member State but does not satisfy the conditions laid down in Article 7(1) of Directive 2004/38 cannot be regarded as a "legal" period of residence within the meaning of Article 16(1)'.

B. Integration and Restriction-defending

The purpose of this section is to show that integration conditionality drawn from EU citizenship law with respect to claim-making has also influenced economic free movement law at the stage of restriction-defending.

Two perspectives collide when a Member State seeks to defend a restriction of free movement rights and/or equal treatment: protection claimed for a (usually national) public interest, on the one hand; and protection produced by integration in the host State, on the other. For the Treaty-based derogations of public health, public policy, and public security, Articles 27–33 of Directive 2004/38 establish a detailed framework that applies in the context of any exercise of free movement rights and, again reflecting the significance of integration, is designed to secure deeper protection for the citizen the longer they remain in the host State. For economic free movement law, 'aims of a purely economic nature cannot constitute an overriding reason in the general interest justifying a restriction of a fundamental freedom guaranteed by the Treaty'.[98] In contrast, to defend exclusion from equal treatment in EU citizenship law, protection of the public finances of the host State is a legitimate aim.[99] In that context, we can see a significant shift over time. Initially, systemic protection of national public finances was acknowledged as a legitimate aim in principle, but individual claims were usually framed as proportionate or 'reasonable' burdens for host States to absorb.[100] More recently, while the Court affirms that 'the assistance awarded to a single applicant can scarcely be described as an "unreasonable burden" for a Member State', it also suggests that 'while an individual claim might not place the Member State concerned under an unreasonable burden, the accumulation of all the individual claims which would be submitted to it would be bound to do so'.[101]

For economic free movement law, the position has also changed over time and protecting national public finances can be legitimate here too if it can be demonstrated that the objectives pursued are not of a *purely* economic nature. According to the Court, 'national legislation may ... constitute a justified restriction on a fundamental freedom when it is dictated by reasons of an economic nature in the pursuit of an objective in the public interest'.[102] On that basis, 'the risk of seriously undermining the financial balance of the social security system may constitute an overriding reason in the public interest capable of justifying the undermining of the provisions of the Treaty concerning the right of freedom of movement for

---

[98] Case C-35/98, *Verkooijen* (EU:C:2000:294), para. 48.

[99] E.g. Case C-200/02, *Zhu and Chen* (EU:C:2004:639), para. 33; Case C-140/12, *Brey* (EU:C:2013:565), para. 55.

[100] E.g. Case C-184/99, *Grzelczyk* (EU:C:2001:458), para. 44; Case C-140/12, *Brey* (EU:C:2013:565), paras 69–72.

[101] Case C-67/14, *Alimanovic* (EU:C:2015:597), para. 62.

[102] Case C-515/14, *Commission v. Cyprus* (EU:C:2016:30), para. 53.

workers'.[103] In *Commission v. Netherlands*, the Court adopted a narrow understanding of this idea: it agreed that 'budgetary considerations may underlie a Member State's choice of social policy and influence the nature or scope of the social protection measures which it wishes to adopt' but held that 'they do not in themselves constitute an aim pursued by that policy and cannot therefore justify discrimination against migrant workers'.[104] However, in its subsequent ruling in *Tarola* and for the first time in a case concerning Article 45 TFEU, the Court characterized as one of the objectives of Directive 2004/38 the aim of 'striking a fair balance between safeguarding the free movement of workers, on the one hand, and ensuring that the social security systems of the host Member State *are not placed under an unreasonable burden*, on the other'.[105]

The language of 'unreasonable burden' is drawn patently from EU citizenship law. Its invocation in *Tarola*—in the context of Article 45 TFEU—mirrors the limiting crossflow dynamics of the claim-making case law discussed in Section 3.A above. To continue with an example also considered there, the language used by the Court for workers in *Givane* came directly from EU citizenship law at the restriction-defending stage of the case too—notably in the very striking statement that '[t]he exercise of the right of residence is, none the less, subject to the limitations and conditions laid down by the EC Treaty and by the measures adopted for its application'—which reflects the wording of Article 21, not Article 45, TFEU.[106]

An intensifying emphasis on 'reasons of an economic nature' to defend restrictions of free movement rights was strongly evident in pre-Brexit negotiations with the UK.[107] In particular, citizenship-oriented public finance logic directly informed the EU/UK February 2016 Decision's defence of proposed restrictions on the free movement of workers (with EU legislative amendments to achieve them mandated in the event of a 'remain' vote in the UK referendum in June 2016).[108]

---

[103] Ibid.

[104] Case C-542/09, *Commission v. Netherlands* (EU:C:2012:346), para. 57. For the Court, '[t]o accept that budgetary concerns may justify a difference in treatment between migrant workers and national workers would imply that the application and the scope of a rule of EU law as fundamental as non-discrimination on grounds of nationality might vary in time and place according to the state of the public finances of Member States' (para. 58).

[105] Case C-483/17, *Tarola* (EU:C:2019:309), para. 50 (emphasis added).

[106] Case C-257/99, *Givane and Others* (EU:C:2003:8), para. 46. In contrast, 'the residence rights provided for migrant workers under [Article 45 TFEU] are not so conditional – the only limitations are those "justified on grounds of public policy, public security or public health", giving narrower scope for rights negation' (O'Brien, n. 63, 1110).

[107] Already in November 2015, UK Prime Minister David Cameron's historic letter to European Council President Donald Tusk, outlining the UK's various EU membership discontents, erroneously conflated freedom of movement with 'immigration'. The text of this letter is available at: https://assets. publishing.service.gov.uk/government/uploads/system/uploads/attachment_data/file/475679/Donald_Tusk_letter.pdf (last viewed 13 April 2023).

[108] The proposals made no clear distinction between directly or indirectly discriminatory restrictions, applying general public interest grounds also to restrictions framed as direct discrimination: see Section D, Decision of the Heads of State or Government, meeting within the European Council, concerning a new settlement for the United Kingdom within the European Union, OJ 2016 C 691/1. See further, see Nic Shuibhne (n. 12).

In one sense, the intensity of (pre-)Brexit political and public concern around social assistance for EU workers may now have passed (or diminished at least), as demonstrated by the outcome of infringement proceedings against Austria, which had unilaterally introduced one of the restrictions proposed in 2016 (indexing exported family benefits to the family's State of residence rather than to the worker's State of employment). AG Richard de la Tour underlined the 'fundamental importance' of the fact that 'migrant workers contribute to the financing of the social policies of the host Member State through the taxes and social contributions which they pay by virtue of their employment there, which justifies the equality of the benefits or advantages granted'.[109] The same point was affirmed by the Court to explain why Austria's indirectly discriminatory restriction of the free movement of workers could not be saved on public interest grounds, since migrant workers 'must ... be able to profit from [their tax and social security contributions] under the same conditions as national workers'.[110]

However, again reflecting Section 3.A in the context of claim-making—and recalling especially that economic activity only 'establishes, *in principle*, a sufficient link of integration with the society of that Member State, allowing [workers] to benefit from the principle of equal treatment, as compared with national workers, as regards social advantages'[111]—note this statement in *Commission v. Austria* at the stage of restriction-defending: 'the risk of jeopardising the financial balance of the social security system does not result from the payment of benefits to workers whose children reside outside Austria, *since those payments are estimated to represent only around 6% of expenditure* in respect of family benefits'.[112] Is a door left open here for reconsideration of the point of principle under different empirical conditions? There is another interesting qualifier in paragraph 105: 'the family benefits and social advantages at issue *are not subject to the adjustment mechanism where the children reside in Austria*, even though it is common ground that there are, between the regions of that Member State, differences in price levels comparable in scale to those which may exist between the Republic of Austria and other Member States. That lack of consistency in the application of the mechanism confirms that the justification put forward by the Republic of Austria cannot be accepted'.[113] The Court in *Tarola* arguably sent a similar warning shot, suggesting that circumstances in which economically active Union citizens become an 'unreasonable burden' on host State social security systems are conceivable—even where there is no suggestion that the *Lawrie-Blum* definition of work is not met

---

[109] AG Richard de la Tour in Case C-328/20, *Commission v. Austria* (EU:C:2022:45), para. 143 of the Opinion. See also, the questions referred in Case C-163/20, *AZ* (EU:C:2022:600) and Case C-574/20, *XO* (EU:C:2023:27).

[110] Case C-328/20, *Commission v. Austria* (EU:C:2022:468), para. 109.

[111] Case C-542/09, *Commission v. Netherlands* (EU:C:2012:346), para. 65 (emphasis added).

[112] Case C-328/20, *Commission v. Austria* (EU:C:2022:468), para. 107 (emphasis added).

[113] Ibid., para. 105 (emphasis added).

and notwithstanding the fact that 'migrant workers contribute to the financing of the social policies of the host Member State through the taxes and social contributions which they pay by virtue of their employment there'.[114]

Joining the discussions on claim-making and restriction-defending, two key points are important around the role of integration in economic free movement law. First, the relationship between economic activity and citizenship is clearly an entangled one, and it is not always easy to pin down where 'free movement law' stops and 'EU citizenship law' starts. At the same time, second, there is no neatly linear trajectory here: aspects of integration were arguably built into economic free movement law long before Union citizenship was conceived; and while integration is sometimes used as a precondition for equal treatment in the context of economic activity, mirroring its more obviously limiting function in EU citizenship law, legal protection is still extended to Union citizens where links to economic activity seem more formal than substantive (and often very tenuous). Overall, the uneven progression of the case law on free movement of workers does appear to confirm what Jacqueson calls 'a more contractual approach to claims of social benefits'.[115] At the same time, the unpredictability of how (and when) integration requirements apply to equal treatment in the domain of economic activity is a point of note in and of itself. In that light, the planting of provisos and qualifiers—often through the 'in principle' phrase that recurs across the case law—is noteworthy. Such terms can often be overcome in individual cases yet might be considered to serve a wider purpose of comforting nervous Member States with respect to the reach of EU equal treatment: as Ristuccia puts it, 'to somewhat soothe Member States' concerns of opening up their welfare systems too much'.[116]

On one view, better alignment of economic free movement law and citizenship law achieves a more rational and politically resonant emphasis on a person's means rather than, more technically, on their status. The difficulty is that it upends decades of established case law on freedom of movement for workers. It entails applying the extended limitation and condition-setting legislative power expressly written into Articles 20 and 21 TFEU in the context of Articles 45 and 49 TFEU, where it is not written at all.[117] It complicates how free movement rights are extended externally, notably with respect to the EEA. And it ultimately makes economic free movement feel less stable—less status based; and even less rights based. As underlined by Iliopoulou-Penot, it 'becomes essential to understand whether the outcome in one case is tailored to its facts or whether it is an expression of a general underlying principle, which will further inform other rulings'.[118] However,

---

[114] AG Richard de la Tour in Case C-328/20, *Commission v. Austria* (EU:C:2022:45), para. 143 of the Opinion.

[115] Jacqueson (n. 88), 921.

[116] Ristuccia (n. 59), 893.

[117] See again (n. 106) and related text.

[118] Iliopoulou-Penot (n. 2), 1009.

ECONOMIC ACTIVITY AND EU CITIZENSHIP LAW   111

the Court does not make that an easy task. The extent to which case law qualifiers transplanted from EU citizenship law and directed at evidencing *sufficient* integration open space in economic free movement law for elevating means over status is therefore important to notice—and to question.

4. Equal Treatment II: Anomalies Produced by the Interplay of Legal Sources

If more limited equal treatment of free movers might attract a certain degree of political relief, how that was achieved with respect to the right to move and reside conferred by Article 21 TFEU remains subject to significant legal criticism. One reason concerns how the concept of lawful residence determined by Articles 7(1) (b) and 24 of Directive 2004/38 conditions access to equal treatment in the host State, displacing Article 18 TFEU even in situations of lawful residence under national law as confirmed recently in *CG*.[119] Thus, even though, as noted in Section 3 above, Article 21 TFEU does attach particular weight to limitations and conditions in EU legislation, the role of equal treatment under Article 18 TFEU and also as a general principle of EU law has diminished, raising questions about the anomalies produced when different legal sources interact. Adding to that discussion, this part of the chapter shows that access to equal treatment in economic free movement is not straightforward either, through anomalies produced by the interplay of primary rights and secondary law in Section 4.A[120] and through the interaction of provisions in Directive 2004/38 and Regulation 492/2011 respectively in Section 4.B.

A. Interplay of Primary Law and Secondary Law

In economic free movement law, rights continue to be sourced directly from primary law in certain situations not covered by EU legislation. Retaining the status of worker after economic activity has ceased provides a good example. Initially, the Court was stricter: for example, in *Förster*, it held that '[t]he conditions of

---

[119] Case C-709/20, *CG* (EU:C:2021:602); for criticism, see Haag (n. 23); O'Brien, 'The Great EU Citizenship Illusion Exposed: Equal Treatment Rights Evaporate for the Vulnerable (*CG v The department for communities in Northern Ireland*)', 46 *European Law Review* (2021) 801; and Reynolds, 'Playing Politics so the UKSC Doesn't Have to: the CJEU Ruling in Case C-709/20 *CG v Department for Communities in Northern Ireland*', UK Constitutional Law Association blog, https://ukconstitutional law.org/2021/08/03/stephanie-reynolds-playing-politics-so-the-uksc-doesnt-have-to-the-cjeu-ruling-in-case-c-709-20-cg-v-department-for-communities-in-northern-ireland/ (last viewed 13 April 2023).

[120] On the interplay between primary law and secondary law in EU citizenship law more generally, see Muir, 'EU Citizenship, Access to "Social Benefits" and Third-country National Family Members: Reflecting on the Relationship between Primary and Secondary Rights in Times of Brexit', 3 *European Papers* (2018) 1353.

112 NIAMH NIC SHUIBHNE

entitlement to the worker's right to remain in the host Member State are set out *exhaustively* in Article 2 of Regulation No 1251/70.'[121] However, in *Saint Prix*, the Court altered course. In Section 2 above, it was noted that Article 7(3) of Directive 2004/38 now sets out the situations in which a worker retains that status following the end of their economic activity in a host State.[122] But the Court held in *Saint Prix* that 'it does not follow from either Article 7 of Directive 2004/38 … or from the other provisions of that directive' that, because of a temporary break from work for the purposes of childbirth, 'a citizen of the Union who does not fulfil the conditions laid down in [Article 7] is, therefore, systematically deprived of the status of "worker", within the meaning of Article 45 TFEU'.[123] For the Court, '[t]he codification, sought by the directive, of the instruments of EU law existing prior to that directive, which expressly seeks to facilitate the exercise of the rights of Union citizens to move and reside freely within the territory of the Member States, *cannot, by itself, limit the scope of the concept of worker* within the meaning of the FEU Treaty.'[124] As a result, 'it cannot be argued … that Article 7(3) of Directive 2004/38 lists exhaustively the circumstances in which a migrant worker who is no longer in an employment relationship may nevertheless continue to benefit from that status'.[125] Thus, notwithstanding the limiting power expressly given to the EU legislator by Article 21 TFEU, the Court confirms in *Saint Prix* that Directive 2004/38 cannot cut into rights conferred directly by Article 45 TFEU—rendering the status of worker *more* fundamental, in effect.[126]

However, while it might be hierarchically logical that rights are drawn from Article 45 TFEU to fill gaps in secondary legislation, the problem is that the Court only does it *sometimes*—as captured perfectly by the title of Kramer's analysis of *Alimanovic* ('Had they only worked one month longer!').[127] I am not suggesting that childbirth and maternity leave are not good reasons to consider going beyond

---

[121] Case C-158/07, *Förster* (EU:C:2008:630), para. 27 (emphasis added).

[122] See again (n. 27).

[123] Case C-507/12, *Saint Prix* (EU:C:2014:2007), para. 31.

[124] Ibid., para. 32 (emphasis added).

[125] Ibid., para. 38.

[126] A suggestion of the significance of rights conferred directly by the Treaties can also be seen in Article 52(2) of the Charter of Fundamental Rights, which provides that '[r]ights recognised by this Charter for which provision is made in the Treaties shall be exercised under the conditions and within the limits *defined by those Treaties.*' Note also Spaventa's astute observation that '[o]n the one hand, the Court seems ready to accept the consequences of Directive 2004/38: an updated instrument incorporating all of the case law of the Court including the proportionality principle, moves the "battleground" of citizenship to the interpretation of these provisions … On the other hand, and at the same time, in relation to the economic free movement provisions, the Court rejects the possibility that Directive 2004/38 could act as a straightjacket for its interpretation of the Treaty provisions: much as it was the case before the Directive was adopted, the purposive interpretation of the Treaty rights is unaffected by codification' (Spaventa, 'Earned Citizenship – Understanding Union Citizenship through its Scope', in Kochenov (ed.) (n. 3), 204 at 208).

[127] Kramer, 'Had They Only Worked One Month Longer! An Analysis of the *Alimanovic* Case [2015] C-67/14' European Law Blog (2015), https://europeanlawblog.eu/2015/09/29/had-they-only-worked-one-month-longer-an-analysis-of-the-alimanovic-case-2015-c-6714/ (last viewed 13 April 2023).

Article 7(3) of the Directive in order to facilitate the retaining of worker status under Article 45 TFEU directly.[128] It is also true that lines have to be drawn somewhere and that the legislator is normally best placed to draw them. However, considering *Alimanovic* alongside *Saint Prix* highlights two things. First, 'if mother and daughter Alimanovic had only worked one month longer, Germany should have granted them *unlimited* access to social assistance' because of the entirely open-ended wording of Article 7(3).[129] The significance of status over means thus recurs here, as does a reminder that while the legislator might be best placed to draw appropriate lines, it does not always draw them well. The second problem is the risk of arbitrary decision-making, to which the Court becomes vulnerable whenever it decides that it will—and when it will not—go beyond legislative provision: the irregular patterns, the lack of predictability.

Two questions further illustrate the complex interplay of primary rights and secondary legislation in a citizenship-infused economic free movement law: first, how primary law expands legislative protection for jobseekers; and second, whether the rights protected for workers by Regulation 492/2011 are extended to self-employed persons by the Article 49 TFEU directly. First, on jobseekers, it was seen in Section 3 above that following the creation of Union citizenship, the Court conceived the jobseeker as bearing a 'hybrid' legal status, with both citizen and worker components—or, in primary law terms, with both Article 21 and Article 45 TFEU components. As a result, having initially excluded jobseekers from equal treatment with respect to social and tax advantages under Article 7(2) of Regulation 492/2011, the Court later expanded the reach of equal treatment by combining Articles 21 and 45 TFEU.[130] However, it added an integration requirement on the basis that 'it is legitimate for the national legislature to wish to ensure that there is a genuine link between an applicant for an allowance in the nature of a social advantage ... and the geographic employment market in question'.[131]

Further conditions were later established in Directive 2004/38. First, Article 7(3) provides that workers who become unemployed in the host State but continue to seek employment there retain worker status (and thus full equal treatment) indefinitely, but only if they had worked in the host State for more than one year and became unemployed involuntarily; however, if someone is employed for less than one year before involuntary unemployment, worker status is only retained

---

[128] Indeed, the European Parliament called attention (to no avail) to this very gap in its assessment of the Commission's original proposal for the Directive: Opinion of the Committee on Women's Rights and Equal Opportunities attached to the European Parliament Report of 23 January 2003 on Commission proposal (COM(2001) 257), A5-0009/2003, amendment 8, p. 89.

[129] Kramer (n. 127) (emphasis added). Unpacking the similarities and differences between the *Alimanovic* and *Saint Prix* cases in more detail, see further Ristuccia (n. 59), 886–888.

[130] For Kramer, 'equal treatment of the work seeker is a manifestation of Union social citizenship based upon the *potential* assimilation of Union citizens into the welfare system of the host society on the basis of future economic contribution' (n. 6), 183 (emphasis in original).

[131] Case C-138/02, *Collins* (EU:C:2004:172), para. 67.

for six months (returned to in Section 4.B below). Second, Article 24(2) of the Directive excludes jobseekers from entitlement to social assistance. Initially, the Court sought to sustain its *Collins* reasoning, notwithstanding the adoption of the Directive, by ruling in *Vatsouras and Koupatantze* that '[b]enefits of a financial nature which, independently of their status under national law, are intended to facilitate access to the labour market cannot be regarded as constituting "social assistance" within the meaning of Article 24(2).'[132] However, by focusing in *Alimanovic* on the 'predominant function of the benefits at issue', which was 'in fact to cover the minimum subsistence costs necessary to lead a life in keeping with human dignity', the Court held that such benefits 'cannot be characterised as benefits of a financial nature which are intended to facilitate access to the labour market of a Member State'.[133]

Taking that case law together, an infusion of primary law did not end up defeating the limits put in place by Directive 2004/38. Although in *Martínez Sala*, the Court ruled that 'a person who is genuinely seeking work *must also be classified as a worker*',[134] equal treatment with respect to social and tax advantages was based on *both* Articles 21 and 45 TFEU in *Collins*. That means that the exclusion from equal treatment expressed in Article 24(2) of the Directive can be linked to the limitation and condition-setting legislative mandate in Article 21 TFEU and, importantly, that the Article 45 TFEU element of the jobseeker's hybrid status does not defeat it. In contrast to *Saint Prix*, the Directive *can* cut into rights only *partly* based on Article 45 TFEU—with respect to social assistance at least. Conversely, in *G.M.A.*, returned to below, the Court extended special treatment to jobseekers, inexplicably complicating the residence rights based on Articles 6 (up to three months) and 7 (more than three months) of the Directive.

In *Antonissen*, where the Court had confirmed that residence rights for jobseekers in a host State are conferred directly by Article 45 TFEU,[135] the contested national regulations provided that a jobseeker could be deported after six months if they had not yet found employment or were not carrying out another occupation. The Court ruled that '[i]n the absence of a Community provision prescribing the period during which Community nationals seeking employment in a Member State may stay there, a period of six months, *such as that as laid down in the national legislation at issue in the main proceedings, does not appear in principle to be insufficient* to enable the persons concerned to apprise themselves, in the host Member State, of offers of employment corresponding to their occupational qualifications and to take, where appropriate, the necessary steps in order to be engaged.'[136] Post-*Antonissen*, Directive 2004/38 does now 'prescrib[e] the period

---

[132] Joined Cases C-22/08 and C-23/08, *Vatsouras and Koupatantze* (EU:C:2009:344), para. 45.
[133] Case C-67/14, *Alimanovic* (EU:C:2015:597), paras 45–46.
[134] Case C-85/96, *Martínez Sala* (EU:C:1998:217), para. 32 (emphasis added).
[135] As established previously in Case 48/75, *Royer* (EU:C:1976:57), para. 31.
[136] Case C-292/89, *Antonissen* (EU:C:1991:80), para. 21 (emphasis added).

during which [Union] nationals seeking employment in a Member State may stay there'—but not in a straightforward way. Rather, by codifying the more qualitative conditions of stay established in *Antonissen*,[137] Article 14(4)(b) of the Directive is framed as a right not to be deported (rather than as a right to reside per se): it provides that 'an expulsion measure may in no case be adopted against Union citizens or their family members if: ... the Union citizens entered the territory of the host Member State in order to seek employment. In this case, the Union citizens and their family members may not be expelled for as long as the Union citizens can provide evidence that they are continuing to seek employment and that they have a genuine chance of being engaged'.

In *G.M.A.*, the Court turned the *example* of the six-month period (in national regulations) in *Antonissen* into a period with legal implications much more generally, notwithstanding the clear three months/more than three months right to reside distinction set by Articles 6 and 7 of the Directive.[138] Recalling that 'freedom of movement for workers forms one of the foundations of the European Union and, therefore, the provisions establishing that freedom must be interpreted broadly', the Court held that when a jobseekers enters a host State, 'that citizen's right of residence falls, from the time of his or her registration as a jobseeker, within the scope of Article 14(4)(b) of Directive 2004/38'.[139] The Court acknowledged that 'according to its wording, Article 6 of Directive 2004/38 applies without distinction to all Union citizens, irrespective of the intention with which those citizens enter the territory of the host Member State' and thus that 'even where a Union citizen enters the territory of a host Member State with the intention of seeking employment there, his or her right of residence is also covered, during the first three months, by Article 6 of Directive 2004/38'.[140] However, citing *Antonissen* 'to that effect', the Court underlined that 'the effectiveness of Article 45 TFEU is secured in so far as EU legislation or, in its absence, the legislation of a Member State gives persons concerned *a reasonable time* in which to apprise themselves, in the territory of the host Member State, of offers of employment corresponding to their occupational qualifications and to take, where appropriate, the necessary steps in order to be engaged'.[141]

This period of reasonable time 'starts to run from the time when the Union citizen concerned has decided to register as a jobseeker in the host Member State',

---

[137] Ibid., paras 21–22.

[138] Overriding the logical view that the approach in *Antonissen* 'was taken over in Directive 2004/38' (Verschueren, n. 72, 205).

[139] Case C-710/19, *G.M.A. (Demandeur d'emploi)* (EU:C:2020:1037), paras 25 and 34; building on Case C-67/14, *Alimanovic* (EU:C:2015:597), para. 52. For very interesting examples of different Member State practices and conditions with respect to residence rights for jobseekers, see Welsh, 'A Genuine Chance of Free Movement? Clarifying the "Reasonable Period of Time" and Residence Conditions for Jobseekers in *G.M.A*', 58 *Common Market Law Review* (2021) 1591.

[140] Case C-710/19, *G.M.A. (Demandeur d'emploi)* (EU:C:2020:1037), para. 35. Accordingly, no further conditions can be imposed on jobseekers during the first three months of residence (para. 36).

[141] Ibid., para. 26 (emphasis added).

i.e. it is disconnected from the (parallel) right to reside for up to three months under Article 6; the 'reasonable period of time' clock starts to tick once the jobseeker registers as such in the host State, even if that decision is taken within the first three months of residence.[142] As a result, after the first three months of residence (to respect Article 6's guarantee of a right to reside 'without any conditions or any formalities other than the requirement to hold a valid identity card or passport') and during the 'reasonable time' (in respect of which six months seems 'reasonable'), jobseekers may be required to demonstrate that they are seeking employment but not (yet) that they have a genuine chance of being engaged.[143] While conceding that the ruling in *Antonissen* had not 'fix[ed] a minimum duration of the "reasonable period of time"', the Court found that *Antonissen* did establish 'that a period of six months from entry into the territory of the host Member State, such as that at issue in the case which gave rise to that judgment, did not appear capable of calling that effectiveness into question.'[144] Thus, while the Court does not quantify a six-month test definitively, it is hard to see how Member States will not do so in national regulations and practices. Contrary to the undoubted intention of providing *more* support for jobseekers, the strong temporal signal might work against certain jobseekers, who need more time to realize their employment goals.[145]

Article 14 of the Directive is a flawed text: Articles 14(1) and 14(2) speak of *having* a right to reside; Article 14(4) provides a 'derogation' from those provisions not in terms of a (different) right to reside but of protection from expulsion. Yet the Court reads the notion of 'derogation' extremely broadly and carves out an autonomous residence space for jobseekers that is not easily connected to the timeframes of Articles 6 and 7 (which are valued profoundly in the case law more generally[146]). As noted above, the Court did refer to Article 21 TFEU in its ruling, but it is the jobseeker's character as an economic actor of the future, and thus the rights conferred by Article 45 TFEU, that enabled reading more into the Directive than is arguably really there. As the Court affirmed in *Saint Prix*, 'a person who is genuinely seeking work *must also be classified as a worker*', reengaging the right to reside

---

[142] Ibid., para. 37.

[143] The latter requirement may be imposed after the reasonable period has elapsed, and it entails, on the basis of 'the evidence adduced to that effect by the jobseeker in question', carrying out 'an overall assessment of all relevant factors such as, for example, ... the fact that the jobseeker has registered with the national body responsible for jobseekers, that he or she regularly approaches potential employers with letters of application or that he or she goes to employment interviews'; the 'situation of the national labour market in the sector corresponding to the occupational qualifications of the jobseeker in question' must also be considered, whereas, '[b]y contrast, the fact that that jobseeker refused offers of employment which did not correspond to his or her professional qualifications cannot be taken into account for the purpose of considering that that person does not satisfy the conditions laid down in Article 14(4) (b) of Directive 2004/38' (ibid., para. 47).

[144] Ibid., para. 40.

[145] See further Welsh (n. 139), 1607–1610, discussing 'groups who face systemic barriers that can make the process of seeking employment more complex and time-consuming' (1607).

[146] See again, Joined Cases C-316/16 and C-424/16, *B and Vomero* (EU:C:2018:256), paras 51–54.

in Article 45(3) TFEU directly, as established in *Antonissen* in the first place.[147] Overall, the ruling in *G.M.A.* therefore shows that, beyond the more fraught question of eligibility for social assistance, the worker element of the jobseeker's hybrid status still carries sufficient primary law weight to modulate limitations and conditions in secondary law. However, trying to reconcile the interplay of legal sources in *Alimanovic*, *Saint Prix*, *Jobcenter Krefeld*, and *G.M.A.* proves challenging.

Turning next to the rights of self-employed persons, Directive 2004/38 refers to both workers and the self-employed across several of provisions, notably in Article 7(1)(a) since they 'have' the right to reside for more than three months without the need to fulfil any further conditions. However, self-employed persons are not mentioned in Article 7(3) with respect to retaining 'worker' status. Nevertheless, in *Gusa*, the Court held that self-employed persons do fall within the scope of Article 7(3), drawing a comparison between involuntary unemployment for workers and cessation of self-employed activity 'due to an absence of work for reasons beyond the control of the person concerned, such as an economic recession'.[148] In this way, the Court tempered 'the traditional binary divide between employment and self-employment, between subordinated labour and independent or autonomous work'.[149] Alongside analysis of the scheme of the Directive overall, and, more specifically, its aim of cohering free movement legislation as well as 'strengthening the fundamental and individual right of all Union citizens to move and reside freely', the Court uses language familiar from Section 3 above to rationalize the decision: treating employed and self-employed persons differently 'would be particularly unjustified in so far as it would lead to a person who has been self-employed for more than one year in the host Member State, and who has contributed to that Member State's social security and tax system by paying taxes, rates and other charges on his income, being treated in the same way as a first-time jobseeker in that Member State who has never carried on an economic activity in that State and has never contributed to that system'.[150]

The Court made no reference to primary law in *Gusa*. In contrast, in *Dakneviciute*, it did need to draw from rights protected by the Treaty to extend the *Saint Prix* ruling to self-employed persons. It held that 'Articles 45 and 49 TFEU afford *the same legal protection*, the classification of the economic activity thus being without significance.'[151] Being forced to cease self-employed activity for reasons of childbirth might deter the exercise of free movement in the first place, justifying retention of status and thus the protection of Article 49 (and Article 18) TFEU.[152]

---

[147] Case C-85/96, *Martínez Sala* (EU:C:1998:217), para. 32; see later e.g. Case C-507/12, *Saint Prix* (EU:C:2014:2007), para. 35. See also, Case C-292/89, *Antonissen* (EU:C:1991:80), para. 13.

[148] Case C-442/16, *Gusa* (EU:C:2017:1004), para. 31.

[149] Verschueren (n. 72), 202. More narrowly, Article 48 TFEU enables the EU legislator to 'make arrangements ... for employed and self-employed migrant workers' in the field of social security.

[150] Case C-442/16, *Gusa* (EU:C:2017:1004), paras 40 and 44.

[151] Case C-544/18, *Dakneviciute* (EU:C:2019:761), para. 31 (emphasis added); confirming Case C-363/89, *Roux* (EU:C:1991:41), para. 23.

[152] Case C-544/18, *Dakneviciute* (EU:C:2019:761), paras 32–33.

118 NIAMH NIC SHUIBHNE

To what extent, though, does Article 49 TFEU deliver 'the *same* legal protection', especially in the absence of a self-employment equivalent to Regulation 492/2011? In other words, to what extent are EU rights for workers constituted by the Regulation itself, meaning that they cannot be applied in the context of self-employment?

For example, the residence rights based on Article 10 of the Regulation have not been extended to the children of former self-employed persons.[153] However, equal treatment with respect to minimum income benefits—a social and tax advantage under Article 7(2) of the Regulation for workers—has been extended to self-employed persons through the direct application of Articles 18 and 49 TFEU.[154] Reflecting on the underpinning right to equal treatment, '[a]lthough the principles in the case-law ... were indeed developed ... specifically regarding the rule of equal treatment enshrined in both Article 45 TFEU and Article 7 of Regulation No 492/2011, *those principles do not apply solely to employed migrant workers* but also apply, mutatis mutandis, in respect of Article 49 TFEU, to self-employed migrant workers.'[155] Interestingly, while the Court cited earlier case law 'to that effect' for this proposition,[156] the cited ruling was based solely on Articles 45 and 49 TFEU—it had not addressed Article 7 of the Regulation at all.

As lawful residents in a host State 'on the basis of' Article 7(1)(a) of Directive 2004/38, Article 24(1) of the Directive establishes another legislative guarantee of equal treatment separately from the Regulation—and another reason to consider the Court's 'in principle' provisos and integration requirements discussed in Section 3 above somewhat questionable, for workers and self-employed persons alike. At a general level, and reflecting expected source of law hierarchy, the Court has confirmed that '[s]ince Article 24(1) of Directive 2004/38 expressly provides that it applies only "subject to such specific provisions as are expressly provided for in the Treaty and secondary law", that provision cannot apply independently if a specific rule on non-discrimination laid down by the FEU Treaty is applicable to the situation in question.'[157] In that light, and differently from economically inactive citizens who cannot have recourse to the Treaty's economic freedoms, 'the *principle* of non-discrimination on the ground of nationality' takes precedence over Article 24(1) of the Directive for the self-employed, since that wider principle is 'given effect, in the area of freedom of establishment, by the specific rule laid down in Article 49 TFEU.'[158]

Is there any difference in reality? Not formally, since self-employed persons are lawfully resident on the basis of the Directive anyway, as required by Article 24(1).

---

[153] Joined Cases C-147/11 and C-148/11, *Czop and Punakova* (EU:C:2012:538), para. 33. For discussion of how the protection extended by Article 12(3) of Directive 2004/38/EC differs, see Ristuccia (n. 59), 900–901.

[154] E.g. Case C-299/01, *Commission v. Luxembourg* (EU:C:2002:394), para. 12.

[155] Case C-168/20, *BJ and OV* (EU:C:2021:907), para. 85.

[156] Case C-174/18, *Jacob and Lennertz* (EU:C:2019:205).

[157] Case C-168/20, *BJ and OV* (EU:C:2021:907), para. 69.

[158] Ibid., para. 71 (emphasis added).

ECONOMIC ACTIVITY AND EU CITIZENSHIP LAW   119

But substantively, the priority given to equal treatment grounded in primary law serves as a reminder that the particular circumstances—the means—of the economically active should not be probed since no further conditions apply to lawful residence once self-employed capacity is established within the meaning of Article 49 TFEU.[159] And yet, means-oriented provisos proliferate. For example, in *Tarola*, the Court observed that worker status is retained 'indefinitely' for situations within the scope of Articles 7(3)(a), 7(3)(b) and 7(3)(d) of the Directive.[160] However, just one year previously, in *Prefeta*, the principles established in *Saint Prix* for retention of status in the context of pregnancy and childbirth were expressed more generally—and with a catch, with the Court ruling that 'the possibility for an EU citizen who has temporarily ceased to pursue an activity as an employed or self-employed person of retaining his status of worker on the basis of Article 7(3) of Directive 2004/38, as well as the corresponding right of residence under Article 7(1) of the directive, *is based on the assumption that the citizen is available and able to re-enter the labour market* of the host Member State within a reasonable period'.[161] The Court then addressed the relationship between Article 7(3) of the Directive and Regulation 492/2011 on the free movement of workers:

> Article 7(3)(a) of Directive 2004/38 concerns the situation of an EU citizen who is temporarily unable to work as the result of an illness or accident, which implies that that citizen will be able to pursue an activity as an employed or self-employed person again once that temporary inability to work has come to an end. Moreover, Article 7(3)(b) and (c) of that directive requires economically inactive EU citizens to register as jobseekers with the relevant employment office and Article 7(3)(d) of the directive requires such persons, under specific conditions, to embark on vocational training. Article 7(3) of Directive 2004/38 therefore covers situations in which the EU citizen's re-entry on the labour market of the host Member State is foreseeable within a reasonable period. Consequently, the application of that provision may not be dissociated from that of the provisions of Regulation No 492/2011 governing the eligibility for employment of a Member State national in another Member State, that is, Articles 1 to 6 of that regulation.[162]

Articles 1–6 of the Regulation do not formally apply to self-employed persons, creating risks of some divergence of approach in practice. The confusion is amplified by the Court's reference to the 'assumption' about re-entering the labour market in

---

[159] It also demonstrates again the very significant distinction in reality that relatively minor factual differences can produce. For example, commenting on *Jobcenter Krefeld*, Ristuccia remarks that the ruling 'builds on the restrictive reading of the Directive in order to reinforce the rights of those who manage to escape it' (n. 59), 902.

[160] Case C-483/17, *Tarola* (EU:C:2019:309), para. 44.

[161] Case C-618/16, *Prefeta* (EU:C:2018:719), para. 37 (emphasis added).

[162] Ibid., paras 38–39.

120   NIAMH NIC SHUIBHNE

Prefeta (in paragraph 40) of *Tarola—just* before the reference to retaining worker status 'indefinitely' (in paragraph 44). The *Prefeta* case thus not only raises complicated interplay of primary and secondary law, but also calls for more specific consideration of how the Directive and the Regulation intersect.

B. Directive 2004/38 and Regulation 492/2011

As recital 4 expresses, a major incentive for the adoption of Directive 2004/38 was its purpose of 'remedying th[e] sector-by-sector, piecemeal approach to the right of free movement and residence'. This 'single legislative act' thus completely repealed and replaced five different measures. However, exceptionally, only the provisions of Regulation 1612/68 concerning family members were replaced: in all other respects, the Regulation remained in force (as reaffirmed through the subsequent adoption of Regulation 492/2011). Over time, however, the Directive and Regulation continuing to have legal force in parallel has produced complexities. One example was already touched on in this chapter, i.e. residence rights under Article 10 of the Regulation for the children of Union citizens who previously worked in the host State. As the Court stated in *Ibrahim*, 'there is nothing to suggest that, when adopting Directive 2004/38, the European Union legislature intended to alter the scope of Article 1[0] ..., as interpreted by the Court, so as to limit its normative content from then on to a mere right of access to education'.[163] As a result, 'the children of a national of a Member State who works or has worked in the host Member State and the parent who is their primary carer can claim a right of residence in the latter State on the sole basis of Article [10] of Regulation [492/2011], without being required to satisfy the conditions laid down in Directive 2004/38'.[164] As seen in Section 3 above, the equal treatment rights that then follow materially distinguish the situation of the former economic actor now residing on the basis of Article 10 via their school-going children from 'inactive' Union citizens.[165]

However, the separation of the Directive and Regulation achieved in *Ibrahim* can bring problems later on. According to Article 16(1) of the Directive, a Union citizen (and/or their family members) must have 'resided legally for a continuous period of five years in the host State' in order to qualify for permanent residence rights. The meaning of 'resided legally' is indicated in recital 17 of the Directive, i.e. residing in the host State 'in compliance with the conditions laid down in this Directive' by either being a worker or self-employed, or otherwise fulfilling the sufficient resources and medical insurance conditions in Article 7(1)(b) (or Article 7(1)(c) for students). Thus, if equal treatment as regards social assistance

---

[163] Case C-310/08, *Ibrahim* (EU:C:2010:89), para. 45.
[164] Ibid, para. 50.
[165] Case C-181/19, *Jobcenter Krefeld* (EU:C:2020:794).

is extended via *Jobcenter Krefeld*, the relevant period of residence will not then qualify for permanent residence. Similarly, even 'a period of residence which complies with the law of a Member State but does not satisfy the conditions laid down in Article 7(1) of Directive 2004/38 cannot be regarded as a "legal" period of residence within the meaning of Article 16(1)'.[166] In contrast, economically still-active Union citizens, or those retaining that status under Article 7(3) of the Directive or Articles 45 or 49 TFEU, will in principle be able to satisfy the requirement of compliance with Article 7 (though it has not yet been tested whether a citizen whose five-year period of residence is based in part on Article 14(4)(b) of the Directive also qualifies).

Another uncertainty about the relationship between the Directive and the Regulation concerns the rights of family members. As noted above, it is generally presumed that Articles 2 and 3 of the Directive occupy this field, so to speak, but there is an open question about residence rights for unmarried partners. Article 3(2)(b) of the Directive makes limited provision for partners with whom Union citizens have a 'durable relationship, duly attested'. In terms of the resulting obligation on a host Member State, Article 3(2) requires only that it 'shall, in accordance with its national legislation, facilitate entry and residence' for these partners. Article 3(2)(b) does not confer residence rights in any circumstances. But it is not clear whether the classically established *Reed* obligation not to treat the non-married partners of Union citizens who *work* in the host State (and thus, recalling the discussion above, those who are self-employed there too) differently from the non-married partners of nationals of that State was overridden by Article 3(2) of the Directive. As emphasized above, the adoption of Directive 2004/38 amended only the provisions of Regulation 1612/68 that addressed family members directly. It left untouched Article 7(2) of the Regulation—now Article 7(2) of Regulation 492/2011—which was the provision from which the Court drew residence rights for non-married partners in *Reed* on the basis of non-discrimination on the grounds of nationality.[167] In fact, the Court developed the Article 7(2) solution in *Reed* because such partners could not be treated in the same way as spouses on account of the rights extended to the latter by the family member provisions of the original Regulation.

The reasoning applied in *Depesme and Kerrou* might provide some indirect guidance but perhaps not resolution of the question. In that case, in the context of financial aid for university studies, the Court had to consider whether the definition of family members in Article 2 of Directive 2004/38 should also inform the concept of family member for the purposes of equal treatment of workers under Article

---

[166] Joined Cases C-424/10 and C-425/10, *Ziolkowski and Szeja* (EU:C:2011:866), para. 47.

[167] Case 59/85, *Reed* (EU:C:1986:157), paras 25–29. The Court emphasized that 'the possibility for a migrant worker of obtaining permission for his unmarried companion to reside with him where that companion is not a national of the host Member State, can assist with his integration in the host State and thus contribute to the achievement of freedom of movement for workers' (para. 28).

7(2) of Regulation 492/2011. More specifically, the question was whether the child of a frontier worker's spouse was included. The Court observed that '[t]here is nothing to suggest that the EU legislature intended to establish, as regards family members, a watertight distinction between the scope of Directive 2004/38 and the scope of Regulation No 492/2011, under which family members of a Union citizen, within the meaning of Directive 2004/38, would not necessarily be the same persons as the family members of that citizen when he is considered in his capacity as a worker.'[168] It also referred to recital 1 of Directive 2014/54, 'under which the free movement of workers "is further developed by Union law aiming to guarantee the full exercise of rights conferred on Union citizens and the members of their family" [so] that the expression "members of their family" should be understood as having the same meaning as the term defined in point (2) of Article 2 of Directive [2004/38], which applies also to family members of frontier workers.'[169]

The point about ensuring synergies across Directive 2004/38 and the Regulation is an important one. However, applying that synergy in *Depesme and Kerrou* enhanced rather than retracted the rights of the worker involved in the case. Moreover, unmarried partners do not fall within the scope of Article 2 of the Directive—within its definition of 'family members'—in the first place. Can Article 3(2)(b), which provides a right to a procedure rather than a right of residence, override a right to reside construed as a social and tax advantage under Article 7(2) of the Regulation? The emphasis placed on the autonomy of the equal treatment guarantees protected by the Regulation in *Jobcenter Krefeld* would suggest not. There, the Court stated that 'the fact that JD had become economically inactive during that period *cannot lead to the result that the principle of equal treatment laid down in Article 7(2) of Regulation No 492/2011 becomes inapplicable*.'[170] Moreover, '[t]he same is true, in a situation where the children and the parent who is their primary carer have a right of residence based on Article 10 of Regulation No 492/2011, with respect to the right to equal treatment as regards entitlement to the social advantages laid down in Article 7(2) of that regulation.'[171]

These statements in *Jobcenter Krefeld* were concerned mainly to establish a right to reside under the Regulation, from which a guarantee of equal treatment then followed. However, they are noted here to underline the 'specific expression' of the latter right that Article 7(2) is deemed by the Court to construct. A qualifier might be read into the statement that 'the derogation from the principle of equal treatment, provided for in Article 24(2) [of the Directive], is applicable only in

---

[168] Joined Cases C-401/15 to C-403/15, *Depesme and Kerrou* (EU:C:2016:955), para. 51.

[169] Ibid., para. 53. Directive 2014/54/EU on measures facilitating the exercise of rights conferred on workers in the context of freedom of movement for workers, OJ 2014 L 128/8. Article 2(2) of Directive 2014/54/EU establishes that its scope is identical to that of Regulation 492/2011/EU.

[170] Case C-181/19, *Jobcenter Krefeld* (EU:C:2020:794), paras 46–47.

[171] Ibid., para. 50.

situations that fall within the scope of Article 24(1), namely situations where the right of residence is based on that directive, and not in situations where that right has an independent basis in Article 10 of Regulation No 492/2011'.[172] Could Article 3(2)(b) of the Directive really be construed as a 'derogation' from equal treatment for workers in the same way, even by analogy? According to AG Pitruzella in *Jobcenter Krefeld*, a 'legitimate objective pursued by the EU legislature … cannot, by itself, justify transferring a rule of secondary legislation to a different legislative context'.[173] Also in *Jobcenter Krefeld*, the Court underlines that Article 7(2) of the Regulation 'is the particular expression, in the specific area of the grant of social advantages, of the principle of equal treatment and non-discrimination on the ground of nationality'.[174] It stated that '[w]hen Directive 2004/38 was adopted, Article [10 of Regulation 492/2011] was neither repealed nor amended. On the contrary, that directive was designed so as to be compatible with Article [10 of the Regulation] and with the case law interpreting that provision. Consequently, that directive cannot, as such, either call into question the independence of the rights based on Article 10 of Regulation No 492/2011 or alter their scope'.[175]

Again, the reasoning is not conclusive: in terms of compatibility-focused design, it could be argued that the Directive was designed to take over the residence rights of family members from the Regulation's repealed provisions. At the same time, neither residence nor procedural rights for unmarried partners were ever written into the repealed provisions of Regulation 1612/68; and the language of the key provision for *Reed*-based rights—Article 7(2)—was 'neither repealed nor amended' by the Directive. In the different context of *Saint Prix*, Iliopoulou-Penot establishes a point that may yet be decisive on the *Reed* versus Directive 2004/38 question: 'a legislative definition (such as that of the former worker of Art. 7(3) of the Directive) cannot water down the (more inclusive) scope of the constitutional category of a worker, which remains under the interpretative authority of the Court'.[176] It is therefore important to remember that neither Regulation 492/2011 nor—before the Directive—Regulation 1612/68 refers to a right to reside for workers: the basis of that right rests in Article 45(3)(c) TFEU—in primary law, bringing us back full circle to that dimension of anomalies produced by the interplay of sources. What we can therefore see across the discussion in Section 4 overall is that there are strands of both separation and conflation across the Treaty and legislative provisions that aim to determine the rights of Union citizens generally and economically active citizens more specifically—which again conspire to render the

---

[172] Ibid., para. 65.
[173] AG Pitruzella in Case C-181/19, *Jobcenter Krefeld* (EU:C:2020:377), para. 39 of the Opinion.
[174] Ibid., para. 74.
[175] Ibid., para. 64.
[176] Iliopoulou-Penot (n. 2), 1018.

124 NIAMH NIC SHUIBHNE

protection classically developed for the latter both *more* and *less* fundamental in different circumstances.

5. Conclusion

This chapter has explored the intersection of economic free movement law and EU citizenship law, primarily to understand the influence of the latter on the former. It has shown, in essence, the extent to which EU citizenship law has implications for the application and development of economic free movement law, with two apparently discordant trends seeming to manifest in parallel: intensively protecting Union citizens when a connection (including a historic connection) can be made to economic activity, promoting legal protection based on status, on the one hand; yet, at the same time, transplanting provisos and qualifiers from citizenship law to economic free movement law, promoting legal protection based on means, on the other. In both dimensions, a fragmented understanding of the purpose of integration requirements and of how different sources of EU law interrelate was evident, the 'simplification' aim of Directive 2004/38 notwithstanding.

Migration of concepts and ideas across different parts of free movement law is not problematic per se. But it becomes problematic when limitations and conditions developed under the extended legislative mandate in Articles 20 and 21 TFEU are transposed to legislation and case law based on Articles 45 and 49 TFEU—often without clear rationale or accommodation of the different Treaty bases, different legislative contexts, and different case law histories in question. In *Gusa*, the Court of Justice spoke about the importance of protecting economically active Union citizens 'in a vulnerable position'.[177] It seems counterintuitive to conclude that EU citizenship law leaves the economically active legally more vulnerable in some respects. And yet, that is sometimes the case. The legal privilege that we presume for economic free movers still exists in relative terms; but it is incomplete[178] and it is fragile, mirroring the fact that while EU legal attention has traditionally focused on the *status* of

---

[177] Case C-442/16, *Gusa* (EU:C:2017:1004), para. 43.

[178] Noting, in particular, Dani's caution that the rights conferred on workers by EU law 'are not meant to protect the individual from the risks of markets, but [to] offer to individuals opportunities to express themselves through markets' (Dani, 'The subjectification of the citizen in European public law' in Azoulai, Barbou des Places, and Pataut (eds), n. 6, 55 at 63).

the mover, political attention has shifted more to the mover's *means*. Again, closer alignment of the legal and political worlds is no bad thing in and of itself. But it has obvious risks for legal stability, both systemically and for affected individuals; and it tends to produce less than convincing reasoning when the relevant legal parts do not easily offer what might be a politically preferred outcome. In *Brey*, AG Wahl observed that '[t]he idea that a Union citizen could say *"civis europeus sum"* and invoke that status against hardships encountered in other Member States was famously pioneered 20 years ago', before asking whether 'that status can be relied upon today, against the economic difficulties of modern life'.[179] He was mainly concerned with economically inactive citizens, noting the circumstances of the *Brey* case itself. But his words now have sharper resonance for economic free movers too. In 2019, a Council Recommendation emphasized the importance of access to social protection for workers and the self-employed, but it is premised on Article 153 TFEU and is entirely silent on the specific situation and needs of workers and self-employed persons who are nationals of another Member State.[180]

In *Commission v. Austria*, Austria's defence relied in part on the fact that in the 2016 Decision capturing the UK's 'renegotiation' of its EU membership, indexation of family benefits was 'fully compatible with the Treaties' according to the European Council and that the Commission had also considered it to be compatible with Article 48 TFEU.[181] Responding to that submission, the Court issued a stunning statement: recalling not only that the 2016 Decision never entered into force, but that if the Commission had proposed an amendment to Regulation 883/2004, and 'if such an amendment had been adopted by the EU legislature, it would have been invalid under Article 45 TFEU'.[182] The legal/political tensions that shape the free movement of persons in EU law[183] are perfectly captured in the history

---

[179] AG Wahl in Case C-140/12, *Brey* (EU:C:2013:337), para. 1 of the Opinion. See similarly, AG Pitruzzella in Case C-181/19, *Jobcenter Krefeld* (EU:C:2020:377), para. 1 of the Opinion: 'As I prepare this Opinion, the European Union is going through an unprecedented public health crisis, to which the Member States have responded by demonstrating equally unprecedented solidarity as regards health-related matters. In the present case, it is the limits of social solidarity which the Court is called upon to clarify'.

[180] Council Recommendation of 8 November 2019 on access to social protection for workers and the self-employed, OJ 2019 C 387/1. See further, Nic Shuibhne, 'The "Social Freedom"? The Free Movement of Persons in EU27', in S. Garben and I. Govaere (eds), *The Internal Market 2.0* (2020) 111.

[181] Case C-328/20, *Commission v. Austria* (EU:C:2022:468), para. 41.

[182] Ibid., para. 57.

[183] For thoughtful accounts, see Iliopoulou-Penot (n. 2), 1030–1035; and Seubert, 'Shifting Boundaries of Membership? The Politicisation of Free Movement as a Challenge for EU Citizenship', 26 *European Law Journal* (2019) 48. Addressing the wider economic and political context of indexation specifically, see Blauberger, Heindlmaier, and Kobler, 'Free Movement of Workers under Challenge: the Indexation of Family Benefits', 18 *Comparative European Politics* (2020) 925.

behind and eventual ruling in *Commission v Austria*. However, as this chapter has shown, the risks to economic free movement are not only political in nature. It is becoming harder to distinguish free movement and migration more generally;[184] and it is becoming harder to sustain a status-based protection that does not also take account of means. Fundamentally, there is a legal problem too: EU citizenship law does not always protect Union citizens when they exercise the economic free movement rights protected—since the very beginning—by the EU Treaties.

---

[184] Note the remark already in 2014 about 'how different but related issues (EU migration, migration generally, employment standards and the exclusion of sections of the population from the employed or employable class) have become confused in the minds of commentators and the general public alike' (Editorial comments, 'The Free Movement of Persons in the European Union: Salvaging the Dream while Explaining the Nightmare', 51 *Common Market Law Review* (2014) 729, at 732). It is also worth remembering that transitional restrictions on the free movement of persons in the context of Union accession have not focused on a distinction between economically active and economically inactive citizens, with the free movement of self-employed and self-sufficient citizens privileged over the free movement of workers. See more generally, the contribution to this volume by Barbou des Places.

5

Free Movement and European Welfare States

Why Child Benefits for EU Workers Should Not Be Exportable

Martin Ruhs and Joakim Palme[*]

1. Introduction

The right to free movement of workers is one of the fundamental pillars of the European Union (EU). This notwithstanding, the conditions under which it occurs have been subject to considerable political debate between EU Member States in recent years. Free movement played a major role in Brexit and it is likely to continue to exert a divisive influence over the EU in the years to come. This makes it important to try to understand the political dynamics driving the tensions around free movement. We argue that the political tensions associated with free movement cannot be understood without paying close attention to the institutions and politics of modern welfare states in Europe. In particular, it is necessary to explore the role of institutional characteristics and reforms of European welfare states as sources of discontent with the current rules for free movement and, in particular, with the current way of coordinating the social protection of mobile workers among EU Member States.

Under the current rules for free movement, EU citizens enjoy the unrestricted right to move to and take up employment in any other EU country and—as long as they are 'workers'—have full and equal access to the host State's national welfare system. While EU workers' access to social protection in host States has always been contentious, the enlargement of the EU and the subsequent rise in intra-EU labour mobility over the past 20 years have generated increasing tensions around the consequences and legitimacy of free movement of workers.[1]

---

[*] For their helpful comments, we are grateful to Niamh Nic Shuibhne, Andreas Bergh, Michael Blauberger, Clare Fox-Ruhs, Johannes Lindvall, Danny Pieters, and Nicolas Rennuy, as well as participants in workshops at the European University Institute (Academy of European Law) and the University of Lund. This paper is based on research funded by the European Union's Horizon 2020 research and innovation programme under grant agreement No. 727072.

[1] See, for example, Ruhs and Palme, 'Institutional Contexts of Political Conflicts around Free Movement in the European Union: A Theoretical Analysis', 25(10) *Journal of European Public Policy*

Martin Ruhs and Joakim Palme, *Free Movement and European Welfare States* In: *Revisiting the Fundamentals of the Free Movement of Persons in EU Law*. First Edition. Edited by: Niamh Nic Shuibhne, Oxford University Press.
© Martin Ruhs and Joakim Palme 2023. DOI: 10.1093/oso/9780198886273.003.0005

128   MARTIN RUHS AND JOAKIM PALME

It should not, therefore, have come as a great surprise when, in recent years, a number of EU Member States, including the UK (when it was still a member), Austria, Denmark, Germany, and the Netherlands proposed to change the current rules on EU workers' access to welfare benefits. In the UK, it is clear that these issues around free movement and access to social protection for EU workers fed into the Brexit debate that ultimately resulted in the UK's decision to leave the EU. The continuing debates in and between the 27 EU Member States make it important to question and analyse whether and why the characteristics of national welfare institutions, including the common welfare reform trends over time, generate tensions with the free movement of workers, and—if there are genuine tensions—how they can be reduced to help ensure the political sustainability of unrestricted intra-EU labour mobility in the future.[2]

In this chapter, we focus on one specific issue that has been at the heart of recent and ongoing debates about EU workers' access to welfare benefits: the exportability of child benefits. Under the current EU rules for free movement and social security coordination across Member States, an EU worker can 'export' family benefits to their children and other family members resident in the home country.[3] While some EU Member States have demanded a change to these rules—and Austria already implemented a more restrictive 'indexation' policy (discussed later)—others appear to prefer that they are maintained.[4] This chapter provides an institutional perspective and analysis of this issue and debate. We argue that the political conflicts about exporting child benefits are, at least in part, due to a fundamental tension between the 'employment-based' institutional logic that regulates EU workers' access to child and family benefits and the 'residence-based' institutional logic that underpins family policy in all Member States.

Under *EU* rules, the right to child benefits for mobile EU workers is grounded in, and dependent on, the employment of the parent (worker) and it does not

---

(2018) 1481–1500; Eick and Larsen 'Welfare Chauvinism Across Benefits and Services', *Journal of European Social Policy* (2021), https://doi.org/10.1177/09589287211023047 (last viewed 10 January 2023).

[2] Ruhs and Palme (n. 1).

[3] See Regulation 883/2004/EC on the coordination of social security systems, OJ 2011 L 166/1 and Regulation 987/2009/EC laying down the procedure for implementing Regulation 883/2004, OJ 2009 L 284/1.

[4] The European Commission's 2016 proposal for the reform of Regulation 883/2004/EC on the Coordination of Social Security Systems noted that 'a significant minority of Member States delegations favoured different coordination of benefits intended to replace income during child-raising periods' (p. 6), and the 'Impact Assessment' of the EC's reform proposals in 2016 (SWD(2016) 460 final/2) listed the EU countries that supported or opposed the reform of various aspects of social security coordination. It should be noted, however, that in this chapter we have a stricter focus on child benefits (and do not include maternity or parental leave benefits). For more recent evidence of Member States' preferences for changing the current rules for free movement, see Palme, Ruhs, Mårtensson, and Danielsson, 'Who Wants to Reform EU Workers' Access to Host Country Welfare States? Welfare States and Migration as Contexts of EU Member States' Policy Positions', *mimeo*, May 2022.

matter where in the EU the child lives (so benefits are 'exportable' in the sense that they can be paid to children who do not live in the same Member State as the working parent). In contrast, under the *national* family policies of (all) Member States, the right to child benefit is based on the residence of the child rather than the employment of the parent. We argue that this clash of principles and associated institutional logics contributes to the political conflicts around the exportability of child benefits that we have observed in the EU over recent years. In European host countries, exportability can easily be seen as unfair because a state's responsibility for the welfare of a child is perceived as being based on the residence of the child (as reflected in national family policies), not the labour-market participation of the parents (as required by current EU rules). This perceived unfairness, associated with clashing national and EU principles, is an overlooked and, in our view, much more important source of the enduring political conflicts about the exportability of child benefits than the fiscal costs for the Member States that provide the benefits.

Our focus in this chapter is on Member States that are net-receivers of EU workers, i.e. most of the EU15 countries that were part of the EU before enlargement in 2004. This is because the political debates and disagreements about free movement in general, and the exportability of child benefits in particular, have been concentrated in these countries. Most EU countries that are net-senders of EU workers (i.e. most of the more recent Member States in Eastern Europe) have been against reforms of the current rules for free movement including the exportability of child benefits. This difference between the national policy preferences of net-receivers and net-senders of EU workers has arguably little to do with the characteristics and/or common long-term trends in welfare institutions and more with the simple economic logic that countries that have to export benefits will be more likely to be against the current system of coordination, while countries that have residents who receive (or 'import') benefits will be more likely to support the status quo.

If we want to reduce the political conflicts about the exportability of child benefits across the EU15 countries, we need to reduce the institutional tension between employment-based EU rules and residence-based (national) family policies that lies at the heart of the current system. To address this issue, we make the case for changing the principles for coordinating EU workers' access to social protection, which would mean, as a consequence, that the exportability of child benefits would no longer apply. It is the country where the child (family member) lives, rather than the country where the working parent/spouse ('breadwinner') is employed that should bear the responsibility for providing child benefits. In addition to reducing political conflicts about the exportability of child benefits that have the potential to threaten the future political sustainability of unrestricted EU labour mobility and broader processes of European integration, we believe that there is also a strong normative case, from a child's rights perspective, for why child benefits should be the responsibility of the country where the child lives.

130 MARTIN RUHS AND JOAKIM PALME

The chapter is divided into four main sections. We begin, in Section 2, with an overview of EU rules and of recent debates between Member States about the exportability of child benefits as related to EU workers. This includes a brief discussion of the recent European Court of Justice (ECJ) ruling[5] against Austria's practice of indexing child benefits for EU workers. We explain how the discussion and reasoning underlying the ECJ ruling on indexing child benefits relate to our broader argument in this chapter. Section 3 first provides our analysis of the institutional tensions underlying political conflicts about the exportability of child benefits, and it then makes the case for reducing these tensions by changing the principles for coordination and effectively ending the exportability of child benefits. In Section 4, we address four potential objections to our proposal, namely, that ending the exportability of child benefits for EU workers would violate the principle of equal treatment; that it is unfeasible because of a need for treaty change; that it would be unfair because some countries would then need to provide benefits for children even though the family's main earner is working and paying taxes abroad; and that there is no need to change the current rules because only 'a few' EU countries have demanded policy change. The chapter concludes with a brief discussion of long-term care benefits, which is an emerging and similar issue in debates about social security coordination in the EU.

2. The Exportability of Family Benefits: Current Rules and Recent Debates

A. EU Rules and Regulations

Free movement is a fundamental aspect of European integration. It was set out as a major goal of the European Community in the Treaty of Rome (1957) and fully implemented in 1968 when EU Council Regulation 1612/68[6] and Directive 68/360[7] removed restrictions on the movement of Community workers and their families. The right to free movement has also been a cornerstone of 'EU citizenship', which was established by the Maastricht Treaty in 1992. Under Article 45 of the Treaty on the Functioning of the European Union (TFEU), free movement of workers means that any EU citizen is entitled to move and freely take up employment in any other EU country. The beneficiaries of this freedom also include jobseekers, i.e. EU citizens who move to another EU country to look for a job. For economically inactive

---

[5] Case C-328/20, *Commission v. Republic of Austria* (EU:C:2022:468).
[6] Regulation 1612/68/EEC on freedom of movement for workers within the Community, OJ 1968 L 257/13.
[7] Council Directive 68/360/EEC of 15 October 1968 on the abolition of restrictions on movement and residence within the Community for workers of Member States and their families, OJ 1968 L 257/13.

groups (such as retired people), the right to free movement and residence within the EU is conditional on having health insurance and sufficient resources such that they will not become an 'unreasonable burden' on the host State.[8] However, as Directive 2004/38 confirms, family members of EU citizens working in another EU Member State are also entitled to reside and work in that State, irrespective of their own nationality.

With regard to access to the welfare state, the right to equal treatment for EU citizens living in another EU Member State is dependent on whether they are economically active or not, the degree of their integration in the host State, and the type of benefit claimed.[9] For EU citizens who move to another EU Member State for the purpose of employment, access to the welfare state depends on having the legal status of a 'worker'. To be considered a worker by EU law, a person must pursue 'effective' and 'genuine' economic activity.[10] EU *workers* are entitled to equal access to all social rights granted to nationals of the host State.

While social security is a Member State competence, the EU rules on the coordination of social security systems aim to coordinate mobile EU citizens' access to social security systems in different Member States. The current coordination rules are set out in Regulation 883/2004 and its implementing Regulation 987/2009.[11] They currently apply to the following benefits: sickness, maternity and equivalent paternity benefits; old-age pensions, pre-retirement and invalidity benefits; survivors' benefits and death grants; unemployment benefits; family benefits; and benefits in respect of accidents at work and occupational diseases. According to the European Council's website for social security coordination,[12] the current rules are based on four key principles:

- *one country only*: citizens are covered by the legislation of one country at a time, so they only pay contributions in one country;
- *equal treatment*: citizens have the same rights and obligations as the nationals of the country where they are covered;
- *aggregation*: when citizens claim a benefit, their previous periods of insurance, work, or residence in other countries are taken into account, if necessary;
- *exportability*: citizens entitled to a cash benefit from one country may generally receive it even if they are living in a different country.

---

[8] Costello and Hancox, 'The UK, EU Citizenship and Free Movement of Persons', *Migration Observatory Policy Primer* (2014), COMPAS, Oxford. See also, Art. 7 of Directive 2004/38/EC on the right of citizens of the Union and their family members to move and reside freely within the territory of the Member States, OJ 2004 L 158/77.

[9] Costello and Hancox (n. 8).

[10] See, for example, CJEU, Case C-66/85, *Deborah Lawrie-Blum v. Land Baden-Württemberg* (EU:C:1986:284).

[11] See n. 3.

[12] See https://www.consilium.europa.eu/en/policies/rules-social-security-systems/ (last viewed 12 December 2022).

Chapter 8 of Regulation 883/2004 on the coordination of social security systems includes EU regulations on the coordination of family benefits (Articles 67 to 69). Article 67 stipulates that: 'A person shall be entitled to family benefits in accordance with the legislation of the competent Member State, including for his family members residing in another Member State, as if they were residing in the former Member State.' (Also, see Article 7 of Regulation 883/2004.) This means that, for example, an Italian worker employed in Austria, with a non-employed spouse and children living in Italy, is able to 'export' family benefits obtained in Austria to his/her family members in Italy. As family benefits can be based on different grounds (employment, receipt of a pension, or residence), it is possible that more than one Member State may be required to pay family benefits to a family whose members live and work across different EU countries. To deal with this issue, Article 68 of Regulation 883/2004 sets out the priority rules that determine the 'primarily competent Member State':

1. Where, during the same period and for the same family members, benefits are provided for under the legislation of more than one Member State the following priority rules shall apply:
   (a) in the case of benefits payable by more than one Member State on different bases, the order of priority shall be as follows: firstly, rights available on the basis of an activity as an employed or self-employed person, secondly, rights available on the basis of receipt of a pension and finally, rights obtained on the basis of residence.

In other words, when deciding which Member State is responsible for providing child benefits, the country of employment of the parent takes priority over the country of residence of the child. This EU rule thus suggests that the basis for the right to a family benefit is work (*lex loci laboris*) rather than residence (*lex loci domicilii*).[13] As we show later in the chapter, the latter has become the basis of family policy-making in all EU Member States (i.e. child and other family benefits are paid to residents only), and this discrepancy between EU and national principles underpinning access to rights is what causes the institutional tension in the current system.

---

[13] Regulation 492/2011/EC on the freedom of movement for workers in the European Union, OJ 2011 L 141/1, stipulates that EU workers must be treated in the same way as national workers with regard to employment conditions and 'social and tax advantages'. Article 7(1) and (2), in Section 2, entitled 'Employment and equality of treatment', provides:

1. A worker who is a national of a Member State may not, in the territory of another Member State, be treated differently from national workers by reason of his nationality in respect of any conditions of employment and work, in particular as regards remuneration, dismissal, and, should he become unemployed, reinstatement or re-employment.
2. He shall enjoy the same social and tax advantages as national workers.

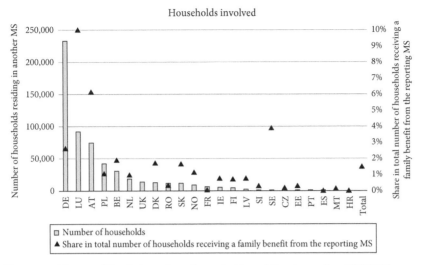

Figure 5.1 Export of family benefits to households residing in another EU/EFTA country in 2018, households involved (based on a survey of MSs on the export of family benefits).

Source: Reproduced from Frederic De Wispelaere, Lynn De Smedt, and Jozef Pacolet, *Export of Family Benefits; Report on the Questionnaire on the Export of Family Benefits, Reference Year 2018*, p. 9 © European Commission 2019. Reproduced here under the Decision 2011/833/EU.

As we will explain in the next section, these institutional tensions and the associated clash of principles can lead to political conflicts within and between EU Member States because of a perception that exporting child benefits is 'unfair' and against the residence-based principle that underlies host country citizens' access to child benefits, rather than because of a concern about the fiscal costs of providing child benefits for children residing abroad. It is, nevertheless, relevant to note that there are large differences in the average annual family benefit per person across EU Member States. According to a recent review of the export of family benefits in the EU,[14] in 2018 the figure was highest in Luxembourg (5,879 euros per year) and lowest in the Czech Republic (348 euros per year). Figures 5.1 and 5.2, taken from the same review, show the family benefits exported to other Member States, in terms of both the number of households and the amounts involved.

---

[14] F. De Wispelaere, L. De Smedt, and J. Pacolet, *Export of Family Benefits. Report on the Questionnaire on the Export of Family Benefits, Reference Year 2018* (2019) European Commission.

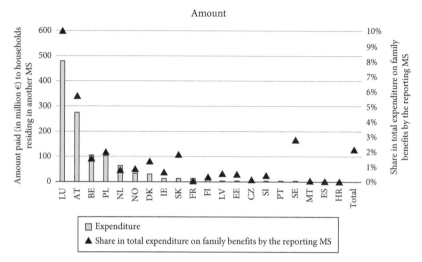

Figure 5.2 Export of family benefits to households residing in another EU/EFTA country in 2018, amounts (million euros).

Source: Reproduced from Frederic De Wispelaere, Lynn De Smedt, and Jozef Pacolet, *Export of Family Benefits; Report on the Questionnaire on the Export of Family Benefits, Reference Year 2018*, p. 9 © European Commission, 2019. Reproduced here under the Decision 2011/833/EU.

B. Recent Debates between EU Member States

The free movement of mobile EU workers and their access to welfare benefits in the host Member State used to be much less controversial than it is today. Although the introduction and full implementation of free movement for workers during the 1950s and 1960s was accompanied by considerable political debates among European countries,[15] once fully established the principle of free movement was relatively stable and largely unchallenged by individual EU Member States until the early 2000s. This is partly because the scale of intra-EU labour mobility used to be much lower, and the social protection systems of EU Member States were based on similar principles. The welfare systems of most of the six founding EU Member States (Belgium, France, Germany, Italy, Luxembourg, and the Netherlands) were characterized by contributory and earnings-related social insurance including derived family benefits and health care based on an insurance model. As the EU expanded in the 1970s, 1980s, and 1990s, the relative scale of intra-EU labour mobility remained relatively low but the diversity of welfare states in the EU increased considerably, not only through the inclusion of countries with more liberal market economies and welfare systems, such as the UK and Ireland, but also of the Nordic

---

[15] Maas, 'The Genesis of European Rights', 43(5) *Journal of Common Market Studies* (2005) 1009–1025.

countries with their universal systems, and of Greece, Portugal, and Spain who can be described as being part of the 'Mediterranean Corporatist Model' of welfare regimes,[16] with a strong emphasis on pensions and comparatively low family benefits.

The EU enlargements in 2004 and 2007 were different from previous enlargements in that they led to *both* a further increase in the diversity of welfare systems in the EU and a large increase in the number of mobile EU workers employed in many EU15 countries.[17] The significant intra-EU labour mobility from eastern to western European countries since 2004 has been largely driven by the considerable differences in average incomes and living standards between the EU15 countries and the more recently joining Member States. The rapid rise in the scale of intra-EU labour mobility over the past 20 years, especially in the mid and late 2000s, contributed to an increase of the political salience of the issue of welfare benefits for EU workers. Specifically, the exportability of family benefits to children residing abroad became a more important and controversial issue in public debates, especially in higher-income Member States employing relatively large numbers of mobile EU workers from lower-income EU countries. At the same time, the economic downturn that began in 2008 was a further factor that contributed to the emergence of political demands by some EU Member States, most notably the UK, to change the current EU rules.[18]

For example, in a joint letter sent to the European Council in 2013, the Ministers of Interior of Austria, Germany, the Netherlands, and the UK called for a review of the payment of social security benefits to recently arrived EU migrants who had never been employed in the host State before. While the letter did not specifically mention family benefits, it argued that 'arrangements at national or EU levels that allow those who have only recently arrived in a Member State and have never been employed or paid taxes there to claim the same social security benefits as that Member State's own nationals are an affront to common sense and ought to be reviewed urgently'.[19]

Three years later, a few months before its referendum on continued EU membership in June 2016, the UK secured an agreement with the other 27 EU Member States that included an 'emergency brake' that would have enabled any Member State to restrict EU workers' access to non-contributory in-work benefits for a

---

[16] Österman, Palme, and Ruhs, 'Illusions of Difference: Variations of the Fiscal Effects of EU Migrants Across European Welfare Regimes', *Politics & Society* (forthcoming).

[17] With the exception of the UK, Ireland, and Sweden, all EU15 Member States imposed transitional restrictions on the employment of workers from the new EU Member States. These temporary restrictions had to be (and were) lifted within seven years.

[18] See, for example, Cameron, 'Free Movement within Europe Needs to Be Less Free', *Financial Times*, 26 November 2013, https://www.ft.com/content/add36222-56be-11e3-ab12-00144feabdc0 (last viewed 15 August 2022).

[19] See http://docs.dpaq.de/3604-130415_letter_to_presidency_final_1_2.pdf (last viewed 12 September 2022).

maximum period of four years under certain conditions.[20] The agreement also included 'a proposal to amend Regulation (EC) No 883/2004 of the European Parliament and of the Council on the coordination of social security systems in order to give Member States, with regard to the exportation of child benefits to a Member State other than that where the worker resides, an option to index such benefits to the conditions of the Member State where the child resides'. Because the UK voted to leave the EU, this agreement never came into force. If the UK had voted to stay in the EU and the agreement had come into force, *all* EU Member States would have been able to index child benefits for EU workers when their children resided in another EU Member State.

Although ultimately rejected, the UK–EU discussions and the agreement reached before the Brexit referendum in June 2016 opened the door to further debates among EU Member States about the need to reform the rules for EU workers' access to social security including family benefits. In December 2016, the European Commission presented a proposal to revise existing regulations on the coordination of social security systems.[21] Neither ending the export of child benefits, nor the indexation of child benefits (as agreed in the 2016 UK–EU agreement), was included as a potential option in the Commission's reform proposals. In the ensuing debate, which continues and remains unresolved today, EU Member States have been divided on the issue of whether and how to include restrictions of child and other family benefits for EU workers in the reform of social security coordination. In 2017 and 2018, the Ministers of Labour of Austria, Denmark, Germany, Ireland, and the Netherlands sent letters to the European Commission that again called for the indexation of child benefits for EU workers with children in another EU Member State. The 2017 letter argued that:

> We explicitly support the principle of freedom of movement in the EU. However, we believe that it is necessary to adjust rights arising as a consequence of this principle to reflect changing circumstances and to ensure that this will continue to enjoy acceptance amongst our EU citizens.[22]

The 2018 letter also emphasized the need for continued public support for the principle for free movement and additionally couched the argument for indexation in terms of 'fairness':

---

[20] See Decision of the Heads of State or Government, meeting within the European Council, concerning a new settlement for the United Kingdom within the European Union, OJ 2016 C 691/1.

[21] See Proposal for a Regulation of the European Parliament and of the Council amending Regulation (EC) No 883/2004 on the coordination of social security systems and Regulation (EC) No 987/2009 laying down the procedure for implementing Regulation (EC) No 883/2004 (Text with relevance for the EEA and Switzerland). COM/2016/0815 final.

[22] See https://www.ft.dk/samling/20161/almdel/BEU/bilag/299/1781050/index.htm (last viewed 12 September 2022).

> We would like to reiterate our explicit support to the principle of free movement in the EU. In order to maintain public support for the principle of free movement the rules must be perceived as fair. We do not consider it fair that family benefits are paid out in full in a country where the value of those benefits is worth twice or even three times as much as in the country which pays them.[23]

We recently surveyed EU Member States to ask about their own 'national policy positions' in EU negotiations on whether and how to reform the current rules on free movement and EU workers' access to welfare benefits, and to provide 'peer assessments' of other Member States' policy preferences on these issues.[24] This survey confirmed that the States that wrote the letters described above remain among the leading countries demanding a change to the current rules. The average peer assessments of the 21 countries who responded to our survey in late 2019 and early 2020 suggest that the Member States that have the strongest preferences for limiting mobile EU workers' access to social protection in host countries include Austria, Denmark, Luxembourg, and the Netherlands, as well as the UK (which are all perceived to have policy positions that fall between wanting to 'limit strongly' or 'limit somewhat' EU workers' access to benefits), followed by Belgium, Finland, France, Ireland, Germany, and Sweden (which are perceived as tending towards wanting to 'limit somewhat' the benefits of EU workers). When describing their own policy preferences, the UK plus five out of the 20 Member States in our survey said they would prefer to limit mobile EU workers' access to child benefits: Austria, Denmark, Ireland, Latvia, and the Netherlands. Our open-ended survey questions and follow-up interviews indicate that the key point of controversy concerning child benefits relates to their exportability to other Member States.

Frustrated with the lack of progress in EU negotiations about what it saw as a necessary reform of the current EU rules for exporting child benefits, on 1 January 2019 the Austrian government at the time (a coalition government between the Conservatives and the right-wing Freedom Party) unilaterally introduced a mechanism that indexed the amount of family benefits, child tax credits, and family tax credits for EU nationals who work in Austria and have children living in another Member State. The European Commission considered this mechanism to violate the current rules for social security coordination in Regulation 883/2004 (which, among other things, prohibit discrimination on grounds of nationality) and also for free movement of EU workers (and more specifically, Article 7(2) of Regulation 492/2011, which demands and re-enforces equality of treatment for EU workers for 'social and tax advantages'). It therefore initiated an infringement procedure against

---

[23] See https://www.ft.dk/samling/20171/almdel/BEU/bilag/386/1914108.pdf (last viewed 12 September 2022).
[24] Palme et al. (n. 4).

138 MARTIN RUHS AND JOAKIM PALME

Austria in late January 2019.[25] Given Austria's continuation with its policy of indexation in 2019 and 2020, the European Commission referred Austria to the Court of Justice of the EU in July 2020.[26]

In January 2022, the Advocate General proposed that the ECJ declare the Austrian practice of adjusting family benefits, child tax credits, and family tax credits unlawful, because it constitutes indirect discrimination based on nationality and violates the principle of equality of treatment of EU workers.[27] In June 2022, the ECJ essentially agreed with the Opinion of the Advocate General and issued its ruling against Austria, declaring that 'the adjustment of family allowances and of various tax advantages granted by Austria to workers according to their children's State of residence is contrary to EU law' because the 'adjustment mechanism constitutes indirect discrimination on grounds of nationality which, in any event, is not justified' and it also 'violates the EU Regulation on freedom of movement for workers within the European Union'.[28]

In the context of this chapter, the ECJ analysis of indirect discrimination and unequal treatment is particularly interesting and relevant. In its judgment, the ECJ points out that indirect discrimination on grounds of nationality is permissible only if it is objectively justified (para. 103). Austria's justification for introducing the indexation mechanism used the language of restoring 'fairness' but it was mainly couched in terms of reducing 'financial distortions'. This can be seen clearly in the ECJ judgment's explanation of the Austrian arguments and positions:

> The Republic of Austria submits that family allowances were introduced at a time when there was less labour migration. Due to increased movement of workers within the European Union, the indiscriminate export of family allowances and the child tax credit led to increasing distortions in the Austrian system of family benefits. The adjustment mechanism makes it possible to address those distortions by taking into account differences in price levels between the Member States as published by Eurostat. It is therefore not simply a cost-saving measure. (para. 38)

> [The Republic of Austria argues that . . .] that mechanism was intended to restore the function of supporting the maintenance of children and the fairness of the social system. In order to attain that socio-political objective, it was necessary to abolish benefits showing surpluses or shortfalls due to the undifferentiated application of the amounts of family allowances. (para. 87)

In its ruling the ECJ states and explains why it does not consider Austria's justification to meet the criterion of an 'objective justification' of indirect discrimination:

---

[25] See https://ec.europa.eu/commission/presscorner/detail/EN/IP_19_463 (last viewed 12 December 2022).

[26] Case C-328/20, Commission v. Austria (EU:C:2022:468).

[27] AG Richard de la Tour in Case C-328/20, Commission v. Austria (EU:C:2022:45).

[28] Court of Justice of the European Union, Press Release No. 102/22, https://curia.europa.eu/jcms/upload/docs/application/pdf/2022-06/cp220102en.pdf (last viewed 24 May 2023).

... the unequal treatment resulting from the adjustment mechanism cannot be justified by the objective, relied on by the Republic of Austria, of ensuring the supportive function and the fairness of the social system. (para. 106)

... the Court of Auditors report shows neither that there is a risk of serious undermining of the financial balance of the system that could be remedied only by the establishment of an adjustment mechanism, nor that the adjustment mechanism is capable of simplifying the management of family benefits and social and tax advantages. (para. 107)

In those circumstances, and as the Advocate General stated in point 146 of his Opinion, it must be held that the difference in treatment according to the place of residence of the child of the worker concerned established by the adjustment mechanism is neither appropriate nor necessary for the purposes of ensuring the supportive function and the fairness of the social system. (para. 111)

We agree that the fiscal consequences of exporting child benefits to other countries are relatively minor for most EU Member States, and that it is hard to argue that exportability of family benefits needs to be restricted because of adverse effects on the public finances of host countries. Whether or not there is an unfairness in terms of the amounts paid to children who live in a Member State that is different from where the EU worker is employed is, in our view, more debatable. In any case, the argument and mechanism for (de facto) ending the exportability of child benefits that we develop in the next section is different: the reason why the current rules (and, more specifically, the underlying institutional tensions) create political conflict is a perception of unfairness grounded in *principles* (residence- versus employment-based benefits) rather than financial concerns. In other words, when it comes to the perceived fairness of EU workers' access to benefits for children abroad, the key question is not whether these benefits need to be indexed/ adjusted but whether they should be exportable at all. We suggest that this question has not been considered and settled by the ECJ ruling and will continue to persist if left unaddressed.

3. Political Tensions about Exporting Family Benefits: Institutional Sources and how to Address them

It is clear and widely agreed that there continue to be strong political tensions around mobile EU workers' full access to the welfare state, and also that family benefits are the most disputed part of the current system.[29] However, there is less

---

[29] Eick and Larsen (n. 1).

140 MARTIN RUHS AND JOAKIM PALME

agreement about the sources of this discontent and hence no common approach to the question of what to do about the current situation.

In a recent paper, Blauberger et al. provide an interesting analysis of the Austrian approach to the problem, i.e. to index benefits in relation to the cost of living in the State where the children of the EU worker are living.[30] The paper asks why the indexation of child benefits, a seemingly small and technical issue, has become so politically salient. While their analysis includes a discussion of both the economic aspects involved and issues of fairness, Blauberger et al. interpret fairness only in terms of 'distributional concerns' and 'welfare chauvinism', and they dismiss these explanations of political demands for indexation of child benefits for EU workers as weak. From our perspective, it is striking that Blauberger et al. do not talk about the role of institutions, and specifically the fairness concerns that arise from the clash of institutional logics at the heart of the current system. In the following, we try to develop an argument as to why it is important to pay attention to fairness concerns and political tensions due to institutional factors, especially in the EU countries that are net-receivers of EU workers (the focus of our chapter).

A. Institutional Sources of Conflict

The institutional logic underlying the current EU rules for social security coordination has been informed by how family policy was organized in the original (six) Member States more than half a century ago, when the principle of free movement was fully established and the implications for social security coordination were codified in Regulation 1408/71 (now repealed and replaced by Regulation 883/2004). At that time, family benefits in the (then) Member States were primarily based on the employment of, and contributions from, the (typically male) breadwinner and usually paid to the fathers of children.[31] Families without a breadwinner would usually have to rely on second tier means-tested safety nets. The logic of such a system is that benefits for family members are 'derived' from the entitlement 'earned' by the breadwinner in the family. We argue and show below that this logic has increasingly come into conflict not only with the different institutional logics of the systems of social protection (including family policies) in the northern and Anglo-Saxon parts of Europe but also with how the systems in the original EU Member States have developed over time.

The Appendix to this chapter compares the basic principles of child benefit policies in EU countries. It shows that in all Member States, family support is provided

---

[30] Blauberger, Heindlmaier, and Kobler, 'Free Movement of Workers under Challenge: the Indexation of Family Benefits', 18 *Comparative European Politics* (2020) 925–943.

[31] J. Wennemo, *Sharing the Costs of Children, Doctoral Dissertation Series No. 25, Swedish Institute for Social Research* (1994).

to families/children based on residence and without employment (contributory) requirements. Italy was the last country to abolish the principle of employment when it introduced the Single Universal Allowance in 2022. According to Vidotto and Lucangeli: 'For the first time in its history, Italy introduces a universal child allowance: a "historical act" in the words of the Minister for Family and Equal Opportunities, Elena Bonetti. The new allowance overcomes inconsistencies of the previous system by not discriminating based on employment status.'[32] In other words, in all EU countries, family policy is now about protecting all residents and not just workers. That the employment-based and contributory model with derived rights for family members has been abolished in all Member States shows that there is a clear clash of ideas and principles between national family policies based on residence (and, therefore, non-exportability), on the one hand, and, on the other hand, EU regulations that require child and other family benefits to be exported to EU workers' family members abroad based on the principle of employment (and thus 'contribution').

We are not the first to highlight this tension between employment-based EU rules for social security coordination and residence-based national family policies. In fact, the European Commission explicitly acknowledged (but did not propose specific policies to address) this tension in the 'Impact Assessment' accompanying the EC's 2016 proposal for reforming Social Security Coordination:

> Such perceptions of unfairness are sustained (reinforced) both by the non-contributory nature of family benefits that are predominantly financed wholly or partially through general taxation and the fact that in the majority of Member States entitlement to family benefits is on the basis of legal residence whereas under the EU social security rules priority is awarded to the State of economic activity. This results in a tension between the EU social security rules and principles of national legislation .... [33]

Our approach to the free movement issue is based on the working hypothesis that the institutional context, in terms not only of the welfare state arrangements but also labour market regulation, has consequences for how free movement actually works on the ground and also for how it is perceived by policy-makers as well as the public in general. From this institutional perspective, it is also important to recognize that there can be significant interactions between family policies and labour market institutions in shaping the effects and political controversies around free movement in particular countries. For example, the tension between

---

[32] See Vidotto and Lucangeli, ' "A Historical Act" – The Single Universal Allowance in Italy', 8 April 2022 https://blogs.lse.ac.uk/socialpolicy/2022/04/08/a-historical-act-the-single-universal-allowance-in-italy/ (last viewed 12 December 2022).

[33] SWD (2016) 460 final/2, p.126. https://eur-lex.europa.eu/resource.html?uri=cellar:3aa0bc5e-c1e6-11e6-a6db-01aa75ed71a1.0001.02/DOC_4&format=PDF (last viewed 12 December 2022).

142 MARTIN RUHS AND JOAKIM PALME

residence-based family policies and employment-based EU rules is likely to be larger in countries with labour market institutions that help generate a greater demand for and inflow of EU workers into low-wage sectors (e.g. the liberal market economies, such as Ireland) which, in turn, will increase the number of migrants eligible for family (including child) benefits as well as in-work benefits (as happened in the UK before Brexit).

B. Why Does the Institutional Tension Matter and What Should Be Done?

We argue that the clash between the institutional logics of national family policies and EU rules on social security coordination is an important contributor to political conflict and tension around free movement. We know from existing research that institutions with particular characteristics and principles tend to go hand in hand with normative attitudes among the population that support these principles,[34] and this is also likely to apply to family policy-making. EU policies with institutional logics that are fundamentally different from prevailing national policies and norms are likely to be seen as 'fundamentally unfair' by the publics and policy elites of Member States.[35] As a consequence, the clash of institutional logics that we have highlighted above is likely to generate perceptions of unfairness in EU workers' access to family benefits, which should be tied to 'residence', the key principle underlying all Member States' national family policies, and not to employment as required by the EU rules. In our view, this perceived unfairness not only feeds political tension about the exportability of child benefits but also potentially threatens the political sustainability of free movement itself. We therefore think that the institutional tension at the heart of the current system of free movement needs to be addressed and not simply accepted as something that exists but cannot be changed.

In the 2016 Impact Assessment of its reform proposals, the European Commission identified what could be called a second type of 'unfairness' arising from the institutional tension between EU and national rules:

> This results in a tension between the EU social security rules and principles of national legislation and *leads to the perception that Member States of residence are abdicating their social security responsibilities in relation to children resident within their territory to another Member State.* As a consequence of this perceived

---

[34] P. Thornton, W. Ocasio, and M. Lounsbury, *The Institutional Logics Perspective* (2012); and M.R. Lepsius, *Max Weber and Institutional Theory* (2017), edited by C. Wendt.

[35] See, for example, Mårtensson, Österman, Palme, and Ruhs, 'Shielding Free Movement? Reciprocity in Welfare Institutions and Opposition to EU Labour Immigration', 30(1) *Journal of European Public Policy* (2021) 41–63.

FREE MOVEMENT AND EUROPEAN WELFARE STATES · 143

unfairness, there is a risk of negative attitudes towards migration amongst the general population, as are already observed in the public debate in some Member States, which entails a risk that public and political support for the EU social security coordination rules may be undermined with a subsequent negative impact on labour mobility. There is also a risk of unilateral imposition of restrictive measures by Member States. For example, there have been a number of examples of public criticism of the current EU rules on export of family benefits and counter-proposals by senior politicians challenging the concept of export for family benefits.[36]

As we explain later in the chapter, we agree that it is morally problematic for countries not to provide child benefits for children on their territories, especially (but not only) if their national family policies are residence-based. However, in our view and understanding of the issue, this is more of a child-rights concern rather than an issue of unfairness. This is why the focus of our analysis in this chapter is on the first type of unfairness, which is associated with the provision of child benefits by the countries where the mobile EU workers are employed rather than the lack of provision by the countries where their children reside.

In principle, any tensions between the EU system for the free movement of workers and national welfare institutions can be addressed by national-level reform, EU-level reform, or a combination of both.[37] At the national level, the specific welfare institutions that create tensions with free movement could be changed to make them more compatible with the current rules on free movement. In the context of this chapter, national family policies could be made more employment- and contributory-based rather than residence-based. In practice, this is highly unlikely to be a realistic or even desirable response to the institutional tension that we have discussed. This is because residence-based national family policies (and other national welfare institutions), and the particular normative principles associated with them, have historically grown and, at least to a degree, are part of the 'DNA' of national societies and economies.[38] The long-term shift away from employment-based to residence-based family policies in many EU countries would be very difficult to reverse and trying to do so in order to accommodate better the free movement of workers is unlikely to be supported or perceived as increasing fairness by the populations of host States of mobile EU workers. From a redistributive perspective, it is also desirable to base family benefits on more universal and

---

[36] n. 33, p. 126 (emphasis added).

[37] Also see Ruhs, 'Free Movement in the European Union: National Institutions vs Common Policies?', 55(S1) *International Migration* (2017) 22–38; Kramer, van Hooren, and Thierry, 'Responding to Free Movement: Quarantining Mobile Union Citizens in European Welfare States', 25(10) *Journal of European Public Policy* (2018) 1501–1521.

[38] Scharpf, 'The Asymmetry of European Integration, or Why the EU Cannot Be a "Social Market Economy"', 8(2) *Socio-Economic Review* (2010) 211–250.

144 MARTIN RUHS AND JOAKIM PALME

inclusive principles rather than to direct public support exclusively to 'insiders' on the labour market.

We therefore suggest that the EU regulations for the coordination of benefits across EU Member States should be reformed by changing the principles for coordinating EU workers' access to social protection, which would have as a consequence that the exportability of child benefits would no longer apply. Our proposal builds on an idea that was put forward by Pieters in the late 1990s, when Regulation 1408/71 was discussed.[39] The new Regulation 883/2004 missed the opportunity to apply the country of residence principle (*lex loci domicilii*) to child benefits. Pieters' (1997) proposed solution is to use a dual determination of competence. The idea is to change Regulation 883/2004 by applying a clear division between income replacement benefits on the basis of country of work (*lex loci laboris*) and cost compensation benefits such as family allowances, but also health care, elderly care, etc. that would follow from applying the principle of *lex loci domicilii* of the concerned child, patient, elderly person, etc.[40]

Such a policy shift would go beyond the changes that have been demanded by some of the Member States calling for reform of social security coordination. If the EU system for social security coordination is reformed in this way, the 'indexing of child benefits' will not be an issue anymore.

We argue that unless there is a clear-cut distinction made in any reforms between these two kinds of benefits and services (benefits for workers versus benefits for all residents), the tension between free movement of workers and national welfare states (including national family policies) that we have identified in our research will continue and possibly be aggravated by the inclusion of other typically residence-based benefits and services in the system of coordination.

4. Potential Objections

We discuss briefly four types of objections to our proposal to change the principles for coordination of family related benefits to *lex loci domicilii* and thereby effectively removing child benefits from EU social security coordination completely, and de facto ending their exportability.

---

[39] Pieters, 'Final Report concerning the Seminars Organised in the Member States concerning the Application of Co-ordination Regulation (EC) 1408/71', in *The Co-ordination of Social Security at Work. Texts, Cases and Materials* (1999) 25–104; and Pieters, 'A Radical Simplification of the Social Security Co-ordination', in P. Schoukens (ed.), *Prospects of Social Security Co-ordination* (1997) 177–224.

[40] See Palme, 'Social Policy Regimes, Financing and Coordination', in *25 Years of Regulation (EEC) No. 1408/71 on Social Security of Migrant Workers* (1997) 111–30, for a similar argument.

A. Equal Treatment and Non-discrimination

A common objection to the idea of indexing child benefits for EU workers with children abroad—and thus a likely objection to our more radical proposal, which will remove child benefits from coordination and thus end exportability altogether—is that it violates the principle of equal treatment and non-discrimination. Blauberger et al.[41] suggest that one of the reasons why indexation became so politically salient is because, in contrast to ending exportability, indexation seemed more feasible from an EU law perspective and it therefore provided a useful outlet for political pressure over free movement. While we now know, following the recent ECJ decision, that Austria's policy of indexation of child benefits for EU workers is incompatible with EU law, it does not automatically follow, in our view, that our broader (and in some ways more radical) policy proposal, which de facto will end exportability of child benefits, would also be considered to violate non-discrimination and equal treatment. In our view, when considering questions about equal treatment and non-discrimination in the provision of child benefits of EU workers whose children have remained in their home countries, it is important to ask: equality and non-discrimination from whose perspective? Who should be the reference group?

Our proposal implies that workers are treated the same way where they work and live, and children are treated the same way where they live (as children do not work). It can in fact be argued that the current rules violate equal treatment between children living in the same country: in migrant-sending countries with residence-based family policies, children with a parent working in another EU Member State do not enjoy equal treatment when it comes to child benefits, because their benefits are derived from their parent's employment abroad and not from their (i.e. the child's) residence in the home State.

If child benefits were no longer exportable, mobile EU workers with children living with them would be treated in exactly same way as nationals of the host State, i.e. they would be eligible for child benefits for any children that live with them. We hence argue that there is no problem of equal treatment without exportability.

The common argument that family benefits should be exportable because of equal treatment between EU and citizen workers is a perspective guided by the old (presumably male) breadwinner system of derived rights. The same can actually be said about the indexation policy of the Austrian government which does not appear to question the right to export benefits for the EU workers. That part is seen as fair. It is the size of the benefit in the home country of the family members that is argued to be unfair. In contrast, we argue that the fundamental practice of exporting *any* child benefits can be perceived as 'unfair' in countries with national family policies that are residence-based.

---

[41] Blauberger et al. (n. 30).

B. Feasibility

Changing the principles for coordination of family related benefits to *lex loci domicilii* and thereby in effect ending the exportability of child benefits is argued by some to require a change to the EU Treaty. Whether this is indeed the case is, to the best of our understanding (as social scientists without particular legal expertise), not as straightforward as the EU Commission argues and remains an open question until tested by the ECJ. That the Commission believes that treaty change would be required is clarified in the 'Impact Assessment' that accompanied the European Commission's reform proposal in 2016, where the fundamental idea of our proposal was included as a hypothetical option that was 'discarded' because of its presumed incompatibility with the EU Treaty:

> It was also considered that family benefits would be provided by the Member State of residence of child(ren) under its national legislation only, i.e. no export of family benefits. 4 Member States supported this option. This option has subsequently been discarded by the Commission on grounds it is considered incompatible with the Treaty on Functioning of the European Union, in particular as the refusal to export family benefits has already been ruled contrary to Article 45 TFEU. The right to family benefits is granted to workers by reason of their employment in the Member State of employment. Refusing to grant them the right to equal treatment as regards entitlement to family benefit would amount to a violation of primary law.[42]

We do not question the difficulties associated with EU treaty change but our argument is that the current regulation of coordination in fact violates equal treatment. Moreover, our larger research shows that it is not just family benefits for EU workers that are politically contested in the area of free movement but also EU workers' access to certain other types of benefits.[43] We therefore consider Pieters' reform proposal appealing because, by applying the principle of *lex loci domicilii* to child benefits and similar residence-based benefits and services, it would imply the kinds of modernization of coordination that we think are necessary and could potentially be done without the need for treaty change.

The view of the Commission, as expressed in the excerpt from the 2016 Impact Assessment, can be contested. For example, when Pieters[44] first made his case for applying the principle of *lex loci domicilii* to child benefits and similar residence-based benefits and services, his view was that this would not require EU treaty change. In any case, it would be important to get the ECJ's view on this issue. To

---

[42] n. 33, p. 138.
[43] See Palme et al, (n. 4).
[44] Pieters, 'A Radical Simplification' (n. 39).

paraphrase Blauberger et al.,[45] ECJ judges 'read the morning papers' and may, in their assessment of the legal issues at stake, be sensitive to the types of social and political issues and tensions around the exportability of child benefits discussed in this chapter. Furthermore, we argue that they have good reasons to (re-)examine what equal treatment really means when it comes to social protection of mobile EU workers and also where to draw the line for inclusion of benefits in the coordination of social protection of workers.

C. Child Benefits without Parents' Taxes?

The traditional male breadwinner perspective that underpins the current rules for EU social security coordination may also give rise to a related third potential objection that relates to the interests of the origin country. Why, one may ask, should an EU Member State provide benefits for a resident child when the primary breadwinner is working and paying taxes in another EU country? We offer three responses. First, children of EU workers who stay in their home countries are future taxpayers in those countries. This means that any calculation of the fiscal costs and benefits of providing child benefits to children with parents working abroad need to take account of this dynamic element of fiscal effects over time. In a way, child benefits can be considered an 'investment' in future workers who will pay taxes in the countries where they live.

A related second point is that the potential economic concerns of migrant-sending countries—that they need to provide benefits to a family without receiving income tax from them—are in practice alleviated by the remittances that migrants send back to their families. A share of remittances is spent on consumption in origin countries, thus generating tax revenues that could be spent on supporting children.

Our third response is more normative: rather than simply being driven by considerations about material (fiscal) effects, child benefits should be determined by the residence of the child and not by the employment of the parent. Family benefits in general, and child benefits in particular, are about the rights of family/children to basic provision from the country of their residence. Article 24 of the EU Charter on Fundamental Rights stipulates that 'children shall have the right to such protection and care as is necessary for their well-being'.[46] Member States of the EU have also all signed the United Nations Convention on the Rights of the Child (UNCRC). To follow Articles 12 and 24 of the UNCRC, EU countries thus need to

---

[45] Blauberger, Heindlmaier, Kramer, Martinsen, Sampson, Schenk, and Werner, 'ECJ Judges Read the Morning Papers. Explaining the Turnaround of European Citizenship Jurisprudence', 25 *Journal of European Public Policy* (2018) 1422.

[46] See https://fra.europa.eu/en/eu-charter/article/24-rights-child (last viewed 12 December 2022).

see children as actors with their own rights for protection and provision and not as derivatives of their families.[47] This motivates a residence-based perspective on children's rights that is, as we have discussed in this chapter, actually reflected in all EU countries' current family policies but not in the EU regulations for social security coordination.

We do, however, acknowledge that in some EU countries (e.g. Germany, Italy, and the Netherlands), national legislation appears to indicate that, despite being residence-based, child benefits are exportable to other countries. This is, however, perfectly compatible with our proposal, which only concerns EU-level coordination. Germany, Italy, and the Netherlands may choose to reform their national policies but this is not necessary for our reform proposal to become effective.

D. National Preferences for Policy Change: 'Only' in a Minority of Member States?

As we discussed earlier in this chapter, the available evidence suggests that only a handful of EU countries have indicated a preference for changing the current rules around the coordination of child benefits for EU workers, meaning that not all EU15 countries with residence-based family policies have demanded policy change. So, one might argue, whether or not the institutional tension that we have identified leads to national policy pressure for changing the EU rules seems to depend on a number of other domestic factors and actors, such as political parties, the media, and so on. If this is true, one may argue, there is no longer-term 'structural' problem as we suggest, but potentially shorter-term tension caused by particular actors at the national level. As a consequence, there is, the argument goes, no need to change the common EU rules to meet the preferences of particular national actors and interest groups at particular points in time.

However, in our understanding, institutions, such as welfare states, labour market regulations, national and EU norms, and laws, etc. provide an important context within which policy actors make decisions. It is true, of course, that a particular institutional configuration, such as the tension between longstanding EU rules and national family policy norms that we have identified in this chapter, do not lead to political conflicts and pressure for policy change unless they are politicized by a particular set of actors. We argue, however, that the clash between employment-based EU rules and residence-based national family policy rule provides fertile ground for the politicization of the exportability of child benefits beyond the EU countries that have called for policy changes in recent years. In our

---

[47] Palme and Heimer, 'A Taxonomy of Child Policies: Conceptualizing the Missing Step in Defamilization of Social Policy', *Social Politics* (2019) https://doi.org/10.1093/sp/jxz016 (last viewed 12 December 2022).

reading, it is a structural tension at the heart of European policy-making that needs to be addressed before it becomes a wider problem and policy issue (also in relation to other, similar types of benefits) that undermines political support for the free movement of labour and/or the social protection of mobile workers in Europe.

5. Conclusion

The present system of freedom of movement of workers in the EU has generated many important benefits for all involved. It provides the right and freedom for EU citizens to take up employment anywhere in the EU with access to social protection. Both receiving and sending Member States appear to benefit from it economically and, except for the UK before Brexit, there has been no wish among the other Member States to end the free movement of workers per se. Instead, debates about reforming free movement have focused largely on specific aspects of the regulation and coordination of social benefits.

Focusing on the exportability of child benefits, we have explained how and why the current political tension about this issue are related to a fundamental clash between the institutional logics of the EU rules on social security coordination (employment- and contribution-based) and of Member States' family policies (residence-based). Given that free movement of workers and their social protection is something we have reason to value, there are good reasons to change the current system to reduce these institutional tensions. Our proposed solution is to change the principles for coordination and effectively end the exportability of child benefits. This change would contribute to making a clearer distinction in the coordination of benefits for mobile EU workers between the rights of *workers* and the rights of *residents*.

While this chapter has focused on child benefits, it is important to recognize that the same line of argument also applies to some other benefits including long-term care benefits. To further expand the inclusion of elderly care in social security coordination in the context of free movement, which has been part of the 'trilogue' talks between the European Commission, the Council of the EU, and the European Parliament,[48] would increase existing tensions by expanding the coordination to include a component of social protection where there is a great deal of diversity across Member States. The exportability of elderly care services (in-kind benefits) has the potential to create significant tensions, especially in countries without a 'defined contribution' system such as the German *Pflegeversicherung*, not only because of the costs but also due to matters of principle. Therefore, as this is an issue

---

[48] Conversations with employees from the EU Parliament and Commission as well as social partners, September 2019.

relevant to all residents and not only to workers, there are good reasons to also apply the principle of *lex loci domicilii* to elderly care.

More broadly, it is important to recognize that the current situation could get even more complicated if nothing is done to clarify what the protection of workers is about in the context of free movement, and this may have politically destabilizing effects that could threaten the sustainability of the free movement of EU labour as we know it. This process of clarification and debate must, in our view, consider legal aspects and the socio-political effects and dynamics of the free movement of workers and their access to welfare benefits in the European Union. Existing European laws clearly matter and play an important role, not only in terms of constraining policy change but also—in some but not all cases—in providing a normative guide and 'red-lines' with regard to basic rights and principles. At the same time, if a particular institutional configuration generates structural pressures that threaten the political sustainability of the broader project, it is not enough to simply say that 'this is EU law'. Unfortunately, much of the existing analysis and research on the regulation of the free movement of labour in the EU has been divided into disciplinary silos, with limited interactions between legal scholars conducting analysis of the European and national legal underpinning of free movement and social scientists studying the economics and politics of the issue. Our chapter is a call for more (and more open-minded) conversations between legal scholars and social scientists on both the free movement of labour and broader processes of European integration.

Appendix: Child benefits in the EU: (1) basic principle, (2) residence requirement for children, and (3) means-testing, January 2022

Austria

1. Universal scheme for all residents financed by employers' contributions and taxes providing child benefit (*Familienbeihilfe*).
2. The entitlement to child benefit (*Familienbeihilfe*) is not allowed to children residing permanently abroad.
3. The benefit is not means-tested.

Belgium

1. Compulsory social insurance scheme financed by a federal grant and covering children domiciled or residing mainly in the Brussels region/

French-speaking Walloon region/Dutch-speaking region/the German-speaking community.
2. For all federated entities, family benefits are conditional on the child's residence. For Flanders, in principle, both parents are the beneficiaries. For the other entities, the mother is considered as the beneficiary, with a few exceptions. Family allowances are, in principle, not payable for children who are educated or attending classes outside Belgium.
3. The benefit is not means-tested. Entitlement to social supplements is means-tested.

Bulgaria

1. A universal system financed by the State budget providing flat-rate benefits to all beneficiaries.
2. The child must reside in Bulgaria.
3. Only three allowances are means-tested.

Croatia

1. Tax financed scheme covering all residents who satisfy a means test and providing benefits that vary according to income.
2. (a) Croatian citizens residing in Croatia for at least three years.
   (b) Foreign citizens residing permanently in Croatia for at least three years.
   (c) Persons temporarily resident, if eligible for children allowance according to the EU coordination instruments.
   (d) Refugees and foreign nationals with the asylum status and those under subsidiary protection.
3. Means-tested and income graded.

Cyprus

1. Child benefit is a tax-financed universal scheme.
2. The child must be resident in the Republic of Cyprus (except cases where EU Regulation 883/2004 applies). On the basis of the same regulation, the carer may be employed/insured but not residing in the Republic of Cyprus.
3. Income-tested.

Czech Republic

1. Tax-financed universal scheme covering all residents in the Czech Republic.
2. Child and its main carer(s) must be permanent residents in the Czech Republic or citizens of the EU or other persons stipulated by Act No 117/1995 Coll. on State Social Support.
3. Income-tested benefits depending on the age of the children.

Denmark

1. Tax-financed universal scheme covering all residents providing benefits depending on the age of the child and the income of the family.
2. The child must be resident in Denmark.
3. The child and youth benefit (*børne-og ungeydelse*) is reduced for families with a high income.

Estonia

1. Tax-financed universal scheme with flat-rate benefits covering all residents. The benefit amount also depends on the number of children.
2. Estonian citizens and foreigners, who permanently live in Estonia with the child. Permanent residents of Estonia living abroad are entitled to receive family benefits if they reside in Estonia for at least 183 days over 12 consecutive months (as defined by the Income Tax Act).
3. Benefits not means-tested.

Finland

1. Tax-financed flat-rate benefit for children resident in Finland.
2. The child must be resident in Finland.
3. The benefit is not means-tested.

France

1. Universal scheme financed by contributions from employers, from the self-employed, and from a portion of the generalised social contribution (*contribution sociale généralisée, CSG*).
2. Child resident in France.

Germany

1. Tax-funded scheme with fixed amounts for tax exemption of the parental income to the amount of certain needs of a child for all parents and for the promotion of family, insofar as child benefit is not used for tax exemption.
2. The child must reside in Germany or in another EU or European Economic Area (EEA) Member State or in Switzerland. In general, persons who are resident in Germany or are liable to income tax without limitations are eligible.
3. The allowance is not subject to a means test.

Greece

1. Tax-financed scheme providing child benefit for those residing legally and permanently in Greece under certain conditions.
2. Legal and permanent residence in Greece for at least five years before the year of submission of the application.
3. Income-tested.

Hungary

1. Tax-financed universal scheme covering all residents.
2. Benefits are dependent on residence in Hungary of the children.
3. Benefits are not means-tested.

Ireland

1. Tax-financed flat-rate universal scheme covering all resident children.
2. Child must be normally living with and being supported by recipient.
3. The benefit is not means-tested.

Italy

1. In 2022, Single Universal Allowance for children was introduced financed mainly by the employers' contributions, partly by workers' contributions, and tax-financed.

3. Since July 2015, allowances are reduced for families with a high income.

March 2022 marks a big step forward for children in Italy. For the first time in its history, Italy introduces a universal child allowance: a 'historical act' in the words of the Minister for Family and Equal Opportunities, Elena Bonetti. The new allowance overcomes inconsistencies of the previous system by not discriminating based on employment status. Moreover, it will guarantee a minimum child benefit to any Italian household that applies for it; no condition attached.[49]

2. The child can be either resident in Italy, in another EU country, or in a third country having concluded a social security agreement with Italy providing for family benefits. Third country nationals who have been residing on the Italian territory for at least two years, even if not on an ongoing basis, or having been employed in Italy on an open-ended or fixed-term contract, for a minimum period of six months, are also covered as long as the claiming parent is subject to the relevant income tax under Italian legislation.
3. The amount of the benefit depends on the means of the family unit, as assessed, and takes into account the number and age of dependent family members and disabled children.

Latvia

1. Tax-financed universal scheme covering all permanent residents.
2. Children must have received their personal identity number in Latvia, which is granted upon registration in the Population Register. This registration is not conditional on (permanent or temporary) residence or on nationality.
3. Benefits are not means-tested.

Lithuania

1. Tax-financed universal scheme with benefits granted to all residents and additional means-tested benefits linked to the age and number of children.
2. The child must be a permanent resident in Lithuania, or have a temporary residence permit in Lithuania.
3. Only supplemental benefit is means-tested.

---

[49] See n. 32.

Luxembourg

1. Universal tax-financed scheme. Child's own right linked to residence.
2. Each child residing continuously in Luxembourg and with a legal residence there. Benefits exported in accordance with Community law.
3. No variation with income.

Malta

1. A universal system financed by general taxation providing an allowance to all Maltese citizens whose children reside in Malta.
2. Children must be residents.
3. Income-tested.

Poland

1. Tax-financed universal scheme covering all residents.
2. The condition of residence of the child must be fulfilled only in relation to foreigners who: (a) do not have EU or EEA countries or Swiss citizenship; (b) stay in the territory of Poland; (c) hold the refugee status or residence permit.
3. Only supplemental benefit is means-tested.

Portugal

1. Universal protection system for all inhabitants financed by taxes. Individual right of the child related to residence.
2. Child residing in Portugal or in a situation assimilated to that of resident in accordance with the legislation.
3. The amounts vary according to the household income.

Romania

1. Social assistance scheme, universal, tax-financed, providing both cash and in-kind benefits, including State Allowance for Children and Family Support Allowance.
2. Domicile or residence in Romania.
3. Only for the supplement (Family Support Allowance).

Slovakia

1. Tax-financed universal scheme providing flat-rate benefits and covering all residents with dependent child/ren.
2. The entitled person must be a permanent or temporary resident.
3. Benefits are not means-tested.

Slovenia

1. Tax-financed.
2. The child must have permanent or temporary residence and actually reside in Slovenia.
3. Income-tested benefits depending on income and number of children in the family.

Spain

1. Tax-financed non-contributory benefits with benefits depending on income, age, number of children, and degree of disability.
2. Both the beneficiary and the child must be resident in Spain.
3. No benefit if the family income exceeds a certain level of income.

Sweden

1. Tax-financed, compulsory, and universal scheme covering all resident parents and children.
2. The child must be resident in Sweden.
3. The benefits are not means-tested.

The Netherlands

1. Tax-financed universal scheme covering all residents.
2. Entitlement to benefits depends on the place where the applicant is living or working. Both child benefit and child-related allowance are also paid for children living in an EU or EEA country or Switzerland or in a country with which the Netherlands has a social security agreement. For transfer of child benefit outside the EU, EEA or Switzerland, the benefit amount is lowered

according to the price level in the country concerned, but it cannot be increased.

3. General Child Benefit Act: no means test. Act on Child-related Allowance: Means-tested benefit.

Source: Mutual Information System on Social Protection (MISSOC) database: https://www.missoc.org/missoc-database/comparative-tables/results, unless indicated otherwise.

6

Brexit and the Free Movement of Persons

What Is EU Citizenship Really About?

Eleanor Spaventa[*]

1. Introduction

In the aftermath of the Brexit referendum, both the EU and the UK government declared that the rights of UK/EU citizens who had moved before withdrawal would be guaranteed so that the lives of those who had exercised their Treaty rights would not be disrupted.[1] Unfortunately, though, this promise has not been met, or not in full anyway. The reasons for this failure are diverse: first of all, and as we shall see in more detail in Sections 2 and 3, Union citizenship confers residence rights only when given conditions are met. When those are not met, however, EU law offers comparatively little protection leaving those affected by Brexit in a vulnerable situation since if they are unable to gain the more protective Brexit status, they face the full force of national immigration law. Second, political choices, both at EU and at UK levels, left some citizens exposed. In particular, the European Commission took the view that since the Treaties cease to apply upon withdrawal from the EU, British citizens lost Union citizenship and the corresponding rights on 1 February 2021. For this reason, British citizens resident in the EU have become third country nationals,[2] albeit with rights as agreed with the UK in the Withdrawal Agreement. In doing so, the Commission excluded any special status for former EU citizens who had moved exercising their Treaty rights before the UK withdrawal.[3] On the

---

[*] I am grateful to the participants at the summer school and the Authors' Workshop held at the EUI Academy of European Law in Florence, and to Niamh Nic Shuibhne and Fulvia Ristuccia for comments.

[1] See the letter by Prime Minister T. May triggering Article 50, *United Kingdom Notification under Article 50 TEU*, Document XT 20001/27, BXT 1, 29 March 2017, https://data.consilium.europa.eu/doc/document/XT-20001-2017-INIT/en/pdf (last viewed 15 April 2023) where the Prime Minister states as her second 'proposed principle for the discussions' between the EU and the UK that both put citizens first; and the *European Council (Art. 50) guidelines following the United Kingdom's notification under Article 50 TEU*, point 8, where the Council identifies citizens' rights as 'the first priority for the negotiations', https://www.consilium.europa.eu/en/press/press-releases/2017/04/29/euco-brexit-guidelines/ (last viewed 15 April 2023).

[2] See the Commission's note on a no-deal Brexit, which indicates that a no-deal Brexit would trigger the application of national rules even for those British citizens who had moved before withdrawal https://ec.europa.eu/commission/presscorner/detail/en/ip_19_5509 (last viewed 15 April 2023).

[3] On former EU citizens as a 'category' see Spaventa, 'Mice or Horses? British Citizens in the EU 27 after Brexit as "Former EU Citizens"', 44 *European Law Review* (2019) 589.

Eleanor Spaventa, *Brexit and the Free Movement of Persons* In: *Revisiting the Fundamentals of the Free Movement of Persons in EU Law*. First Edition. Edited by: Niamh Nic Shuibhne, Oxford University Press. © Eleanor Spaventa 2023.
DOI: 10.1093/oso/9780198886273.003.0006

other hand, the British government, led at the time by Mrs May who had coined and implemented the 'hostile environment' strategy in relation to immigration,[4] wanted to transition EU citizens to existing immigration rules, simply providing a privileged access to residence/settlement under UK law. But, and this has been a longstanding aim of the British government, the UK wanted to exercise some control over which EU 'immigrants' would be allowed to stay, in particular in relation to those at the margins of society—whether involved in petty criminal behaviour or not managing to have a clear and secure economic and/or working status. In this regard, already before the referendum, the British government had introduced a new policy directed at deporting homeless EU citizens and introduced the 'misuse of Treaty rights' category, which would carry a ban on re-entry for a year. Before this policy was found to be unlawful by the High Court,[5] the forced return of EU citizens almost trebled between 2012 and 2016 (so before the referendum).[6] The political priorities of both negotiating parties were therefore consistent with their stated aim of not disrupting the lives of citizens only up to a point and this is reflected in the final deal that was reached in relation to citizens' rights in the Withdrawal Agreement.[7] The Trade and Cooperation Agreement between the EU and the UK,[8] in contrast, does not grant any meaningful right to free movement to each other's citizens, but for safeguarding the Common Travel Area (CTA) for UK and Irish nationals.[9]

This contribution aims to critically consider the challenges posed to the very notion of Union citizenship by the Brexit process. In order to do so, I will first sketch the legal framework introduced by the Withdrawal Agreement (Section 2), highlighting its most problematic deficiencies. I will then turn to the consequences

---

[4] See 'Theresa May interview: "We're going to give illegal migrants a really hostile reception"', *The Telegraph*, 25 May 2012, https://www.telegraph.co.uk/news/0/theresa-may-interview-going-give-ille gal-migrants-really-hostile/ (last viewed 15 April 2023).

[5] *R (Gureckis) v. Secretary of State for the Home Department* [2017] EWHC 3298 (Admin), available on https://www.judiciary.uk/wp-content/uploads/2017/12/r-gureckis-v-sshd-ors-20171214.pdf (last viewed 15 April 2023).

[6] See Home Office statistics, https://www.gov.uk/government/statistics/immigration-statistics-year- ending-march-2021/how-many-people-are-detained-or-returned (last viewed 24 April 2023). The hostile environment policy was first announced in 2012 and in the last quarter of 2011 the total of returns (enforced, voluntary and refused entry at the border) was 638, by the beginning of 2016 (year of Brexit referendum) it had risen to 1,767. The number of returns then oscillated but always in the thousands, and in the second quarter of 2021 after the end of the transition period, so when EU citizens lost free movement rights, reached 3,653.

[7] Agreement on the Withdrawal of the United Kingdom of Great Britain and Northern Ireland from the European Union and the European Atomic Energy Community, OJ 2019 C 384 I/01, hereinafter the 'Withdrawal Agreement' or WA.

[8] Trade and Cooperation Agreement between the European Union and the European Atomic Energy Community, of the one part, and the United Kingdom of Great Britain and Northern Ireland, of the other part, OJ 2021 L 149/10, thereinafter 'Trade and Cooperation Agreement' or TCA.

[9] And even safeguarding the CTA is proving difficult not least because the UK is proposing to introduce pre-entry travel clearance for EU citizens crossing the Irish border, https://www.theguardian.com/ politics/2021/dec/09/uk-proposes-us-style-waivers-for-eu-citizens-crossing-irish-border (last viewed 15 April 2023).

of loss of status, and loss of rights, for the very meaning of Union citizenship. In particular, after having considered the problems facing those citizens who are not able to gain Brexit status (Section 3), I focus on the broader consequences for Union citizenship arising from the choices made in the Withdrawal Agreement. Thus, in Section 4, I argue that there are two approaches to Union citizenship— a minimalistic approach, where Union citizenship simply confers some (minimal) rights on those who are economically inactive; and a more fundamental/identitarian approach, where Union citizenship truly constitutes a new status for its beneficiaries. Both approaches are legally and politically plausible, but the assimilation of British citizens resident in the EU to third country nationals indicates that the EU institutions have adopted a minimalistic reading of Union citizenship. Furthermore, the denial of rights to free movement for British citizens covered by the Withdrawal Agreement indicates that the point of reference for rights to free movement is not the internal market as a whole, but simply the Member State of destination of the free mover (Section 5). This minimalistic approach seems to have been endorsed also by the Court in the recent *Préfet du Gers* ruling,[10] where it was held that British nationals, even if they had moved before the date of withdrawal, lost the status of Union citizen and all rights associated with that status (including free movement rights) on the date of withdrawal. This interpretation might well have broader consequences for the way we construe and understand Union citizenship which would no longer be a 'fundamental status' but rather just a slightly 'privileged' status.

2. The Withdrawal Agreement

Part II of the Withdrawal Agreement, the first part to be finalized, provides for citizens' rights. For ease of reference, I will refer to UK citizens residing within the EU and EU citizens residing in the UK as of the end of the transition period (31 December 2020) as 'Brexit citizens', unless it is necessary to explicitly refer to either category.

As mentioned above, the stated aim of the negotiating parties was that those EU/UK citizens who had exercised their Treaty rights before a given point in time[11] would not be affected in a negative way by Brexit. To this end, the Withdrawal

---

[10] Case C-673/20, *EP v. Préfet du Gers* (EU:C:2022:449).

[11] The Leave campaign had declared that it would seek to guarantee rights for EU citizens (insofar as their guarantees could be trusted) up to the day of the referendum (https://www.cer.eu/insights/brit ain-will-struggle-make-eu-migrants-%E2%80%98go-home%E2%80%99 (last viewed 15 April 2023)). Mrs May refused to give any assurance without reciprocity (https://euobserver.com/brexit/134511 (last viewed 24 April 2023)), and then wavered between the day of notification, the day of withdrawal, or another unspecified date (https://www.theweek.co.uk/brexit/85959/brexit-theresa-may-reveals-fair-and-serious-offer-on-eu-citizens-rights (last viewed 24 April 2023)). The indivisibility of the four freedoms, a red line for the EU, also meant that if the UK wanted and needed a transition period in relation to the other freedoms, it would have to accept that free movement of persons continued until the end of transition. On the other hand, the Leave campaign deceitfully claimed that EU citizens' rights would be

Agreement reproduces, and in certain cases improves,[12] the regime provided for by Directive 2004/38 on the right to reside of Union citizens.[13] The choice to mirror the existing regime must be understood in the context of the desire to maintain, insofar as possible, the existing situation and it has clear advantages: it incorporates not only several provisions of the Directive, but also the rich body of case law that has been developed by the Court in the past decade or so.[14] However, this choice also has its shortcomings: in particular, the Directive confers rights which are conditional on the citizen meeting certain requirements, i.e. being economically active or having sufficient resources and comprehensive health insurance;[15] and it cannot be invoked against the Member State of origin, so that it cannot be applied to citizens coming back to the home State after having exercised their right to move (so-called circular situations).[16] Furthermore, the EU took the decision not to grant 'special' rights to British citizens in the EU beyond what provided for in the WA. We will start by looking at the personal scope of the Citizens' part of the Withdrawal Agreement (2.A) and then turn to its material scope (2.B).

A. The Personal Scope of the Withdrawal Agreement— Brexit Citizens

The Withdrawal Agreement applies to those who have exercised their right to reside in the UK/EU pursuant to EU law up to the end of the transition period (31 December 2020) and continue to reside in the host State thereafter.[17] Article 13

protected after Brexit, see *The Guardian*, 22 June 2016 (https://www.theguardian.com/uk-news/2016/jun/22/will-europeans-be-free-to-stay-in-the-uk-after-brexit (last viewed 15 April 2023)).

[12] See e.g. the longer period (five years instead of two) of allowed absences for permanent residents before losing the status of permanent residence (Article 15 WA); the lighter administrative burden and best effort by administrative authorities in relation to application for post-Brexit residence (Article 18 WA).

[13] Directive 2004/38/EC of the European Parliament and of the Council of 29 April 2004 on the right of citizens of the Union and their family members to move and reside freely within the territory of the Member States amending Regulation 1612/68/EEC and repealing Directives 64/221/EEC, 68/360/EEC, 72/194/EEC, 73/148/EEC, 75/34/EEC, 75/35/EEC, 90/364/EEC, 90/365/EEC and 93/96/EEC, OJ 2004 L 158/77.

[14] The relevant case law remains binding on British courts if delivered before the end of the transition period (Article 4 WA); thereafter, and for eight years, British courts can make a preliminary reference to the Court of Justice (Article 158 WA).

[15] See primarily Article 7 of Directive 2004/38/EC.

[16] In circular situations, EU citizens have analogous rights as those granted by Directive 2004/38/EC albeit through the application of Article 21 TFEU rather than the Directive, see e.g. Case C-456/12, *O and B* (EU:C:2014:135); Case C-673/13, *Relu Adrian Coman and Others v. Inspectoratul General pentru Imigrări and Ministerul Afacerilor Interne* (EU:C:2018:385).

[17] Article 10 WA; on the state of implementation in EU countries and in the UK see Fifth joint report on the implementation of residence rights under part two of the Withdrawal Agreement (22 September 2021) https://ec.europa.eu/info/strategy/relations-non-eu-countries/relations-united-kingdom/eu-uk-withdrawal-agreement/citizens-rights_en#joint-reports-on-the-implementation-of-residence-rights; and 6th Joint Report (https://ec.europa.eu/info/system/files/final_sixth_joint_report_on_residence_rights.pdf (last viewed 15 April 2023)). For a critical overview of the problems in the UK, see

WA then specifies that EU and UK nationals 'shall have the right to reside in the host State under the limitations and conditions' provided for in Articles 21, 45 or 49 of the Treaty on the Functioning of the European Union (TFEU) and the relevant provisions of Directive 2004/38. In relation to the latter, it should be noted that Article 13(1) WA expressly refers to short-term residence (i.e. unconditional residence for the first three months of stay), so as to ensure that even those citizens who have moved just before 31 December 2020 are covered by the WA provided that after the first three months they then become either economically active or economically independent. Furthermore, work-seekers are also protected by the WA beyond the first three months of stay if they are still looking for a job and have a genuine chance of being employed.[18]

In this respect, it is important to recall the recent ruling in *G.M.A.*[19] which, having being delivered just before the end of the transition period (not by coincidence, in the writer's opinion) is binding also on the UK, including on British courts. In that case, the Court held that beyond the first three months, the Member State is required to give the work-seeker a 'reasonable period of time' to acquaint herself with the employment opportunities available and that this time only starts from when the EU citizen looking for work has signed up to the local unemployment office. It is only after this reasonable period of time has elapsed that the work-seeker is required to also show, in order to continue to stay lawfully in the host State, that she has a genuine chance of being employed. In the context of Brexit, this means that a person who has arrived just before the end of transition and was still looking for a job before the 30 June 2021 (time limit for registration when not extended[20]) falls in theory within the scope of the Withdrawal Agreement. And yet, and unfortunately, Article 18 WA, which regulates the issuance of residence documents, only refers to proof of engagement/activity; and proof of sufficient resources and comprehensive health insurance in order to acquire said documents,

---

Sumption, *What Now? The EU Settlement Scheme after the Deadline* (2021), https://migrationobservat ory.ox.ac.uk/resources/commentaries/what-now-the-eu-settlement-scheme-after-the-deadline/ (last viewed 15 April 2023); on the difficulties encountered by British citizens in France, see also the survey conducted by the EU Rights Clinic (Kent University), (2022), https://blogs.kent.ac.uk/eu-rights-clinic/ (last viewed 15 April 2023). The WA also protects, at least to a certain extent frontier workers, who also fall within the personal scope of the WA, see Article 10(1)(c) and (d). Unfortunately, however, their rights are limited to the state where they worked/resided at the end of transition (because of the lack of free movement rights for Brexit citizens, see later). Furthermore, frontier workers are at risk of losing status more easily, for instance in the case in which they voluntarily take periods off work in circumstances not provided for by Union law. They are at particular risk exactly because the State of residence (which issues the documents) and that of work are different.

[18] See also Article 14(4)(b) of Directive 2004/38/EC.
[19] Case C-710/19, *G.M.A. v. Belgium* (EU:C:2020:1037).
[20] Article 18(1)(b) WA. It is utterly disappointing, and a sign of the state of the relationship between the UK and the EU, that the deadline was not modified for all applicants (in the EU and in the UK) pursuant to Article 18(1)(c) WA, given the impact created by the various lockdowns on the administrative capacity of the Member States/UK.

being silent about work-seekers.[21] There is therefore a grey zone in respect to work-seekers, and one where no doubt denial of rights might become an issue.[22]

It has been mentioned that in order to qualify for protection under the Withdrawal Agreement, citizens must have resided in the host State pursuant to EU law (Article 10 WA), whereas in the case of the right to reside the formulation is more precise and citizens must reside according to the limitations and conditions of the listed provisions (Article 12 WA), i.e. economic activity or sufficient resources and comprehensive health insurance. Article 10 WA brings within the scope of the WA those Brexit citizens whose right to stay in the host country derives from EU law, but not directly from the Treaty free movement provisions or Directive 2004/38.

For instance, Articles 24(2) and 25(2) WA specify that, consistently with established case law, children of workers/self-employed persons who have left the host State have the right to stay in the host State to pursue their education and from this right derives (explicitly in the case of the Withdrawal Agreement, implicitly in the case of EU law) the right to reside of the primary carer of the person in education. In *Jobcenter Krefeld*,[23] again delivered shortly before the end of transition, the Court clarified that such carers are also entitled to equal treatment in relation to social and tax advantages, including income support. It is not clear from that ruling whether in order to be so entitled the carer should also be the former worker (this was the case in the facts of *Jobcenter Krefeld*). The wording of the Withdrawal Agreement seems to suggest, however, that there is no such limitation as the primary carer would become a person residing pursuant to EU law as per Article 10 WA, who would then be entitled to the right to equal treatment in respect of all matters covered by the TFEU.[24]

This said, there are important omissions (all intentional) from the protection afforded by the Withdrawal Agreement: thus, and as mentioned, in order to qualify for special Brexit status, the stay prior to the end of the transition period must be *pursuant to EU law*. In *Dano*, the Court of Justice interpreted the condition that economically inactive citizens must possess sufficient resources as constitutive of the rights conferred by EU law, so that a citizen who does not satisfy

---

[21] This might well have been the case because the drafting of the WA precedes the ruling in *G.M.A.*, even though the Commission has long pushed for a more generous interpretation of Article 14(4)(b) of Directive 2004/38/EC so that work-seekers would have a longer period before having to show genuine chances to find a job.

[22] In any event, it should be considered that there are problems in relying on judicial review for the assertion of EU rights as in most cases (vulnerable) claimants might not go to court, even in those places where there is an active network of NGOs (like the UK); and work-seekers who have just arrived might well be more likely to accept the authorities' decisions without challenging them.

[23] Case C-181/19, *Jobcenter Krefeld – Widerspruchsstelle v. JD* (EU:C:2020:794).

[24] For a very thought-provoking analysis of this case see Ristuccia, 'The Right to Social Assistance of Children in Education and their Primary Carers: *Jobcenter Krefeld*', 58 *Common Market Law Review* (2021) 877; see also Tecmenne, 'Migrant Jobseekers, Right of Residence and Access to Welfare Benefits: One Step Forward, Two Steps Backwards?', 46 *European Law Review* (2021) 765.

164   ELEANOR SPAVENTA

that requirement not only falls outside the scope of the Directive but also outside the protection of the Treaties more generally.[25] The *Dano* case seems, therefore, to be in contrast with earlier case law, and in particular with the *Baumbast* ruling,[26] where the Court held that the principle of proportionality applied also when the Union citizen failed to satisfy in full the requirements of comprehensive health insurance provided for by the precursor to Directive 2004/38. The risk then is that, because of the strict interpretation in *Dano*, national authorities deny the right to stay to Brexit citizens who failed to satisfy the conditions of sufficient resources and comprehensive health insurance. As we shall see also in Section 3, the latter is particularly problematic since it might exclude from the protection conferred by the Withdrawal Agreement those who might have lived in the host State for a long time but were not aware that they should have, or could not afford to take up, private insurance.[27] And, the lack of proportionality assessment in light of the *Dano* ruling might also have a significant effect on those with an irregular working path, including those who having lost their job might not have been aware of the need to register as work-seekers in order to maintain their status as economically active people.[28]

It is true that the Court might well interpret these provisions generously, although (and as we shall see in this chapter) early signs do not allow for optimism[29]—and yet it should be recalled that any case law subsequent to the end of transition (and unless the preliminary reference arose from the UK) is not binding upon the UK.

---

[25] Case C-313/13, *Dano v. Jobcenter Leipzig* (EU:C:2014:2358); and see Thym, 'When Union Citizens Turn into Illegal Migrants: the *Dano* case', 40 *European Law Review* (2015) 249; Spaventa, 'Earned Citizenship: Understanding Union Citizenship through its Scope', in D. Kochenov (ed.), *Citizenship and Federalism in the European Union: the Role of Rights* (2017), also available on http://papers.ssrn.com/sol3/papers.cfm?abstract_id=2497941 (last viewed 15 April 2023); Nic Shuibhne ' "What I Tell You Three Times Is True": Lawful Residence and Equal Treatment after *Dano*', 23 *Maastricht Journal of European and Comparative Law* (2016) 908. The ruling in Case C-181/19, *Jobcenter Krefeld – Widerspruchsstelle v. JD* (EU:C:2020:794) has not had an impact on the ruling in *Dano*, since the claimant in the former derived his right to reside and equal treatment from his children's right to education pursuant to Article 10 of Regulation 492/2011/EU, whereas in *Dano* the issue was whether the claimant, who did not have any other title to reside and did not possess (allegedly) sufficient resources, fell within the scope of EU law. See in particular para. 38 of *Jobcenter Krefeld*.

[26] Case C-413/99, *Baumbast and R v. Secretary of State for the Home Department* (EU:C:2002:493); this was restated a few months before the *Dano* ruling in Case C-140/12, *Brey* (EU:C:2013:565), esp., para. 70. More recently see Case C-247/20, *VI* (EU:C:2022:177), esp. paras 69 and 70.

[27] See Case C-535/19, *A* (EU:C:2021:595) on the host State's duty to affiliate EU migrants to the health system, even though the host State can impose a financial contribution. However, it should be noted that that ruling was delivered after the end of the transition period and hence is not binding upon UK courts. There is disagreement as to whether the NHS, which is free at the point of delivery, would constitute comprehensive health insurance for EU nationals. In Case C-247/20, *VI* (EU:C:2022:177), the Court held that if the Union citizen has been affiliated to the NHS free of charge, then that constitutes comprehensive health insurance, possibly provided that such affiliation did not constitute an unreasonable burden (para. 70), leaving open the possibility of a different assessment if, for instance, free affiliation was for a prolonged period of time.

[28] See Article 7(3)(b) and (c) of Directive 2004/38/EC.

[29] See Case C-709/20, *CG v. The Department for Communities in Northern Ireland* (EU:C:2021:602), discussed below in Section 3.A.

The risk then is to disrupt significantly the lives of citizens who might have built a meaningful and perhaps long-lasting connection with the host States. Whereas the Withdrawal Agreement contains an obligation for the authority examining an appeal against denial of status to ensure that the decision is not disproportionate,[30] it remains to be seen how this requirement will be applied in practice.

Furthermore, the fact that in order to benefit from special Brexit status the citizen must have resided in the host State pursuant to EU law excludes from the scope of the Agreement those citizens who reside in the EU/UK by virtue of *national* rather than EU law:[31] this would be the case, for instance, for those EU citizens who do not fulfil the requirements for lawful residence under EU law (economic activity/independence) but rather derive their residency status from marriage or registered partnership to a citizen of the host State or other host State national law provisions, including perhaps EU citizens in the UK who, pursuant to domestic law, have gained pre-settled status without satisfying the conditions of economic independence/activity. The decision to exclude those residing pursuant to national law might also have significant gender implications since women are more likely to exit the labour market to take up unpaid caring roles within the family, and hence rely on a derivative status pursuant to national law rather than on an autonomous status pursuant to EU law. And, it should be remembered that those falling within the scope of the Withdrawal Agreement might benefit from a more favourable treatment than that afforded by national law, including significant procedural advantages, not least in relation to expulsion.

In relation to dual citizens, i.e. those EU/UK citizens who have acquired the citizenship of the host State, the Court has specified in *Lounes*[32] that the rights conferred by Article 21 TFEU are not lost upon naturalization when the citizen has resided in the host State pursuant to or in accordance with Article 7(1) (i.e. economic activity/independence) or 16 (permanent residence) of Directive 2004/38. In the context of the Withdrawal Agreement, this means that Brexit status is also available to those who have acquired nationality of the home State but only to the extent to which they had previously resided satisfying the conditions in the Directive, with the exclusion, for instance, of those whose residence derived by national law and who were neither economically active or independent (including dual nationality children). So, to give an example, a German national in the UK who before becoming a British national had resided in the UK pursuant to the conditions provided for in the Directive will be covered by the Withdrawal Agreement so that, for instance, her future and existing children would be covered by the Agreement, and so would her spouse (if the conditions in the Agreement are

---

[30] Article 18(1)(r) WA.

[31] With the exception of those who had acquired the right to permanent residence under national law, who are protected also by the WA, see Article 18(1)(h) WA. Following the ruling in *CG*, national rules which afford more generous treatment also fall outside the scope of EU law.

[32] Case C-156/16, *Lounes v. Secretary of State for the Home Department* (EU:C:2017:862).

satisfied). In contrast, a German national who became British but was not residing in the UK pursuant to the Directive but pursuant to UK law (for instance, because the right to reside was granted on the basis of a prior marriage) will not be covered by the Withdrawal Agreement, nor will her children or her (new) spouse.[33] Depending on national law, this might result in a more detrimental treatment: for instance, in the UK, the right to reside of a foreign spouse is conditional upon satisfying a minimum income requirement[34] and the payment of a very high fee, whereas neither is applicable to those protected by the Withdrawal Agreement.

Third, some situations covered by EU law have been excluded from the scope of the Withdrawal Agreement and in particular those situations where the EU citizen is protected against the Member State of nationality. Therefore, the Agreement cannot be invoked in so-called *Ruiz Zambrano* situations, or in circular migration cases, i.e. when own nationals face barriers in returning to their home Member State having exercised their right to move.[35]

Ruiz Zambrano cases occur when the denial of a right to stay to a third country national impacts on the Union citizenship rights of a State's own national by forcing them to leave the territory of the EU altogether.[36] Thus, for instance, the third country national carer of a minor Belgian national residing in Belgium cannot be deported, unless there is a public policy justification, if doing so would force the minor to follow the carer and hence leave the territory of the EU. Those cases are excluded from the scope of the Withdrawal Agreement, and it is not difficult to understand the reasons behind such an exclusion. After all, in those cases there is no movement and the citizens' rights derive from Article 20(1) TFEU, which establishes Union citizenship and is not included in the Agreement, rather than Article 21 TFEU, which provides for the right to move and reside of Union citizens. Moreover, claims against the Member State of origin seeking to establish the derivative residence rights of a third country national family member are particularly sensitive, and many Member States, including the UK, have not been happy with the *Ruiz Zambrano* interpretation seeing it as an undue interference with the States'

---

[33] As mentioned in n. 29, if the applicant had acquired a permanent right to reside under domestic law, then they would be entitled to Brexit status; however, when citizenship is acquired through family ties, rather than naturalization, it might be granted without the claimant having met the conditions to be granted a permanent right to reside.

[34] At the time of writing, the minimum income requirement is higher than what a full-time worker would earn on the minimum wage, and it is further increased for each child. So, for instance, family reunification of a spouse and two children is conditional upon a minimum income requirement of £22,644 per year and of a fee of £1,538 if the application is from outside the UK and £1,048 if it is from within for each member of the family (in our example, £4,614 if applying from outside the UK and £3,144 if applying from within). See https://www.gov.uk/uk-family-visa (last viewed 15 April 2023).

[35] Case C-456/12, *O and B* (EU:C:2014:135); Case C-673/13, *Relu Adrian Coman and Others v. Inspectoratul General pentru Imigrări and Ministerul Afacerilor Interne* (EU:C:2018:385).

[36] Case C-34/09, *Gerardo Ruiz Zambrano v. Office national de l'emploi* (EU:C:2011:124). The Treaty can also be invoked against the Member State of nationality in relation to barriers to move *from* their own country. However, those are not relevant in the case of the Withdrawal Agreement since the latter only applies to those who had already exercised their Treaty rights before the end of transition.

ability to determine their own immigration rules. For this reason, *Ruiz Zambrano* cases have been excluded from the scope of the Withdrawal Agreement, which, like Directive 2004/38, seeks to secure the post-Brexit right to *continue residing* in the *host* State (EU or UK as the case might be).

Furthermore, this omission is predominantly symbolic given that, on the one hand, the UK has decided to protect *Ruiz Zambrano* situations anyway;[37] and that, on the other hand, the *Ruiz Zambrano* case law continues to apply in the EU by virtue of EU law. In fact, in this latter case, it adds an additional layer of protection to British parents of EU children, since those cannot now be refused a right to stay in the child's home State if to do so would force the child to go back to the UK, i.e. a third country, and therefore affect the substance of their EU rights.

The failure to recognize circular situations, i.e. the protection of citizens returning to their Member State of nationality after having exercised Treaty free movement rights, can be ascribed to the same approach—a deep hostility towards the application of EU law to its own citizens. Again, the UK has recognized in domestic law the right of its own citizens to return with their families, but only for a limited period of time.[38] More disconcerting, however, is the European Commission's approach—whereas I would argue that EU citizens returning from the UK to their own Member State continue to be protected by the Treaty if they moved to the UK on the basis of exercising Treaty rights at that time, the Commission believes such situations to fall altogether outside the scope of EU law.[39]

As indicated above, Brexit status is available to those who were resident in the UK/EU before 31 December 2020 and *continue to reside* there after that date. In line with the provisions of Directive 2004/38, the residence of those who have not yet acquired the right to permanent residence[40] is interrupted in the case of absences of more than six months in a year unless the absence is of longer duration for reasons of compulsory military service.[41] Absences for up to a consecutive year do not interrupt the five-year period if the absence is due to 'important reasons', such as childbirth, vocational training, study, or posting.[42] Owing to the pandemic, many otherwise eligible citizens might have returned to and stayed in (whether

---

[37] See *Immigration Rules Appendix EU*, https://www.gov.uk/guidance/immigration-rules/immigration-rules-appendix-eu (last viewed 15 April 2023), EU11 and following; family members of British citizens returning to the UK must have applied by 29 March 2022 (five years from notification of withdrawal). If the British citizen and her family have not yet returned by then, her family does not benefit from the more favourable immigration regime.

[38] See *Immigration Rules Appendix EU*, https://www.gov.uk/guidance/immigration-rules/immigration-rules-appendix-eu (last viewed 15 April 2023) EU 1 and following, and see Home Office guidance https://www.gov.uk/settled-status-eu-citizens-families/eligibility (last viewed 15 April 2023).

[39] Commission Notice Guidance Note relating to the Agreement on the Withdrawal of the United Kingdom of Great Britain and Northern Ireland from the European Union and the European Atomic Energy Community. Part Two—Citizens' Rights, OJ 2020 C 173/01, point 1.2.2.3.

[40] The right to permanent residence accrues after five years of lawful residence pursuant to the provisions of Directive 2004/38/EC or a shorter period when so provided: see Article 16.

[41] Article 16(3) of the Directive.

[42] Ibid.

willingly or due to circumstances) their Member State of nationality for a period exceeding the six months provided for in the Directive/Withdrawal Agreement. Yet given that the list of 'important reasons' is not exhaustive, absences due to the pandemic should be covered by the exceptions;[43] it is thus particularly regrettable that no special provision has been made in this regard.[44] And, of course, the pandemic has also had detrimental effects on the time limit for application for Brexit status (six months), given that it has caused great disruption to the operation of public administrations both in the UK and in the EU.

The right to permanent residence once gained pursuant to the Withdrawal Agreement is lost only through absences of five years, rather than the two years provided by Directive 2004/38. It is not clear, however, how the absence is interrupted, i.e. whether by mere visits, or through re-establishing residence.[45]

Finally, family members of Brexit citizens are also protected by the Withdrawal Agreement provided, if they were not already resident in the host State at the end of transition, the family link already existed before then; furthermore, the Agreement also protects future children, natural or adopted.[46] The definition of family member is the same as that provided for in Directive 2004/38: spouse; registered partner if the partnership is recognized in the host State; children up to the age of 21 or dependent; and dependent relatives in the ascending line.[47] Partners in a durable relationship duly attested (or where the host Member State does not recognize registered partnerships) are also protected if their entry/residence had already been facilitated before the end of transition,[48] and the host Member State continues to be under a duty to facilitate entry/residence provided the relationship was durable before the end of transition.[49]

B. Main Rights Accruing from the Withdrawal Agreement

Brexit citizens derive the right to equal treatment in respect of all matters falling within the scope of Article 18 TFEU, without prejudice to any special provisions

---

[43] This is also the interpretation given by the UK Home Office, see Home Office Guidance *Coronavirus (COVID-19): EU Settlement Scheme - guidance for applicants*, https://www.gov.uk/guidance/coronavirus-covid-19-eu-settlement-scheme-guidance-for-applicants#above (version last updated 18 November 2021) (last viewed 15 April 2023).

[44] Special provisions could be made by the Joint Committee by means of amendment to the WA, pursuant to Article 164(5)(d) which allows amendments inter alia to 'address situations unforeseen' at the time of signature of the WA (November 2019, before the recorded start of the pandemic).

[45] See pending reference C-637/21, *K.R.*, where the national Court enquires about exactly this point in relation to a British citizen who, having grown up in the Netherlands, went to live and work in the UK, only returning for brief visits to see her family in the Netherlands.

[46] Article 10(1)(e)(iii) WA.

[47] Article 10(1) WA.

[48] Article 10(2) WA.

[49] Articles 10(3), (4), and (5) WA.

contained in Part II of the Withdrawal Agreement. In relation to the latter, Article 23 WA reproduces Article 24 of Directive 2004/38 and provides for the right to equal treatment for citizens residing pursuant to the Withdrawal Agreement. As it is the case under the regime provided for in the Directive, States are not obliged to confer entitlement to social assistance to short-term residents or to work-seekers during the extended residence period provided for by Article 14(4)(b) of Directive 2004/38; or maintenance aid for studies for economically inactive people (including students).[50]

More important, and more complex, are the provisions relating to the right to reside. Here, in the writer's opinion, there were competing policy and legal constraints. First of all, and as mentioned previously, both the EU[51] and the UK government had stated that Brexit should not affect existing rights and disrupt the lives of those who had moved to the EU/UK before the end of the transition period. Second, legally, after *Dano*, in EU law the right to reside was conditional upon economic activity or having sufficient resources and comprehensive health insurance. And yet, it was well understood that not all those affected actually met those conditions. For instance, the comprehensive health insurance requirement is not always known. But also, in relation to economically active individuals there are requirements that might not be met by those affected, such as for instance the duty to register with the unemployment office to maintain the status (and rights) conferred by EU law. Similarly, the conditions provided for in Directive 2004/38, as interpreted by the Court, are not necessarily properly implemented at national level.[52] And, there remain grey areas when the economic activity is atypical (for example, on-call and platform workers) or not continuous. The strict application of the conditions provided for by the Directive therefore had the potential of having a disruptive effect on citizens; and yet, even had there been the political will, it would have been difficult for the EU to afford more advantageous conditions to citizens of a withdrawing State than those afforded to EU citizens.

---

[50] The relationship between Article 24(2) of Directive 2004/38/EC and Article 18 TFEU is not altogether clear; in *Dano*, the Court held that Article 18 TFEU was *lex generalis* in respect to Article 24(2) of Directive 2004/38/EC, so that, if the latter did not apply, neither did the former. As a result, Union citizens who did not meet the conditions for residence provided for in Article 7 of the Directive (economic activity or economic self-sufficiency) fell altogether beyond equal treatment protection, at least in relation to social assistance. And yet there are indications that this strict interpretation, confirmed also in the case of work-seekers in *Garcia-Nieto* and *Alimanovic*, is starting to falter. Take, for instance, the above-mentioned case of *Jobcenter Krefeld*, where the Court established the right to equal treatment in respect of all matters pursuant to Article 7(2) of Regulation 492/2011/EU in relation to a carer of a child in education pursuant to Article 10 of the same Regulation. See also Case C-535/19, *A* (EU:C:2021:595) and AG Saugmandsgaard Øe's Opinion in that case (EU:C:2021:114), where he tries to distinguish and limit the application of the *Dano/Garcia-Nieto/Alimanovic* case law.

[51] See n. 1.

[52] In relation to workers see e.g. O'Brien, Spaventa, and De Coninck, 'Comparative Report 2015 – The Concept of Worker under Article 45 TFEU and Certain Non-standard Forms of Employment', upon request of the European Commission, https://ec.europa.eu/social/main.jsp?pager.offset=10&catId=1098&langId=en&moreDocuments=yes (last viewed 15 April 2023).

The balance was therefore not easy to achieve, and the Withdrawal Agreement provides that if the application for residence is denied, the applicant must have access to administrative redress procedures and that those procedures must ensure that the denial of residence is not disproportionate.[53] And yet, this is a meagre consolation for those who might struggle to prove to be covered by the Withdrawal Agreement, even if they have been in the host State for a long time, and it shows one of the limits of the conditional nature of rights granted by Union citizenship.

There are other two very serious limitations to the regime established by the Withdrawal Agreement; first of all, and unlike in EU law, the UK and the Member States may make the application for residence constitutive of the rights provided for in the Agreement.[54] In other words, if the citizen does not apply within six months from the end of the transition period, or the longer deadline where provided, they are set to lose entitlement to Brexit status. The severity of this provision is tempered by the fact that the competent authorities are under an obligation to assess the reasons for failure to respect the deadline and must allow the person concerned a 'reasonable' time to submit an application if there are 'reasonable grounds' for failure to respect the deadline.[55]

Second, the Withdrawal Agreement allows for systematic criminality and security checks on applicants,[56] whereas such systematic checks are not allowed in EU law.[57] Furthermore, while for the purposes of denial of residence and expulsion conduct that occurred before the end of the transition must be evaluated having regard to the constraints imposed by Directive 2004/38 as interpreted by the Court, this is not the case for conduct that occurred after the end of the transition period, which can be evaluated pursuant to national law.[58] It is the combination of systematic criminality checks and the application of national law in relation to conduct that occurred after the end of the transition period which, to my mind, leaves one of the biggest loopholes in the guarantees provided for by the Withdrawal Agreement: the former might serve the purpose of pre-identifying 'undesirables', and the latter allows for expulsion once a further offence is committed even when such an offence would not be enough to trigger the public policy derogation in EU law.[59]

---

[53] Article 18(1)(r) WA.
[54] Article 18(1) WA.
[55] Article 18(1)(d) WA.
[56] Article 18(1)(p) WA.
[57] Article 27(3) of Directive 2004/38/EC.
[58] Articles 20(1) and 20(2) WA. Note that the UK Government has provided that citizens in detention who had not gained permanent residence before going to prison, can only gain pre-settled status if they have been released on or before 31 December 2020 (i.e. the end of the transition period); see https://www.gov.uk/settled-status-eu-citizens-families/what-youll-need-to-apply (last viewed 15 April 2023).
[59] The latest figures from the UK Home Office show that 0.8% (38,900) of applications were refused, 1% were withdrawn or void (51,400), and 1% were invalid (50,600). These figures highlight the magnitude of the problem especially in the UK which has a huge EU population (as of 31 January 2021, 5.06 million applications were received). There is no data as yet in relation to expulsions since, at the time of writing, the implementation period had just expired (March 2021) https://www.gov.uk/gov

3. Failure to Gain Brexit Status

I mentioned previously that the Withdrawal Agreement reproduces the conditional nature of residence rights which characterizes the regime under Directive 2004/38 and, indeed, it has brought to the fore the problematic nature of such conditionality. In this context, I would just like to offer a few critical remarks to place the failure to properly protect affected citizens in its wider context. In particular, part of the scholarship had long highlighted the tensions present in the conditionality requirements:[60] if, on the one hand, the Court famously declared that Union citizenship was going to be the *fundamental status* of Union citizens,[61] its interpretation of the provisions of Directive 2004/38 has been, at times, less citizen-centred and more attentive in simply ensuring a correct transposition of said provisions.[62] This trend is particularly visible in the years preceding the Brexit referendum: the proportionality assessment previously required in order to legitimately limit rights conferred by Union citizenship gave way in favour of a strict application of the conditions contained in secondary legislation, most notably in the *Dano/Alimanovic* rulings,[63] but not only. Here, it is sufficient to recall the interpretation given to the continued residence rights of divorcees, which are severely limited by the Court's insistence that those rights only continue if the application for divorce had been lodged before the main right holder left the host country.[64] Or, the broad application of the notion of public security, and the imposition of a further requirement, that of integration in the host State through good behaviour, to enjoy the enhanced

---

ernment/collections/eu-settlement-scheme-statistics (last viewed 15 April 2023). To the author's knowledge, the EU has not published any aggregated statistics although there are media reports about a certain zeal by the Danish authorities in enforcing the deadline for registration, see https://www.theg uardian.com/politics/2022/nov/25/british-man-deported-denmark-post-brexit-rules (last viewed 15 April 2023).

[60] See e.g. O'Brien, 'Civis Capitalist Sum: Class as the New Guiding Principle of EU Free Movement Rights', 53 *Common Market Law Review* (2016) 937; and C. O'Brien, *Unity in Adversity: EU Citizenship, Social Justice and the Cautionary Tale of the United Kingdom* (2020).

[61] Case C-184/99, *Rudy Grzelczyk v. Centre public d'aide sociale d'Ottignies-Louvain-la-Neuve* (EU:C:2001:458).

[62] On this point see e.g. Nic Shuibhne, 'Limits Rising, Duties Ascending: The Changing Legal Shape of Union Citizenship', 52 *Common Market Law Review* (2015) 889; Spaventa, 'Earned Citizenship: Understanding Union Citizenship through its Scope', in D. Kochenov (ed.), *Citizenship and Federalism in the European Union: the Role of Rights* (2017), http://papers.ssrn.com/sol3/papers. cfm?abstract_id=2497941 (last viewed 15 April 2023).

[63] Case C-67/14, *Jobcenter Berlin Neukölln v. Nazifa Alimanovic and Others* (EU:C:2015:597); see also C-299/14, *Vestische Arbeit Jobcenter Kreis Recklinghausen v. Jovanna García-Nieto and Others* (EU:C:2016:114).

[64] E.g. Case C-218/14, *Singh and Others* (EU:C:2015:476); finally the Court has partially overruled Case C-115/15, *Secretary of State for the Home Department v. NA* (EU:C:2016:487) and has accepted that in the case of domestic violence, in order to protect the victim of domestic violence, divorce proceedings can be initiated within a 'reasonable' time from the departure from the host State of the Union citizen perpetrator of domestic violence. However, the Court also indicated that a three-year time lapse is not 'reasonable', although hopefully this is just an obiter and the personal circumstances that led to the delay will be taken in due regard; see Case C-930/19 *X v. Belgian State* (EU:C:2021:657), paras 43–45.

rights of protection from expulsion on public policy/security grounds available after 5 and 10 years of residence.[65] Directive 2004/38 has therefore had, at least in some instances, a chilling effect on the constitutional interpretation of the rights deriving from Union citizenship.

This said, it is necessary to put this case law in its broader context: first of all, there has not been a case yet on whether the *Baumbast* approach to residence rights, i.e. the need to assess the application having regard to the principle of proportionality at least in relation to the comprehensive health insurance requirement,[66] has been overruled.[67] Rather, *Dano*, *Garcia Nieto*, and *Alimanovic* related to access to welfare provision, where the Court, rightly or wrongly, is striking a balance between the need to protect national welfare systems and the rights of Union citizens.[68] Second, and connected to the first point, Union citizens might, in the EU context, exist in a fluid situation, which might well continue undisturbed until that time in which the citizen applies for some support from the host State. Even then, we have very little guidance on when and how Member States can terminate residence and expel Union citizens. And, in any event, Union citizens who have been expelled might lawfully re-enter the host country at any point.[69] For this reason, even the strict conditionality rule after *Dano*, while very serious in risking a new generation of 'underclass' migrants who might find themselves devoid of social and medical protection, does not necessarily entail the termination of the citizen's stay.

This is not, however, the case in relation to citizens affected by Brexit, especially in those countries that have made application for a residence document constitutive for the enjoyment of rights under the Withdrawal Agreement.[70] Once an application for Brexit status has been refused because the applicant fails to meet the requirements of economic activity/independence, then that citizen is transitioned

---

[65] E.g. Case C-378/12, *Nnamdi Onuekwere v. Secretary of State for the Home Department* (EU:C:2014:213); Joined Cases C-316/16 and C-424/16, *B v. Land Baden-Württemberg*; and *Secretary of State for the Home Department v. Franco Vomero* (EU:C:2018:256).

[66] See Case C-535/19, *A* (EU:C:2021:595) in relation to the duty of the host Member State to affiliate European Union citizens to the public sickness insurance system even when economically inactive subject, if the Member State so decides, to a charge.

[67] See also Case C-93/18, *Bajratari* (EU:C:2019:209), where the Court requires the conditions for residence to be interpreted in relation to the principle of proportionality.

[68] It is not always clear how this balance is struck and which are the relevant criteria to be taken into account; see e.g. Case C-181/19, *Jobcenter Krefeld – Widerspruchsstelle v. JD* (EU:C:2020:794), and Ristuccia, 'The Right to Social Assistance of Children in Education and their Primary Carers: *Jobcenter Krefeld*', 58 *Common Market Law Review* (2021) 877.

[69] However, note that the Court has recently tried to define the boundaries of this right to re-entry, see Case C-719/19, *FS v. Staatssecretaris van Justitie en Veiligheid* (EU:C:2021:506); for an excellent and very critical analysis of this case, see Ristuccia, ' "Cause tramps like us, baby we were born to run": untangling the effects of the expulsion of "undesired" Union citizens: *FS*', 59 *Common Market Law Review* (2022) 889. On expulsion, see also Case C-718/19, *Ordre des barreaux francophones et germanophone et al v. Conseil de Ministre* (EU:C:2021:505). See also abuse of rights doctrine by the UK.

[70] For country by country rules see *Optimised Overview of MS Residence Rights* (European Commission) https://ec.europa.eu/info/sites/default/files/brexit_files/info_site/overview_ms_residence_rights.pdf (last viewed 15 April 2023); 2 out of 27 countries have made application for residence constitutive.

to normal immigration law. This means that her continued stay in the country without a permit might be illegal, and open to sanctions. The same citizen would then be subject to immigration control also in relation to the possibility to work or pursue an economic activity. The severity of the consequences of not meeting the criteria provided for in Directive 2004/38 for Brexit citizens is in no way comparable to what happens in the EU context. True, and this was one of the points made by some of the participants in the EUI Academy, those citizens might not have had a right to stay even before Brexit: and yet, because of the fluid nature inherent in the free movement provisions, they might have stayed in the host country, often in good faith, and have built lives and networks there. And, it should be remembered that, as is the case in the context of Union citizenship more generally, the conditions of economic activity or economic independence might have a gender and disability discrimination effect. Gender, because women are more likely to take unpaid caring roles within the family unit, which might prevent their participation in the labour market, or make that participation patchy with long periods away from paid work. Disability, because the requirement of comprehensive health insurance is particularly punitive for those who have long-term conditions, who might well struggle to enter or stay in the labour market, but who might also find it economically or otherwise impossible to secure comprehensive health insurance.[71] And finally, and as mentioned already above, an increasing number of people might have non-linear employment paths, moving between different statuses.[72] Only time and practice will show how stringently those criteria will be applied by national authorities, although the data coming from the UK is not that comforting.[73]

Another issue to be considered relates to 'Brexit status' itself, i.e. when does a citizen fall within the protection of the Withdrawal Agreement? This problem arose recently in relation to the UK rules applicable to EU citizens who have gained pre-settled status in the UK. Here, some context is necessary—the UK did not have a pre-Brexit registration scheme for EU citizens; this fact coupled with the sheer number of EU citizens resident/present in the UK before the end of the transition period resulted in a titanic administrative task, that of providing more than 5 million EU citizens with the required status.[74] For this reason, the UK started its

---

[71] See in relation to Brexit, O'Brien, 'Between the Devil and the Deep Blue Sea: Vulnerable EU Citizens Cast Adrift in the UK post-Brexit', 58 *Common Market Law Review* (2021) 531.

[72] It should be recalled that worker status is retained only under certain circumstances and requires the former worker to register with the unemployment office; see recently, e.g. Case C-483/17, *Tarola* (EU:C:2019:309); here, it would have been appropriate for the Commission to at least remind the national authorities of the safeguards built into the case law on the definition of 'worker' under EU law.

[73] See statistics provided by the Home Office and note that because of the sizeable number of applicants, a small percentage of refusals result in a significant number of denials (in September 2021 165,550 refusals) https://www.gov.uk/government/statistics/eu-settlement-scheme-quarterly-statistics-september-2021/eu-settlement-scheme-quarterly-statistics-september-2021#:~:text=The%20num ber%20of%20concluded%20applications,were%20granted%20pre%2Dsettled%20status (last viewed 15 April 2023).

[74] The latest Home Office statistics (February 2022) put the figure at 5.33 million EU/EEA citizens, and 437,000 from TCNs/non EEA; https://www.gov.uk/government/collections/eu-settlement-sch

174   ELEANOR SPAVENTA

registration scheme well before the end of the transition period. The UK scheme distinguished between pre-settled status, for those EU citizens who had been in the UK for less than five years at the time of application or who had their application for settled status rejected for lack of evidence; and settled status, a scheme akin to permanent residence. Neither status was/is subject to proving that the period of residence in the UK complied with the requirements of Directive 2004/38,[75] and hence both statuses are more generous than what is required under the Withdrawal Agreement. The question, which arose in the *CG* case, is whether those EU citizens who have been conferred pre-settled and settled status, but who did not meet the conditions provided for in Directive 2004/38 as incorporated in the Withdrawal Agreement, are nonetheless protected.

In *CG*,[76] the claimant was a Union citizen, mother of two young children and victim of domestic violence, living in a woman's refuge in Northern Ireland. She was granted pre-settled status by the British authorities, but when she applied for universal credit, a welfare benefit aimed at ensuring minimum subsistence, she was denied it since she did not fulfil the criteria established by UK law that excluded those who did not meet the conditions provided for in EU law from access to

eme-statistics (last viewed 15 April 2023). Note that the UK applies the same rules to EEA citizens as it does to EU citizens, even though EEA citizens are not covered by the Withdrawal Agreement.

[75] There has been some discussion as to whether, in the case of the UK, comprehensive health insurance (CHI) was required or whether the fact that the NHS was free at the point of delivery meant that EU citizens were automatically insured under British law. The Court of Appeal found that the CHI requirement applied also in the UK; see *Ahmad v. The Secretary of State for the Home Department* [2014] EWCA Civ 988, available on https://www.bailii.org/ew/cases/EWCA/Civ/2014/988.html (last viewed 15 April 2023).The European Commission, on the other hand, took a different view, and before the referendum issued a reasoned opinion for infringement proceedings on this matter, https://ec.europa.eu/commission/presscorner/detail/en/IP_12_417 (last viewed 15 April 2023), which were then discontinued (most likely because of political considerations); however, the Commission has now issued a new letter of formal notice https://ec.europa.eu/commission/presscorner/detail/en/inf_20_1 687 (last viewed 24 April 2023). In the meantime, a similar issue was referred in Case C-247/20, *VI v. Commissioners for Her Majesty's Revenue & Customs* (EU:C:2022:177). The Court found that 'it must be recalled that, although the host Member State may, subject to compliance with the principle of proportionality, make affiliation to its public sickness insurance system of an economically inactive Union citizen, residing in its territory on the basis of Article 7(1)(b) of Directive 2004/38, subject to conditions intended to ensure that that citizen does not become an unreasonable burden on the public finances of that Member State, such as the conclusion or maintaining, by that citizen, of comprehensive private sickness insurance enabling the reimbursement to that Member State of the health expenses it has incurred for that citizen's benefit, or the payment, by that citizen, of a contribution to that Member State's public sickness insurance system …, the fact remains that, *once a Union citizen is affiliated to such a public sickness insurance system in the host Member State, he or she has comprehensive sickness insurance within the meaning of Article 7(1)(b)*' (para. 69, emphasis added).

[76] Case C-709/20, *CG v. The Department for Communities in Northern Ireland* (EU:C:2021:602); see also the UK Supreme Court ruling in *Fratila and another (AP) (Respondents) v. Secretary of State for Work and Pensions* (Appellant) [2021] UKSC 53 which applies the *CG* ruling. For a critical analysis see O'Brien, 'The Great EU Citizenship Illusion Exposed: Equal Treatment Rights Evaporate for the Vulnerable (*CG v. The Department for Communities in Northern Ireland*)', 46 *European Law Review* (2021) 801.

welfare provision (the 'habitual residence test').[77] As CG had never worked or exercised an economic activity, and did not have sufficient resources (or else she would have not been eligible for the benefit which is means-tested), she was not entitled to Universal Credit. The issue for the Court was whether, given that CG was lawfully resident in the UK, she could be discriminated against in this way. The reason why the habitual residence test is indirectly discriminatory is that own nationals and Irish citizens have an automatic and unconditional right to reside in the UK, whereas most EU citizens would have to prove economic activity or economic independence in order to qualify as habitually resident. The Court held that the title of residence in question derived from national law, since Ms CG did not meet the criteria in Directive 2004/38. The Court then re-affirmed the *Dano* reasoning: since CG's residence was not pursuant to Directive 2004/38, the right to equal treatment provided for in Article 24(1) of the Directive did not apply, and neither did Article 18 TFEU because that is *lex generalis* vis-à-vis Article 24(1), so that if the latter does not apply, the former cannot rectify the situation. The Court did find, however, that the Charter of Fundamental Rights applied (unlike in *Dano*) since CG had exercised her Treaty rights and was covered by Article 21 TFEU.[78]

The ruling in *CG* is obviously of great significance for EU citizens in the UK (and for UK citizens in the EU) and it entails two main consequences. First of all, national rules that are more favourable to citizens, including Brexit citizens, in relation to residence rights might have the effect of excluding those citizens from the benefits of the Withdrawal Agreement altogether (e.g. in relation to family reunification; to residence rights of future children; protection from expulsion; etc.). Second, the Court has accepted that Member States are free to discriminate between citizens, they just need to be smart about it. Thus, whereas in *Grzelczyk* the idea was that once residence was conferred, the burden fell on the Member State to terminate residence by demonstrating that granting access to welfare to the economically inactive Union citizen would transform her in an unreasonable burden,[79] in *CG* the Court allows Member States simply to separate the two issues, lawful residency and access to benefits, so that the latter can be denied *whenever* the Union citizen does not satisfy the conditions provided for in Directive 2004/38 (albeit with the minimum safety net provided by the Charter). In this way, the Member State no longer needs to demonstrate that awarding the benefit would transform the citizen into an unreasonable burden, it needs only to grant residence rights more liberally but

---

[77] In order to be able to access benefits, claimants have to prove that the UK, Ireland, or the Isle of Man is their main home, and that they have a right to 'reside' there, which in the case of most EU citizens means satisfying the conditions provided for in Directive 2004/38/EC.

[78] Although given that Article 21 TFEU applies, it becomes more difficult to understand why Article 18 TFEU would not as it always applies if the matter falls within the personal and material scope of the Treaty. On these issues, aptly defining this approach (pre-*CG*) as a 'normative migraine', see Nic Shuibhne (n. 62).

[79] Case C-184/99, *Rudy Grzelczyk v. Centre public d'aide sociale d'Ottignies-Louvain-la-Neuve* (EU:C:2001:458).

then impose strict conditions on access to benefits. Furthermore, this also leads to a bizarre result where, potentially, an EU citizen who is first refused pre-settled (and possibly also settled) status, and then wins an appeal through the application of the 'disproportionality' assessment contained in Article 18(1)(r) WA is in a better position than an economically inactive person who was immediately granted pre-settled or settled status by that same legislation. In the first case, in fact, residence would be pursuant to the Withdrawal Agreement, while in the latter case it would be simply residence pursuant to 'national' law.

And while this is not the forum to further explore the significance of this ruling more generally, its implications for Brexit citizens cannot be overestimated: those with less means might well face a choice between destitution or having to leave the country where they live, perhaps also losing the possibility of returning there once their circumstances have improved, as they would then be subjected to standard immigration law. Furthermore, it is debatable whether the fundamental rights guarantee, that minimum of protection recognized by the Court in *CG*, would actually be applicable in the case of EU citizens in the UK. Here, Article 4(4) WA provides an obligation to follow the interpretation of the Court of Justice only for rulings 'handed down' before the end of the transition period, whereas British courts have to have 'due regard' to case law handed down after that period. The UK Supreme Court in *Fratila*,[80] a case that raised the same legal points as *CG*, considered itself bound by the latter ruling because the facts occurred during the transition period when EU law still applied to the UK. This, however, leaves the question as to whether British courts would take the same view in relation to cases concerning facts that occurred after the end of transition: if yes, then the Charter would be applicable also in those cases; however, if they followed the wording of the Withdrawal Agreement, they might well conclude that the ruling in *Dano* does not compel them to apply the Charter, and limit the fundamental rights assessment to an application of the UK's Human Rights Act.[81]

4. British Citizens in the EU: Competing Visions of Union Citizenship

The deal encapsulated in the Withdrawal Agreement also has further consequences for British citizens specifically, and for our understanding of what Union

---

[80] *Fratila and another (AP) (Respondents) v. Secretary of State for Work and Pensions* (Appellant) [2021] UKSC 53.

[81] The UK Government has tabled a Bill to repeal and replace the Human Rights Act 1989, https://publications.parliament.uk/pa/bills/cbill/58-03/0117/220117.pdf (last viewed 15 April 2023). Furthermore, the Johnson government also sought to curb the powers of review of the judiciary, see Queen's Speech, 10 May 2022, https://www.gov.uk/government/speeches/queens-speech-2022 (last viewed 15 April 2023).

citizenship really entails more generally. In particular, the Withdrawal Agreement fails to confer free movement rights on British citizens who are covered by its provisions, reflecting a transactional view of Union citizenship—after all if EU citizens in the UK face a considerable loss of status and rights, why should that not be the same for UK citizens in the EU? Both should be treated exactly the same and have exactly the same rights. And if the UK refuses, as a matter of principle, any free movement of people, why should the EU grant the same to British citizens? (We will come back to the fallacy in this comparison that unfortunately has driven the Commission's approach in this field, an approach then accepted by the European Parliament and the Council.)

This more limited vision of Union citizenship has been brewing for some time, becoming central to the political, judicial, and scholarly debates in the aftermath of the 'Cameron deal'[82] and the Brexit referendum. In this regard, it is widely accepted that the debate on 'immigration' from EU countries, which became particularly high in the UK post-2004, was one of the contributing factors that led to the outcome of the referendum. It is open to debate whether that was because immigration was weaponized for political expedience or whether it was a genuine concern for voters, but in any event the narrative surrounding free movement shifted rapidly. This shift can be seen, first and foremost, in the 'Cameron deal' where both the Member States and the Commission accepted a regression in workers' rights so as to link access to certain welfare provision (in-work benefits) to length of residence in the UK and allowing for indexation of family benefits for migrant workers whose families lived abroad.[83] Whether these new measures were compatible with the Treaties was never tested since their adoption was conditional upon the UK voting to stay in the EU;[84] however, and in any event, they are indicative of a step back from understanding even the free movement of workers as a 'constitutional' freedom. In this respect, Schmidt[85] has linked the outcome of the referendum

---

[82] The 'Cameron deal' is the deal struck by the then UK Prime Minister, Mr Cameron and annexed to the Council conclusions of the European Council of 18–19 February 2016 (https://www.consilium. europa.eu/media/21787/0216-euco-conclusions.pdf (last viewed 15 April 2023)). Pursuant to the deal, amongst other matters, the UK would have been allowed, had it decided to stay in the EU, to limit access to in-work benefits (i.e. welfare provision aimed at supporting workers whose wages are too low to survive) linking eligibility to length of stay and to index family benefits to the cost of living of the country where the family of the worker resided.

[83] Indexation of family benefits is another matter that has been politically seized, and not only in the UK; see the letter addressed to the Commissioner for Social Affairs in 2018 by representatives for Germany, Austria, the Netherlands, Ireland, and Denmark demanding indexation as a matter of fairness, https://www.ft.dk/samling/20171/almdel/BEU/bilag/386/1914108.pdf (last viewed 15 April 2023). See Blauberger, Heindlmaier, and Kobler, 'Free Movement of Workers under Challenge: the Indexation of Family Benefits', 18 *Comparative European Politics* (2020) 925 https://link.springer.com/article/10.1057/s41295-020-00216-3#Fn6 (last viewed 15 April 2023).

[84] The Commission did, however, bring successful infringement proceedings against Austria for unilaterally providing for indexation of family benefits, see Case C-328/20, *Commission v. Austria* (EU:C:2022:468).

[85] Schmidt, 'Extending Citizenship Rights and Losing it All: Brexit and the Perils of "Over-Constitutionalisation"', in D. Thym (ed.), *Questioning EU Citizenship – Judges and the Limits of Free Movement and Solidarity in the EU* (2017) 7; Nic Shuibhne (n. 62).

178 ELEANOR SPAVENTA

to this prior over-constitutionalization which, in her opinion, had different effects in the UK because of the specificity of its case law based legal system. The 'Cameron deal' then can be seen as the first explicit political move towards this deconstitutionalization, contextual to the same effort undertaken by the Court and visible in the case law recalled above which limits certain rights, and in particular those relating to access to welfare for economically inactive and not-yet-active citizens, to what was determined in Directive 2004/38. And, the shockwaves of the referendum did spark a new, and more critical, debate on the limits of free movement of persons, and whether the extensive interpretation which characterized the case law until *Dano* was in fact sustainable.[86]

It is in the light of this contraction in the vision of Union citizenship that we should understand the Commission's position in relation to the rights of British citizens post-Brexit and its insistence, from the very beginning, that Union citizenship would be withdrawn from British citizens when the UK withdrew from the European Union. The legal underpinning for this approach is deceptively simple: Article 50(3) TEU provides that: 'The *Treaties shall cease to apply* to the State in question from the date of entry into force of the withdrawal agreement or, failing that, two years after the notification' of the intention to withdraw. Given that Union citizenship is a 'creation' of the Treaties, once the latter no longer apply, Union citizenship also ceases to apply, and hence British citizens are no longer Union citizens. In this view, then, Union citizenship is 'transactional in nature', i.e. based on reciprocity, and 'international' rather than supranational in its regulation.

The stress in this interpretation is then on the *additional* nature of Union citizenship, and not on Union citizenship as emerging from a deeper integration process that fosters, and is aimed to foster, deep links of belonging. In this way, the importance of those links of belonging to the identity of those affected is ignored and again, in a transactional way, citizens involved should simply be ferried from Union citizenship to third country national status, easing the journey for those who already reside in the EU by providing as little disruption as possible through the creation of a special status as conferred by the Withdrawal Agreement. Consistently with this approach, then, the Commission has rejected from the very beginning the demands by British citizens resident in Europe that they be conferred free movement rights, again showing a very limited vision of both the internal market and Union citizenship. Hence, in this view, the British citizen has simply moved to *another* Member State, not to *another Member State as part of the internal market*. It is for this reason that, once Union citizenship is withdrawn, the

---

[86] See Nic Shuibhne, 'Reconnecting Free Movement of Workers and Equal Treatment in an Unequal Europe', 43 *European Law Review* (2018) 477. As proven by the 'Cameron deal', Member States are well aware that the most significant welfare transfer, the real example of transnational solidarity, is not that operated in relation to economically inactive citizens, but rather that operated in favour of in-work poor—i.e. those who earn very little and are therefore entitled to rely upon means-tested welfare provision to supplement their earnings.

British citizen remains 'locked' in that Member State,[87] rather than being allowed to move freely within the internal market. In this view then, movement is possible because of the internal market, but it is still movement to *one particular Member State* and it is only in that Member State that the mover's rights are guaranteed— the internal market dimension is therefore downgraded from a constitutional project, to a simple change in 'migratory' status and rights of the beneficiary. And, since rights of free movement are at the very core of the EU integration project, once the country of nationality has withdrawn from such a project, those rights are no longer available. Construed in this way, Union citizenship is truly *additional* to national citizenship—it is not fundamental in nature and it does not confer a new status upon Union citizens. It simply expands to a new constituency—the economically inactive—some of the internal market derived rights:[88] the conditionality of those rights then can be explained in this light. Here, the *Ruiz Zambrano* and *Tjebbes* approaches,[89] whereby Union citizenship can be used to limit the discretion of the Member State of nationality to deport the carers of their own citizens and to withdraw national citizenship, are to be seen simply as a limit imposed on the power of the Member State to exclude their own citizens from the benefits of the internal market, rather than a constitutionalization of Union citizenship per se.

Juxtaposed to this view is one that sees the spatial dimension of Union citizenship rights as embedded in the *European* and not in the national territory; and, at its most *identitarian*, sees Union citizenship as conferring a new and distinct identity. The latter perspective is well encapsulated in an article by Behr in *The Guardian*: 'EU free movement conferred a right to relocate. And, whether Brexiters like it or not, that implied a *right to belong in perpetuity.*'[90] Here, Union citizenship is no longer perceived merely as an international law construct, but rather as the outcome of a *supranational* political project. The stress then is on Union citizenship as a *truly* fundamental status, that changes the relationship between beneficiaries and the EU territory as a whole by creating something more, and radically new—the *additional nature* of Union citizenship is perceived not as a tool to 'protect' national citizenship, but as conferring a fundamentally novel status.

---

[87] And consistently with this approach, Article 10(1)(b) WA provides that the Withdrawal Agreement applies to 'United Kingdom nationals who exercised the right to reside *in a Member State* in accordance with Union law before the end of the transition period and continue to reside *there* thereafter' (emphasis added), hence circumscribing the geographical reach of the protection conferred by the Agreement.

[88] This interpretation is also evidenced by the fact that the indivisibility of the internal market was interpreted as encompassing, in the transition period, residence rights for economically inactive citizens, whereas the 'pure' citizenship rights (i.e. rights of passive and active electoral franchise) were terminated upon withdrawal.

[89] Case C-34/09, *Gerardo Ruiz Zambrano v. Office national de l'emploi* (EU:C:2011:124); Case C-221/17, *M.G. Tjebbes and Others v. Minister van Buitenlandse Zaken* (EU:C:2019:189); and see more recently Case C-118/20, *JY v. Wiener Landesregierung* (EU:C:2022:34); Case C-490/20, *V.M.A. v. Stolichna obshtina, rayon 'Pancharevo'* (EU:C:2021:1008).

[90] R. Behr, 'Brexit rots our rights. How can Theresa May ignore the stench?', *The Guardian*, 13 September 2017, https://www.theguardian.com/commentisfree/2017/sep/13/brexit-rights-theresa-may-eu-uk-brexit-identity (last viewed 15 April 2023) (emphasis added).

180 ELEANOR SPAVENTA

Withdrawal of Union citizenship then becomes an amputation of one's identity and is not seen merely as a loss of rights. In this view, the protection conferred by *Ruiz Zambrano* and *Tjebbes* is part of a constitutionalization of this new status which confers additional claims, including that of inhabiting the European space.[91]

The tension between these two meanings of Union citizenship, minimalistic/transactional versus identitarian/constitutional, which are both legally and politically plausible, is still being played out in the legal sphere—a number of cases having been lodged based on the identitarian vision of Union citizenship and contesting the constitutional legality of its withdrawal from British citizens.[92] As we shall see in more detail (Section 5), in *Préfet du Gers* the Court has openly endorsed a transactional view of Union citizenship, excluding a more generous interpretation of the Withdrawal Agreement for British nationals who had moved before Brexit also on the basis that such an interpretation would create an 'asymmetry' between the rights of UK and EU nationals.[93]

5. Union Citizenship and Territory: Situating Rights in the National Context and its Significance

It has been mentioned previously that the Commission and the citizens affected have radically different views about the spatial dimension of Union citizenship rights. From the Commission's perspective, the 'no loss of rights' rhetoric, the need to protect those citizens who had exercised Treaty rights before withdrawal, is limited to ensuring the rights of British citizens *in the Member State* where they reside at the end of the transition period. This approach, transactional in nature, identifies Union citizenship rights with a conditional right to reside, but most interestingly, with the right to reside in *a given State* rather than in the EU territory at large.

From the British citizens' perspective, however, the spatial dimension of accrued/expected rights is that of the EU, not simply that of the Member State of current residence at the time of Brexit. When British citizens triggered their Treaty rights, they did so in the expectation that they were free to move around the internal market and not be locked in a given State; and, indeed, movement is encouraged in the European integration project.

---

[91] On the significance of the *Ruiz Zambrano* case law for the way we construe the notion of European Union territory, see Nic Shuibhne, 'The "Territory of the Union" in EU Citizenship Law: Charting a Route from Parallel to Integrated Narratives', 38 *Yearbook of European Law* (2019) 1; Azoulai, 'Transfiguring European Citizenship: From Member State Territory to Union Territory', in D. Kochenov (ed.), *EU Citizenship and Federalism: The Role of Rights* (2017) 178.

[92] See cases later in this chapter, and for a summary of Brexit related litigation including on citizens' rights see Peers, *Litigating Brexit: a Guide to the Case Law*, 24 July 2020, http://eulawanalysis.blogspot.com/p/litigating-brexit-guide-to-case-law.html (last viewed 15 April 2023)

[93] Case C-673/20, *EP v. Préfet du Gers* (EU:C:2022:449), para. 72.

So, whether British citizens in Europe, who have been denied free movement rights, face or do not face a loss of rights depends on one's perspective, and the perspective adopted by the Commission has deeper consequences for how we construe Union citizenship more generally. In particular, the decision to deny free movement rights to British Brexit citizens only makes sense if the point of reference is the Member State rather than the EU, i.e. if Union citizenship is embedded only in that State where the EU citizen is currently exercising her rights. If it is so, and the Member State is the point of reference, then it is reasonable to expect that the British Brexit citizen would revert to the status of third country national upon withdrawal, and the regime for British citizens should mirror that for third country nationals. Seen in this light, the denial of free movement rights is justified having regard to the fact that immigration rules are predominantly national in nature, and give access, at least at first, only to the Member State that issued the visa. British citizens, like most other third country nationals in the first five years of their stay, do not enjoy free movement rights even if they were exercising Treaty rights when they had moved.[94]

The lack of free movement rights, though, is primarily a political choice originating from the 'animosity' regarding the British decision not to accept any migratory element in the Trade and Cooperation Agreement with the EU. The narrative here is that of reciprocity, which underpins international relations. But again, in so doing, the Commission erases the internal market as the space of reference for the exercise of Treaty-based rights: the decision not to allow free movement for UK Brexit citizens is more appropriately compared to a potential UK claim to limit the movement of EU Brexit citizens to one of the nations in the UK, rather than to the decision not to allow future free movement. This would have been legally impossible because immigration is not devolved to the constituent nations of the UK, but the comparison shows that the decision not to allow free movement of British Brexit citizens brings a rethink of what Union citizenship really is about, and in a way casts some doubts over the *Ruiz Zambrano* case law.[95] In the latter strand of case law, as mentioned above, the intrusion of EU law into the realm of domestic immigration law is justified by the fact that otherwise the own national might be deprived of her rights conferred by EU law: but those arise in the European, not in the national space. On the contrary, the rights of British Brexit citizens are confined to the national space, and the European dimension is negated. The two approaches then seem difficult to reconcile.

---

[94] Furthermore, it is not clear whether after the first five years, British citizens will enjoy at least the limited rights of movement conferred on third country nationals by the Long-Term Residents Directive; see Council Directive 2003/109/EC of 25 November 2003 concerning the status of third-country nationals who are long-term residents, OJ 2004 L 16/44, Chapter III.

[95] In a different contribution, I tried to offer a different interpretation of the rights accruing from having exercised Treaty rights once the Member State of nationality has withdrawn, see Spaventa (n. 3).

Closely linked to the loss of free movement rights is the loss of the other right traditionally associated with EU citizenship: the right to vote in European Parliamentary and municipal elections. This, in the words of Behr, is part of that right to 'belong', a limited belonging perhaps but belonging nonetheless. Legally, this issue is even more complex: the electoral franchise is decided by national law, and it is only for Union citizens that EU law has something to say.[96] And yet, the right to democratic participation intersects with EU, ECHR, and domestic constitutional law.

This is evidenced by a recent preliminary reference from a French court. In the *Préfet du Gers* case,[97] the claimant is a British citizen living in France who complained about her removal, following the end of the transitional period, from the French electoral roll, disenfranchizing her from the right to vote for the European Parliamentary and local elections. A similar claim had already failed in the French domestic courts:[98] however, Ms EP distinguished her case based on the fact that, unlike the claimants in the other case, she had lived in France for more than 15 years so that, under British law, she had not had a chance to vote for the UK referendum or in the political elections *and* she was now totally disenfranchised, being unable to vote either in the UK or in France. The national court found that the application of Article 127 WA to EP constituted a disproportionate interference with her right to vote. It hence referred preliminary questions to the Court of Justice enquiring as to whether Article 50 TEU and the Withdrawal Agreement must be interpreted as revoking EU citizenship for British nationals who had moved before the end of the transition period and in particular for those who had moved more than 15 years earlier and therefore had lost the right to vote in the UK. Should the answer to the first question be positive, the national court further enquired whether British citizens retained in any case EU citizenship rights if they had moved before the end of transition; if not, whether the Withdrawal Agreement generally is invalid for infringing inter alia Union citizenship rights and the principle of proportionality; and, more specifically whether Article 127 WA, depriving Union citizens and British citizens of the right to vote, is valid.

The Advocate General found that, as argued by the Council, Article 50 TEU, together with the Withdrawal Agreement, has the effect of terminating Union citizenship for British citizens, and that, in this respect, the fact that Ms EP had exercised her Treaty rights was immaterial. The Advocate General then turned to analyse the Council decision concluding the Withdrawal Agreement;[99] in a rather

---

[96] Rights to the electoral franchise, including the right to vote in European Parliament elections, can be vested also upon non-Union citizens, see Case C-145/04, *Spain v. United Kingdom* (EU:C:2006:543).

[97] Case C-673/20, *EP v. Préfet du Gers*, Opinion (EU:C:2022:129), Judgment (EU:C:2022:449).

[98] See also Cour de Cassation Pourvoi n° 20-16.901 (FR:CCASS:2020:C201153).

[99] Council Decision (EU) 2020/135 of 30 January 2020 on the conclusion of the Agreement on the withdrawal of the United Kingdom of Great Britain and Northern Ireland from the European Union and the European Atomic Energy Community, OJ 2020 L 29/1.

cursory analysis, Mr Collins found that the Council Decision could not be 'criticized' for not affording British nationals the right to vote and stand in the EP elections during and after the transition period, since (tautologically) that loss is the consequence of withdrawal and for this reason is compatible with both the Treaties citizenship provisions and Article 40 of the Charter. He further found that the EU institutions did not exceed the bounds of their broad discretion in the conduct of external relations. Perhaps more interestingly for our discussion, Mr Collins also stated that the European Union could not 'secure rights that, in any event, *it was not bound to assert on behalf of persons who are nationals of a State that has left the European Union and who are therefore no longer Union citizens.*'[100]

The Court of Justice very much agreed with Mr Collins' analysis and found that UK nationals had lost their Union citizenship on the date on which the UK became a third state by withdrawing from the EU. In this respect, whether the UK citizen had exercised her Treaty rights before withdrawal was immaterial, and no rights accrued from their previous Union citizen status.

This approach confirms the minimalistic/transactional view of Union citizenship—there is no consideration of the fact that Union citizenship might be a status that transcends the confines of international law nor of any residual responsibility of the EU towards its former citizens. Rather, the responsibility for British citizens, even for those living in the EU as a result of the exercise of their Treaty rights, rests firmly with the UK government.

The *Préfet du Gers* case also raised the problem of the compatibility of the deprivation of the rights of British citizens with the Treaties' Union citizenship provisions. Here, the Court clarified that given that British citizens are no longer Union citizens upon the withdrawal of the UK, they can no longer rely on the rights conferred specifically on Union citizens by the Treaty and the Charter.[101] This also

---

[100] Emphasis added. It is worth recalling the entire paragraph of Mr Collins' Opinion: 'In so far as the third question specifically asks whether the Withdrawal Agreement infringes certain principles underlying EU identity and is disproportionate since it contains no exception to the rule that British nationals lose the rights attaching to Union citizenship, I would make the following brief observations. Since the United Kingdom's sovereign choice to leave the European Union amounts to a rejection of the principles underlying the European Union, and the Withdrawal Agreement is an agreement between the European Union and the United Kingdom to facilitate the latter's orderly withdrawal from the former, the European Union was in no position to insist that the United Kingdom fully adhere to any of the European Union's founding principles. Nor could the European Union secure rights that, in any event, it was not bound to assert on behalf of persons who are nationals of a State that has left the European Union and who are therefore no longer Union citizens. Finally, since Union citizenship depends upon the possession of Member State citizenship, no response other than the exclusion of British nationals from the definition of Union citizens was possible whilst remaining within the scope of the Treaties.' (para. 75, Case C-673/20 *EP v. Préfet du Gers and Institut national de la statistique et des études économiques* (EU:C:2022:129)). Note that, as recalled also by the Court in Case C-673/20, *EP v. Préfet du Gers* (EU:C:2022:449), there is no bar in conferring voting rights to the EP to non-EU citizens; albeit that would normally be a matter for the Member States (see also see Case C-145/04, *Spain v. United Kingdom* (EU:C:2006:543)). It is debatable, and now perhaps irrelevant, whether voting rights could have been granted to British citizens through the Withdrawal Agreement.

[101] See also Dougan, 'So Long, Farewell, Auf Wiedersehen, Goodbye: The UK's Withdrawal Package', 57 *Common Market Law Review* (2020), 631; Hillion, 'Withdrawal Under Article 50 TEU: An Integration-Friendly Process', 55 *Common Market Law Review* (2018) 29.

184   ELEANOR SPAVENTA

means that EU constitutional principles do not apply and that no individual assessment of the circumstances of the UK citizen whose Union citizenship has been withdrawn is required.[102]

However, the broader legal question remains unaltered—which is whether the Withdrawal Agreement provisions are subject to judicial review vis-à-vis the constitutional principles in the Treaties; and if yes, against which principles would this review be allowed (proportionality, the Charter, and the Union citizenship provisions, as the absolute core which cannot be derogated from, or whether it extends to other parts). As mentioned above, Advocate General Collins took for granted that both the Treaties and the Charter apply to the Decision ratifying the Agreement, which is to say to the Agreement per se. This would also indicate that Brexit UK citizens are protected by EU constitutional principles, at least when they fall within the scope of the Withdrawal Agreement.[103] More difficult, however, is the question of whether 'paths not taken' as it were, can be challenged in relation to the EU constitutional principles: in other words, there is a substantial legal difference between the review of a given legislative choice, and the contestation of the political decision not to confer given rights, first and foremost free movement rights. As hard as this might be for the citizens affected, the ruling in *Préfet du Gers* demonstrates the Court's unwillingness to step in and affect the discretion of the EU institutions. However, it would have been important for the very concept of Union citizenship that the Court recognized that British citizens are in a unique position—that the loss of Union citizenship, perhaps legally legitimate, entails also the loss of a particular form of identity. It is regrettable that in *Préfet du Gers* the Court bluntly rejected the relevance of the fact that British citizens who had exercised their Treaty rights before Brexit might be in a special situation, thus limiting if not altogether erasing the constitutional dimension of Union citizenship. By doing so, the Court significantly limited the ambitions of an unprecedented experiment, that of construing a supranational identity.

6. Conclusion

Brexit is challenging the very idea and significance of Union citizenship in three ways: first of all, it brings to the fore the tension between the conditionality requirements associated with Union citizenship rights and the fundamental status

---

[102] See also Case T-252/20, *Silver* (EU:T:2021:347), where the General Court declared the application inadmissible for lack of standing; the appeal is pending in Case C-499/21 P; it is very likely that inadmissibility will be confirmed by the Court of Justice, see e.g. Order of the Court in Case C-755/18 P (EU:C:2019:221). See also, Case T-198/20, *Shindler and others* (EU:T:2021:348), under appeal (C-501/21 P) and Case T-231/20 *Price* (EU:T:2021:349), under appeal (Case C-502/21 P).

[103] I have argued elsewhere that the principle of legitimate expectations offered protection in the event of a no deal, Spaventa (n. 3).

rhetoric which, at least to a certain extent, is also endorsed by the EU institutions. Second, it shows the tensions between different understandings of Union citizenship—transactional/international or identitarian/supranational—and it questions the spatial reference point of Union citizenship, national or EU. Third, it questions the constitutional value of Union citizenship and the extent to which such a status, and the rights associated with it, can be withdrawn from those who had already triggered Treaty rights at the point of withdrawal; and from those who had yet to do so. The three questions are closely linked, even though they might deliver differing answers.

It has been argued that the choices made at a political level in relation to the treatment of Brexit citizens reflect a thin interpretation of Union citizenship, an interpretation that betrays the earlier vision espoused by both the Commission and the Court, as to the absolute innovative nature of a supranational identity. Furthermore, the confinement of the rights of British citizens to the host State of residence at the time of withdrawal also challenges our understanding of what the internal market really is: the moving citizen does not inhabit the internal market as a 'whole', rather she continues to inhabit the territory of the State of destination, albeit subject to special and more privileged rules. Finally, the Court's ruling in *Préfet du Gers* has greatly limited the centrality of Union citizenship as a constitutional status, one that, even though it can be lost upon withdrawal of the Member State of nationality, could be meaningful in the treatment of former Union citizens.

Index

For the benefit of digital users, indexed terms that span two pages (e.g., 52–53) may, on occasion, appear on only one of those pages.

access to work 12, 16n.39, 36
accommodation, substandard 82–83
aggregation of periods mechanism 18
Alimanovic 25, 29–30, 100, 112–14, 116–17, 171–72
allocation or assignment 3
Ankara Agreement 31, 34–35
aspirational justice 74, 78, 80
asylum seekers 13, 16–17
'augmented' wo/men 15, 17–20
Austria 50n.42
    child benefits indexation policy 108–10, 128, 130, 135, 136, 138–39, 140, 145, 150
authorization to enter 29
Azoulai, L. 15–16

Babayev, R. 78
Balibar, E. 38
Barnard, C. 8–9
Behr, R. 179–80, 182
Belgium 10–11, 24, 50n.42, 134–35, 137, 150–51
Benelux countries 10
Blauberger, M. 140, 145, 146–47
Bonetti, E. 140–41
border controls 6–7, 9–10, 20, 21–22, 30
Brexit 6–7, 25–26, 43–44, 127, 128
Brexit and citizenship 158–85
    absences of more than six months in a year 167–68
    children and residence rights in order to pursue education 163
    circular migration 160–61, 166, 167
    citizenship and territory: rights in national context 180–84
    competing visions of citizenship 176–80
    comprehensive health insurance 160–61, 162–64, 169, 172–73
    conditionality requirements 171–72, 178–79, 184–85
    deadlines, failure to respect 170
    denial of residence 170
    dual citizens 165–66
    economically active workers 163, 165–66, 169

economically inactive persons 160–61, 163–64, 168–69, 177–79
expulsion 165, 170
failure to gain Brexit status 171–76
gender implications 165
identitarian/constitutional citizenship 159–60, 179–80, 184–85
job-seekers 161–64, 168–69
minimalistic/transactional citizenship 159–60, 176–77, 178–79, 180, 183, 184–85
residence rights 158–59, 169, 172, 180
short-term residents 161–62, 168–69
sufficient resources 160–61, 162–64, 169
third country nationals 158–60, 166–67, 178–79
Withdrawal Agreement
    personal scope for Brexit citizens 160, 161–68
    rights accruing from 168–70
Withdrawal Agreement 158–70, 177–79, 180, 182–83, 184
Bulgaria 151

Cameron, D. 25–26, 108n.107
'Cameron deal' 177–78
categories of free movement of persons law 2–4, 36–37
Charter of Fundamental Rights (CFR) 12–13, 38, 72–73n.128, 74–75, 78–79, 174–75
Chétail, V. 16–17
child benefits 30–31, 52, 104–5
    see also exportability of child benefits
child education subsidies 18, 36
children and residence rights for education purposes 163
circular migration 160–61, 166, 167
citizenship 4, 6–8, 12, 34
    exportability of child benefits 130–31
    law 1–3
    -oriented integration requirements 3
    posted workers 74
    see also Brexit and citizenship; economic activity and citizenship

188 INDEX

collective agreement 56, 58, 58–59n.73, 60–61, 64–65
Common Travel Area (CTA) for UK and Irish nationals 158–59
compliance gap 23–24
comprehensive health insurance 92–93, 95, 120–21, 130–31, 160–61, 162–64, 169, 172–73
Comte, E. 11
conceptual interdependency 9, 25–30, 37–38
  integration 26, 28–30
  public policy 26–28
conditionality requirements 100–2, 107, 171–72, 178–79, 184–85
conflict rule 53–54
constitutional democracy *see under* posted workers and fair mobility
constitutional principles 183–84
constitutionalization 72–73n.128, 73–74, 75, 77–78, 80, 178–80
  see also over-constitutionalization
construction industry 54–55, 64–65
constructivist perspective 9
continuous employment 104
contributory in-work benefits 30–31
Conway, G. 43n.15
coordination and harmonization distinction 70–72
coordination rules 131, 132, 142–43
Covid-19 pandemic 6–7, 30
Croatia 151
Cyprus 151
Czech Republic 133, 152

Dano 6–7, 25–26, 29–30, 36, 37, 100, 163–64, 169n.50, 171–17, 174–76, 177–78
de-constitutionalization 177–78
de-subjugation 18–19
deadlines, failure to respect 170
deceased worker's family 101–2
Denmark 128, 136, 137, 152
deportation 114–15
  see also expulsion
differential treatment 36–37, 50–51
differentiation, appropriate 3–4
direct effect 58–59n.73, 72–73
disability discrimination 172–73
discrimination
  Brexit and citizenship 175–76
  gender and disability 172–73
  indirect 80–81, 138, 174–75
  problematic 3–4
  see also nationality non-discrimination
disempowerment 82–83

dismissal 99
disproportionality assessment 175–76
domestic interpretation gap 23–24
dual citizens 165–66
Dublin system 16–17
duties, rise of 29–30

Eastern Europe 30–31
economic activity and citizenship 87–126
  Directive 2004/38 and Regulation 492/2011 120–24
  economically active workers 89–90, 91–92, 95, 96–97, 98, 118, 120–21, 124–25
  economically inactive citizens 89–90, 92–93, 95, 96, 103–4, 122
  education, right of access to 120
  equal treatment 87–88, 90, 91–93, 94–95
    and access to education 100
    economic activity as indicator of integration 95–111
    on grounds of nationality 89–90
    legal sources anomalies 111–24
  family members 87–88, 93, 95–96, 101–3, 120–22, 123–24
  free movement 91–95
  frontier workers 103–6, 121–22
  integration 98–102
    as activator of limits in free movement 102–6
    and claim-making 96–106
    conditionality 100–2, 107
    requirements 90, 92–93, 95, 124
    and restriction-defending 107–11
  involuntary unemployment 93n.27, 113–14, 117
  jobseekers 94–95, 96–97, 113–17
  lawful residence 111
  means-dependent 95, 96–97, 124, 125–26
  nationality non-discrimination 92–93, 98, 118, 121, 122–23
  primary and secondary law interplay 111–20
  public interest 107–9
  reasonable time period 115–16
  residence rights 87–88, 90, 93–94, 97, 100, 101–3, 104–6, 114–19, 120–21, 122–24
  self-employed citizens 88–90, 91, 93, 95, 96–97, 98, 113, 117–21, 124–25
  service provider 91
  social assistance and social security 87–88, 95, 96–98, 104–5, 107–8, 109–10, 112–14, 116–17, 120–21, 125–26
  social and tax advantages 91–92, 94–96, 97–99, 105–6, 109–10, 113, 114, 122–23
  status and means disconnection 90

status and means distinction 89–90
status-based protection 95, 97, 124, 125–26
students and maintenance grants 92–93, 96–
  97, 101–2, 103–4, 120–22
temporary break in employment for childbirth
  purposes 106, 111–13, 117–18
temporary break in employment due to illness
  or accident 119
temporary break in employment pending
  trial 106
unmarried partners 121, 122, 123–24
unreasonable burden 107–8, 109–10
economic capacity 4–5
economic competition 43–44
economically active workers 2, 36–37, 131
  Brexit and citizenship 163, 165–66, 169
  economic activity and citizenship 89–90,
    91–92, 95, 96–97, 98, 118, 120–21,
    124–25
economically inactive persons 36–37, 130–31
  Brexit and citizenship 160–61, 163–64, 168–
    69, 177–79
  economic activity and citizenship 89–90, 92–
    93, 95, 96, 103–4, 122
  see also retired people; students
education, access to 100
EEA Agreement 32–33, 94–95
EEC–Turkey Association Agreement 32–33
elderly care services (in-kind benefits) 149–50
elitist nature of free movement 7–8
employment-based rules 129, 139, 140–42, 143–
  44, 148–49
equal treatment 36
  Brexit and citizenship 168–69
  equal pay for equal work 65–67
  exportability of child benefits 130, 131, 137–
    38, 146–47
  non-discrimination 6–7, 145
  posted workers 41, 45, 46–47, 48–50, 52–57,
    58–59, 62–63, 67–68, 69–71, 69n.118, 74,
    80, 82–84
  and social and tax advantages 163
  see also under economic activity and
    citizenship
essential workers 30
Estonia 152
EU15 129, 135
European Committee of Social Rights 61–63
European Convention for Human Rights
  (ECHR) 72–73n.128, 182
European Free Trade Association (EFTA)
  States 32–33
European Social Charter (ESC) 61–62
'Eurostars' 15, 17–18, 70

exceptionalism 4–5
  see also under free movement law and
    emancipation from migration law
exile (mobility category) 14–15
expansionism 34
exportability of child benefits 4, 127–57
  aggregation 131
  Austrian indexation policy 128, 130, 138–39,
    140, 145
  child benefits without parents' taxes 147–48
  country of employment 132
  country of residence 132
  distributional concerns 140
  dual determination of competence 144
  employment-based rules 128, 129, 139, 140–
    42, 143–44, 148–49
  equal treatment and non-discrimination 145
  EU countries and child benefits 150–57
  EU rules and regulations 130–33
  fairness 136, 138, 139, 140, 143–44
  feasibility 146–47
  Impact Assessment (2016) 141, 142–43,
    146–47
  institutional logic 128–29, 149
  institutional tensions 129–30, 132–33, 137–
    44, 148
  lex loci domicilii 144, 146–47, 149–50
  national preferences for policy
    change 148–49
  one country only 131
  political conflicts 127, 128–30, 133, 139–44,
    149
  political sustainability 128, 129, 142
  politicization 148–49
  recent debates between Member
    States 134–39
  residence-based family policies 129, 133, 139,
    140–42, 143–44, 145, 146–49
  Social Security Coordination 141
  unfairness 128–29, 139, 141, 142–43
  welfare chauvinism 140
expulsion 12, 93, 165, 170
  protection from 175–76
external circulation 32

fair mobility see posted workers and fair
  mobility
fairness 1, 4
  posted workers 39–40, 41–44, 74
  see also under exportability of child benefits
family benefits 108–10, 125–26, 177–78
  see also exportability of child benefits
family members 10n.12, 32, 34, 35–36, 37
  Brexit and citizenship 168

190   INDEX

family members (*cont.*)
  economic activity and citizenship 87–88, 93, 95–96, 101–3, 120–22, 123–24
  posted workers 70
family reunification 28–29, 175–76
Favell, A. 15, 17–18, 30–31
Finalarte 49, 52, 54–55, 57, 83–84
financial means questioning 3
Finland 63–64, 137, 152
fiscal and social advantages 36
fixed term contracts 66, 70–71
'flaneur' (mobility category) 14–15
forced labour 82–83
forum shopping 16–17
fragility of free movement of persons 4–5
France 10, 21, 22, 47–48
  Algeria/Algerians 11
  exportability of child benefits 134–35, 137, 152–53
  Overseas Territories 11
  voting rights 182
Fredriksen, H.H. 32–33
free movement of goods 68
free movement law and emancipation from migration law 3, 6–38
  evolution 33–35, 37
  exceptionalism 6–7, 8–33
    conceptual interdependency 9, 25–30, 37–38
    invention: labour mobility 10–12
    particularization: distinctive forms of mobility 14–20
    separation: insulation of free movement law from migration law 12–14
    structural interdependency 9, 20–25, 37–38
    unclear border between free movement and migration 30–33
  progressivism 33–34, 35–38
freedom of establishment 61, 73–74, 88–89, 94, 118
freedom to conduct a business 78–80
freedom to provide services 47–49, 52–56, 57–59, 64–65, 66–68, 73–74, 84–85, 94
Friedman, M. 42
frontier workers 49–50, 103–6, 121–22
fundamental freedoms 74–75, 80, 107–8
fundamental principles 4–5, 34, 58–59, 94–95
fundamental right to strike 58–59, 61, 62–63
fundamental rights 1–2, 34, 44, 45–46, 62, 72–81, 83–84, 85, 176
  see also under posted workers and fair mobility
Fundamental Rights Agency 79–80
fundamental status of citizenship 24–25

fundamental status of nationals 2–3

gender discrimination 172–73
Geneva Convention 27–28
genuine link 105–6, 113
Germany 10–11, 21, 23n.77
  economic activity and citizenship 104–5, 112–13
  exportability of child benefits 128, 134–35, 136, 137, 148, 153
  Pflegerversicherung 149–50
  posted workers 52, 54–55
  Posted Workers Law 64–65
global mobility infrastructure 20
Goedings, S. 11
Greece 134–35, 153
Grzelczyk 32–33, 175–76

habitual residence test 174–75
harmonization
  maximum 56–57, 60–61, 72
  minimum 56–57, 60–61, 72, 84
health insurance *see* comprehensive health insurance
Hillion, C. 32–33
Hoffman, D. 73n.131
housing eligibility 36
human dignity 73–75, 76–77, 81–84, 95–96, 113–14
human rights 13, 43–44, 79
human trafficking 12, 82–83
Hungary 67–68, 69–70, 72, 153

Iceland 32–33
Iliopoulou-Penot, A. 98n.50, 110–11, 123–24
illegal migration 12, 21–22
'immobilized' and 'obliged' wo/men 15–17
impartiality 42
implementation gap 23–24
individual agency and empowerment 74–75, 79–80, 81–84
individual economic autonomy, protection of 78–80
infrastructure of mobility 20
institutional approach 9
institutional logics 4, 128–29, 140, 142, 149
institutional tensions 129–30, 132–33, 139, 142–44, 148
institutionalized life of migrants 16–17
integration 6–7, 26, 28–30, 34
  exportability of child benefits 131
  injunctions 15, 29
  negative 75, 77–78
  positive 75, 77–78, 86

posted workers and fair mobility 45–46
sufficient 105–6
tests 29
through work philosophy 93
see also under economic activity and
citizenship
inter-ethnic conflicts 15
International Labour Organization 61–62
intimidation 82–83
involuntary unemployment 93n.27, 113–14, 117
Ireland 134–35, 136, 137, 141–42, 153
Italy 10–11, 22, 134–35, 148, 153–54
Single Universal Allowance Act
(2022) 140–41

Jacqueson, C. 110
job-seekers 36–37, 49–50, 94–95, 96–97, 113–
17, 119, 130–31
Brexit and citizenship 161–64, 168–69
Juncker, J.-C. 65–66

Kilpatrick, C. 1, 60–61
Kramer, D. 93, 96n.39, 112–13, 113n.130

labour mobility 10–12
Latvia 137
Laval 58–62, 154
lawful residence 111
legal aspects of migration 3, 13
Lithuania 154
living conditions 35
Lobow, A. 84–85
Lucangeli, L. 140–41
Luxembourg 29–30, 133–35, 137, 155

macro-categories 36–37
Maduro, M. 75
Malta 155
marriage 16–17
May, T. 158–59
means-dependence 95, 96–97, 124, 125–26
Mediterranean Corporatist Model 134–35
Messina Conference 10n.14
migrants, institutionalized life of 16–17
circular 160–61, 166, 167
controls 21–22
crisis 22–23
and free movement, unclear border
between 30–33
law *see* free movement law and emancipation
from migration law
normative qualities 3
trajectory 16–17
Miller, N. 23–24

minimum income benefits 117–18
minimum income requirement 165–66
minimum rates of pay and remuneration 60–61,
62–65, 66, 67–68
minimum standards 61, 72
minimum subsistence 113–14, 174–75
mobility, distinctive forms of 14–20
'augmented' wo/men 15, 17–20
'immobilized' and 'obliged' wo/men 15–17
Monnet, J. 35
multiculturalism 15
mutual recognition 76–77

national authorities 20–22, 23, 163–64, 172–73
and margin of discretion 13
nationality 1–2, 3, 4–5, 28–29
nationality indirect discrimination 138
nationality non-discrimination 50–51, 58–
59n.73, 66, 69n.118, 74, 82, 84, 86
economic activity and citizenship 92–93, 98,
118, 121, 122–23
exportability of child benefits 137–38
posted workers 50–51, 58–59n.73, 66,
69n.118, 74, 82, 84
Netherlands 27–28, 29, 128, 134–35, 136, 137,
148, 156–57
New Pact on Migration and Asylum 13
New Settlement of the UK within the EU
(2016) 25–26, 30–31
nomad (mobility category) 14–15
non-essential workers 30
Nordic countries 134–35
normative ghetto 16–17

occupational qualifications 115
on-call workers 169
over-constitutionalization 45–46, 72–81, 84–85,
177–78

part-time workers 66, 70–71
partners in durable relationship 168
pedestrian (mobility category) 14–15
peer assessments 137
pensions 18
permanent residence 26–27, 93, 104–5, 106, 153,
165–66, 168, 173–74
permanent workers 66
Pieters, D. 144, 146–47
pilgrim (mobility category) 14–15
platform workers 169
Poland 155
police controls 21–22
political conflicts and exportability of child
benefits 127, 128–30, 133, 139–44, 149

192 INDEX

political sustainability 4, 128, 129, 142, 150
Portugal 46–48, 57
  Act of Accession 47–49, 83–84
  exportability of child benefits 134–35, 155
  Posted Workers Directive (PWD) 39–40, 55–57, 64–65
  Revised 65–72, 83, 84–86
posted workers and fair mobility 3, 39–86
  collective agreement 56, 58, 58–59n.73, 61, 64–65
  constitutional democracy over-constitutionalization and fundamental rights 72–81
    constitutional protection of free movement 80–81
    individual agency and dignity 74–75, 81–84
    individual economic autonomy, protection of 78–80
    transnational democracy 75–78, 80–82
  democratic constitutionalism 39–41, 43–45, 53–54, 58–59n.73, 72–86
  discontents 61–63
  equal pay for equal work 65–67
  equal treatment 41, 45, 46–47, 48–50, 52–57, 58–59, 62–63, 67–68, 69–71, 69n.118, 74, 80, 82–84
  exclusion of posted workers from notion of worker 46–55
  fairness 41–44
  Finalarte 49, 52, 54–55, 57, 83–84
  fundamental right to strike 58–59, 61, 62–63
  fundamental rights 44, 45–46, 74, 83–84, 85
  individual human dignity 73–74, 76–77
  Laval 58–62
  maximum harmonization 56–57, 60–61, 72
  minimum harmonization 56–57, 60–61, 72, 84
  minimum rates of pay and remuneration 60–61, 62–65, 66, 67–68
  nationality non-discrimination 50–51, 58–59n.73, 66, 69n.118, 74, 82, 84, 86
  Posted Workers Directive (PWD) 39–40, 55–57, 64–65
  posting as case study 45–46
  readjusted case law 63–65
  Revised Posted Workers Directive (RPWD) 65–72, 83, 84–86
  Rush Portuguesa 46–53, 54, 55–56, 57
  transnational constitutional democracy 84–86
  working conditions 61, 62–63, 70–71, 80–81
pre-settled status 173–76

precarious and exploitative employment relationships 82–83
pregnancy and childbirth 118–19
primacy 72–73
primarily competent Member State 132
primary carer of person in education and residence rights 163
primary law 13
  economic activity and citizenship law 90, 106, 123–24
  posted workers 58–59, 64, 67–68, 77–78
  and secondary law interplay 111–20
private international law (PIL) rules 51–52
progressivism 33–34, 35–38
proportionality test
  Brexit and citizenship 163–64, 171–72, 182, 184
  economic activity and citizenship law 104, 112n.126
  posted workers 54, 76
protectionism 77–78, 80
public health 107, 108n.106
public interest
  Brexit and citizenship 166–67, 170–72
  economic activity and citizenship 107–9
  posted workers and fair mobility 67, 68–69, 79–81, 86
public policy 22–23, 26–28
  economic activity and citizenship 107, 108n.106
  posted workers and fair mobility 56–57, 61
  threat to 22–23, 26, 28
public security 26–27, 28, 107, 108n.106, 171–72

re-employment 99
reasonable time period 115–16, 162–63
reciprocity 178, 181
refugees 16–17, 151
regulatory power 43–44
reinstatement 99
remuneration 99
  see also minimum rates of pay and remuneration
repatriation 12
residence, denial of 29, 170
residence, length of 37, 177–78
residence permits 20, 21, 29, 102–3, 154, 155
residence rights
  Brexit and citizenship 158–59, 169, 172, 180
  of divorcees 171–72

economic activity and citizenship 87–88, 90, 93–94, 97, 100, 101–3, 104–6, 114–19, 120–21, 122–24
  of future children 175–76
residence status from marriage or registered partnership 165
residence termination, protection against 28–29
residence-based family policies 129, 133, 139, 140–42, 143–44, 145, 146–49
retired people 130–31
Revised Posted Workers Directive (RPWD) 65–72, 83, 84–86
Ristuccia, F. 110, 119n.159
Romania 155
rule of law 43–44, 45, 73–74
Ruiz Zambrano 166–67, 178–80
Rush Portuguesa 46–53, 54, 55–56, 57

Salazar, N.B. 19
Scharpf, F.W. 84n.169
Schengen area 20–21, 22–23
Schengen Borders Code (SBC) 9–10, 13–14, 21–23, 28
Schmidt, S.K. 84–85, 177–78
Schuman Plan 10
Schuman, R. 35
Scott, J. 1
seasonal workers 48–51
secondary law 12–13
  Brexit and citizenship 171–72
  economic activity and citizenship law 90, 122–23
  posted workers 50–51, 66, 67–68
secondary movements 15–16
selective mobility 30
self-determination 74
self-employed workers 2, 88–90, 91, 93, 95, 96–97, 98, 113, 117–21, 124–25
settled status 173–74, 175–76
Shaw, J. 23–24
short-term residents 161–62, 168–69
Slovakia 156
Slovenia 156
social advancement 35–36, 91–92, 101–2
  see also upward social mobility
social assistance and social security 87–88, 95, 96–98, 104–5, 107–8, 109–10, 112–14, 116–17, 120–21, 125–26
social dumping 55–56, 65–66, 85
social justice 43–44, 85
social protection 3, 17, 36
  see also exportability of child benefits; social assistance and social security

social rights 6–7, 28–29, 41, 62, 131
social and tax advantages 91–92, 94–96, 97–99, 105–6, 109–10, 113, 114, 122–23, 137–38
sociological obstacles 30–31
solidarity 1, 6–7, 17, 19, 38, 83, 85
Spaak Report 11
Spain 134–35, 156
'special relationship' 32–33
Spijkerboer, T. 20
status-based protection 95, 97, 124, 125–26
structural interdependency 9, 20–25, 37–38
  impact of migration controls on free movement 20–23
  unclear separation of free movement and migration in national law 23–25
students 2, 16–17, 36–37, 92–93, 120–21
  maintenance grants 93, 96–97, 101–2, 103–4, 121–22, 168–69
  refusal to grant aid to 29–30
subsidiarity principle 66n.106
sufficient resources 130–31, 160–61, 162–64, 169
sufficiently close connection 104
surveillance 16–17
Sweden 60–61, 137, 156
  Lex Laval 61–63
systematic criminality and security checks 170

temporary agency workers 56–57, 66, 70–71
temporary break in employment
  for childbirth purposes 106, 111–13, 117–18
  due to illness or accident 119
  pending trial 106
third country nationals 9–10, 13–14, 15–16, 20–21, 22–23, 24–25, 28, 29, 30, 31, 32, 34
  Brexit and citizenship 158–60, 166–67, 178–79, 181
  posted workers 47, 49
tourist (mobility category) 14–15
Trade and Cooperation Agreement (EU-UK) 158–59, 181
traditional non-European ethnic immigrants 15
transnational constitutional democracy 75–78, 80–82, 84–86
transposition, application and enforcement of free movement rules 23–24
Turkish workers 31–33, 34–35, 106
Tusk, D. 25–26, 108n.107

unemployment 11, 99
  involuntary 93n.27, 113–14, 117

194 INDEX

United Kingdom
  economic activity and citizenship 108–9,
    125–26
  exportability of child benefits 128, 134–36,
    137, 141–42, 149
  Human Rights Act 176
  posted workers 57
United Kingdom-European Union
    agreement 136
United Nations Convention on the Rights of the
    Child (UNCRC) 147–48
unmarried partners 121, 122, 123–24
unreasonable burden 107–8, 109–10, 130–31,
    175–76
upward social mobility 36–37, 79–80

Valcke, A. 23–24
Vidotto, V. 140–41

vocational training 101–2, 119, 167–68
voting rights 182–83

wage theft 82–83
Waldron, J. 43n.15
welfare chauvinism 140
welfare systems 1–2, 7–8, 25–26
  see also exportability of child benefits
Withdrawal Agreement *see under* Brexit and
    citizenship
Witte, F. de 18–19, 74, 80n.160
women's autonomy 36
work permits 20, 52–53
workers *see* economically active workers
working conditions 35–36, 61, 62–63, 70–71, 80–81
working hours, excessive 82–83

yellow card procedure 66n.106